Journey through the afterlife

ANCIENT EGYPTIAN BOOK OF THE DEAD

Journey through the afterlife

ANCIENT EGYPTIAN

BOOK OF THE DEAD

Edited by John H. Taylor

THE BRITISH MUSEUM PRESS

This book is published to accompany the exhibition
at the British Museum from 4 November 2010 to 6 March 2011

This exhibition has been made possible with the assistance of the
Government Indemnity Scheme which is provided by the Department
for Culture, Media and Sport and administered by the Museums,
Libraries and Archives Council.

First published in 2010 by the British Museum Press
A division of the British Museum Company Ltd
38 Russell Square, London WC1B 3QQ
www.britishmuseum.org

A catalogue record for this book is available from the British Library

ISBN (hardback) 978 0 7141 1989 2
ISBN (paperback) 978 0 7141 1993 9

Designed by Price Watkins
Printed in Italy by Printer Trento

Frontispiece: The god Osiris enthroned.
Papyrus of Ani, 19th Dynasty, *c.* 1275 BC. EA 10470/4.
Opposite: The Chantress Anhai.
Papyrus of Anhai, 20th Dynasty, *c.* 1100 BC. EA 10472/5.

Papers used in this book are natural, recyclable products made from
wood grown in sustainable forests. The manufacturing processes
conform to the environmental regulations of the country of origin.

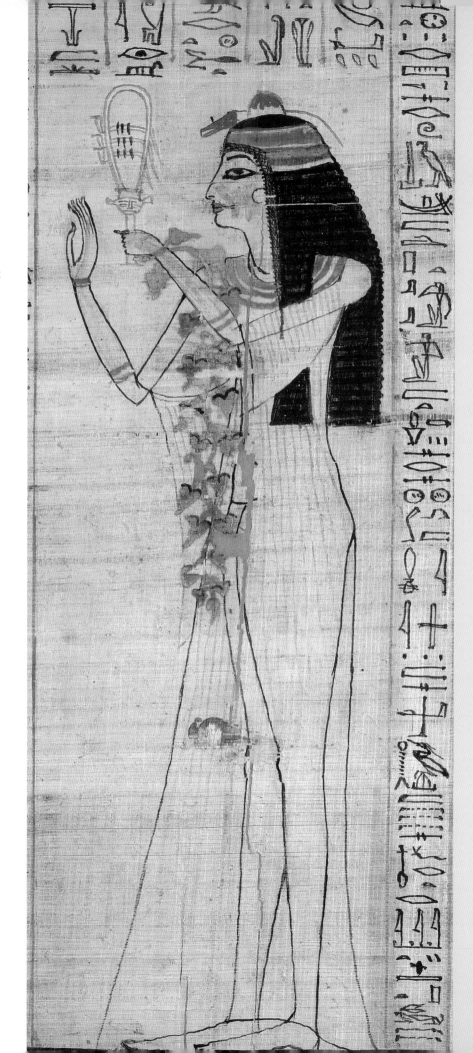

CONTENTS

SPONSOR'S FOREWORD

BP is delighted to support this BP Special Exhibition, which draws on the unequalled collections of the British Museum and other major world institutions.

Journey through the Afterlife: Ancient Egyptian Book of the Dead opens up the mysterious world of the ancient Egyptian afterlife. Making use of the latest research, the exhibition reveals the hopes and fears of one of the world's most remarkable civilizations.

Over the last ten years, BP has been proud to support a number of special exhibitions at the British Museum and the promotion of wider access to arts and culture worldwide.

Bob Dudley
Group Chief Executive, BP

DIRECTOR'S FOREWORD

THE eternal question of what happens to us when we die was one to which the ancient Egyptians devoted much thought; indeed they have left more writings on this subject than any comparable society of antiquity. The conviction that the individual could survive death was so deeply rooted in the Egyptian psyche that it became one of the mainstays of their culture. Caring for the dead was a duty common to all members of society; to neglect that duty was a contravention of *Maat* – the governing principle of Right and Truth, which maintained the cosmos in order. Hence it comes as no surprise that the quest for immortality features heavily in material culture, of which writing and art are two of the main expressions.

For the Egyptians, the creation of written documents, paintings and sculptures was more than the making of a record. Word and image contained magical power which could make extraordinary things happen – not least, they could help a man or woman in the hazardous passage from death to afterlife. Texts and images placed in the tomb equipped the dead with the means of achieving their own salvation, giving them guidance, instructions and special powers to overcome all perils on the difficult journey. Among this magical armoury the collection of illustrated spells which we call the Book of the Dead has a special place. It stood at the culmination of a long development. The older Egyptian mortuary texts present an afterlife formulated for kings, and which for a long time remained mainly for them. But the Book of the Dead reveals the hopes and fears of a broader spectrum of people – men and women of different ranks. For the first time the dead are judged, and the idea is clearly articulated that admittance to paradise does not depend solely on status, but on personal conduct, on being morally upright. This notion brought with it a new set of concerns – what if one's record in life was less than perfect? With their usual pragmatism, the Egyptians devised ways to escape punishment by the gods, but the fact that they felt a need to do so is revealing of a new stage in human psychology, a new notion of just behaviour.

Besides marking a key moment in the development of ethics, the Book of the Dead is a monument of art and writing. Copies of the spells on papyrus include some of the Egyptians' highest achievements in calligraphy and drawing. A few images will be familiar – the weighing of the heart, the paradise of the Field of Reeds – but there is much of great interest besides. This exhibition allows the visitor to experience this rich source in depth, to see the well-known images in their true context, and to compare one manuscript with another. The many variations in the words and illustrations show that these were far from fossilized ancient formulae being slavishly reproduced. The creative process was open-ended, and the scribe and artist producing a new papyrus roll could add their own creative touches.

The collections of the British Museum provide an unsurpassed basis for such an exhibition, containing as they do a comprehensive range of Book of the Dead documents including some of the most celebrated papyri of all – those of Ani, Hunefer and Anhai. Because of the requirements of conservation, only a small part of this rich material can ever be on long-term show. So this exhibition offers a rare opportunity to present the Museum's holdings in greater depth. The broader selection presented here has been augmented by a number of outstanding pieces, generously lent by other museums.

The timing of this exhibition is auspicious, as scholarly research on the Book of the Dead proceeds apace, opening to us new levels of understanding and revealing hitherto unnoticed patterns in the arrangement of the documents and the manner of their creation. We are most grateful to our generous sponsors BP for making possible this enthralling glimpse into the fears, hopes and beliefs of ancient Egypt.

Neil MacGregor
Director, British Museum

ACKNOWLEDGEMENTS

THE idea of creating an exhibition on the subject of the Book of the Dead was suggested several years ago by Vivian Davies, and he has consistently supported the project at every stage of its development.

Both the exhibition and the catalogue reflect the long-term dedication and effort of a large number of colleagues in the British Museum. In the Exhibitions department thanks are owing to Carolyn Marsden-Smith, Sarah Scott, Neil Casey, Caroline Ingham, Paul Goodhead, Chloe Luxford, Carol White and Peter Ruocco. The Museum's conservators have been particularly busy. We are grateful to David Saunders, head of Conservation and Scientific Research, for making their services available, and for the work done by Alice Rugheimer, Lynne Harrison, Nicola Newman, Barbara Wills, Kat Oliver, Rachel Swift, Fleur Shearman, Karen Birkhölzer, Pippa Cruikshank and Nicole Rode. The greatest debt is owed to Bridget Leach, our indefatigable papyrus conservator, who with the assistance of Helen Sharp has conserved and re-mounted a huge number of sheets of papyrus, including all ninety-six frames of the Greenfield Papyrus. Janet Ambers and Caroline Cartwright have contributed scientific data on the objects. Giovanni Verri gave up his time generously to take infra-red photographs of papyrus EA 10478, enabling previously illegible texts to be read for the first time.

The guidance of the Museum's organics conservators and scientists has been crucial in the process of selecting objects for inclusion in this exhibition. It is only in relatively recent years that the vulnerable nature of many of the papyri, on account of the light-sensitive pigments on their surfaces, has come to be fully appreciated. Priority must be given to the long-term preservation of these fragile documents, and to this end it has been judged that many interesting coloured papyri should not be displayed until some reliable solution to this problem has been found. Choosing items which could be exhibited safely has been a lengthy process, involving detailed discussions between curators and conservators, often on a case-by-case basis. The result, we feel, offers a representative cross-section of the treasures of the British Museum collection without compromising the future survival of these irreplaceable artefacts.

Dudley Hubbard devoted a great deal of time and effort to the photography of the objects and responded to repeated requests for further views and details. Thanks are also owing to John Williams and Michael Rowe for additional photographs. In Learning and Audiences Stuart Frost provided valuable input on the information structure of the exhibition. A special word of thanks should go to Olivia Buck, who created the copy for many of the text panels and labels, working from often rough drafts and incomplete information. In the Department of Ancient Egypt and Sudan much important work has been done by Richard Parkinson, Elisabeth O'Connell, Claire Messenger, Evan York and Simon Prentice.

The exhibition owes a great deal to colleagues from around the world, too numerous to mention individually. We are particularly grateful to all those institutions which have lent items from their collections, and to their staff – Guillemette Andreu-Lanoë and Marc Etienne (Musée du Louvre, Paris), Maarten Raven (Rijksmuseum van Oudheden, Leiden), Rita Freed and Lawrence Berman (Museum of Fine Arts, Boston), Gisele Pierini (Musée d'Archéologie Mediterranéenne, Marseilles) and Gillian Greenaway (Reading Museum Service). Special thanks are owing to Irmtraut Munro, Rita Lucarelli and Barbara Lüscher for taking time from their busy schedules to contribute the essays which appear in this volume. I have profited from having had privileged access to the work of many scholars who are diligently collecting, documenting and collating Book of the Dead manuscripts and making observations and deductions which are changing our understanding of that fascinating source. I am all too aware that to digest all this new work and to summarize and re-present it in a synthesis such as this risks omission, distortion and misinterpretation. I hope I have avoided these pitfalls, but for any imperfections in interpretation I alone am responsible.

The catalogue owes much to the tireless editorial work of Coralie Hepburn, Laura Lappin and Jane Lyons, and the design skills of Ray Watkins. Axelle Russo located numerous photographs and Charlotte Cade carefully colour corrected the illustrations. Alex Samuel provided valuable help with the checking of proofs at a particularly busy time.

We are grateful to our sponsors BP for providing the funding which has made this exhibition possible.

A note on the translations of passages from the Book of the Dead which appear in this book is in order. There are many variations in the original wording of the spells, making a 'standard edition' virtually impossible to achieve, and different scholars often translate the same text in widely divergent ways. As more and more copies of the texts are made available for study some of the obscure passages in the spells are becoming clearer, but there is still a long way to go before all ambiguities are removed. In the absence of a more up-to-date English translation of the entire corpus, I have adopted Raymond Faulkner's renderings of many of the spells, which are based on the papyrus of Ani. I have adapted these selectively, either where alternative manuscripts and more recent scholarship have suggested a more accurate translation or where a more contemporary wording seemed warranted for the sake of clarity.

John H. Taylor

CHRONOLOGY

EARLY DYNASTIC PERIOD

1st Dynasty *c.* 3100–2890 BC

2nd Dynasty *c.* 2890–2686 BC

OLD KINGDOM

3rd Dynasty *c.* 2686–2613 BC

4th Dynasty *c.* 2613–2494 BC

5th Dynasty *c.* 2494–2345 BC

6th Dynasty *c.* 2345–2181 BC

FIRST INTERMEDIATE PERIOD

7th/8th Dynasties *c.* 2181–2125 BC

9th/10th Dynasties *c.* 2160–2130 BC, *c.* 2125–2025 BC

MIDDLE KINGDOM

11th Dynasty *c.* 2125–1985 BC

12th Dynasty *c.* 1985–1795 BC

13th Dynasty *c.* 1795–1650 BC

SECOND INTERMEDIATE PERIOD

14th Dynasty *c.* 1750–1650 BC

15th Dynasty (Hyksos) *c.* 1650–1550 BC

16th Dynasty *c.* 1650–1550 BC

17th Dynasty *c.* 1650–1550 BC

NEW KINGDOM

18th Dynasty *c.* 1550–1295 BC

19th Dynasty *c.* 1295–1186 BC

20th Dynasty *c.* 1186–1069 BC

THIRD INTERMEDIATE PERIOD

21st Dynasty *c.* 1069–945 BC

22nd Dynasty *c.* 945–715 BC

23rd Dynasty *c.* 818–715 BC

24th Dynasty *c.* 727–715 BC

25th Dynasty (Nubian or Kushite) *c.* 747–656 BC

LATE PERIOD

26th Dynasty (Saite) 664–525 BC

27th Dynasty (Persian Kings) 525–404 BC

28th Dynasty 404–399 BC

29th Dynasty 399–380 BC

30th Dynasty 380–343 BC

PERSIAN KINGS 343–332 BC

MACEDONIAN KINGS 332–305 BC

PTOLEMAIC PERIOD 305–30 BC

ROMAN PERIOD 30 BC–AD 395

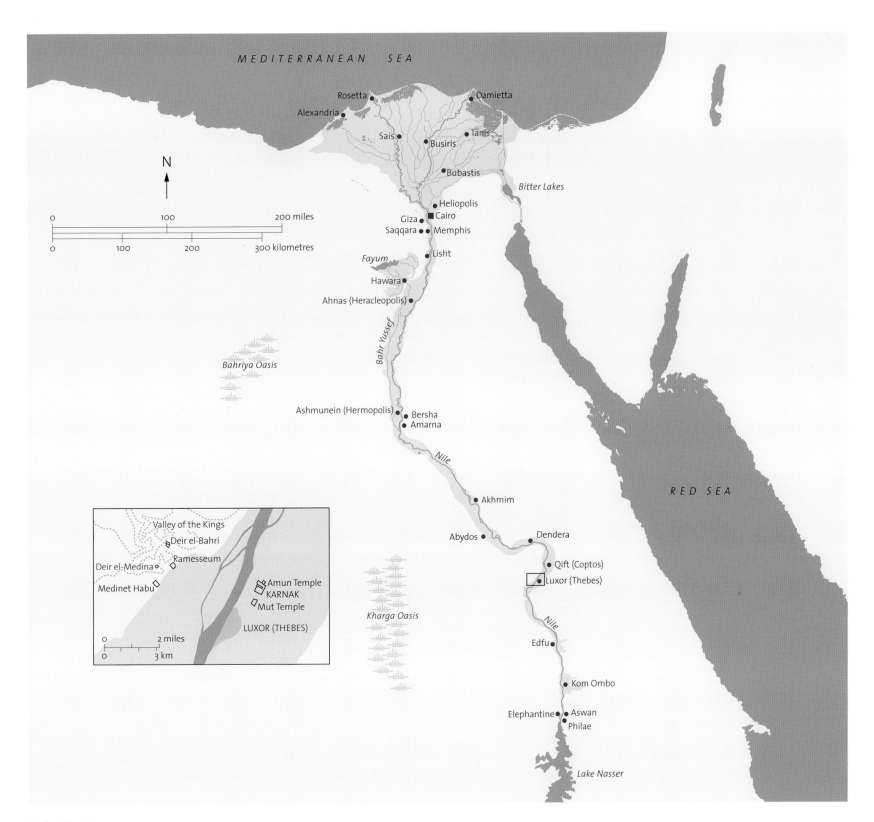

Ancient Egypt

PREFACE

T HE ancient Egyptians lived in one of the most fertile and secure places in the ancient world. Their home, the Nile valley, was protected by natural defences, and was well watered and rich in resources. It was a land of contrasts: the 'Black Land' (the fertile region inundated by the Nile) was the antithesis of the 'Red Land' – the arid and lifeless desert which bordered the cultivated areas. Yet under a stable system of centralized government there flourished a highly organized society in which everyone knew his place. For those at the lower end of the social ladder life may often have been harsh, but for the elite it was a paradise which they did not wish to leave.

Death, which put a stop to this happy existence, was therefore a challenge to the Egyptians' conception of the ideal. More than perhaps any other society they directed a vast amount of their material culture to counteracting death. An ancient text addressing those who might visit a tomb begins: 'O you who love life and hate death'. Of all ancient societies none was more concerned to defeat death than the ancient Egyptians. But attitudes to death were many and varied: it was also accepted as a transition that had to be passed through to reach eternal life. Their hopes were fixed on a blissful afterlife, but although they visualized this hidden realm in intricate detail, reaching it was not straightforward. The transition from life to after-life was a passage fraught with dangers and challenges. Supernatural help would be needed in a variety of situations: to ensure there was air to breathe and water to drink, to drive back dangerous creatures, to persuade the gods that one deserved eternal life. For over 3,000 years the Egyptians used many cultural approaches in their efforts to live forever. The special treatment which they applied to the dead body and the construction of some of the most elaborate tombs ever built are only the most conspicuous witnesses to their concern. Sacred writings also played a key role. Ancient Egypt has yielded more literature on the themes of death and immortality than perhaps any other comparable culture in history, vast collections of spells which constitute the oldest comprehensive expression of human thought about the survival of the individual. The evolution of these ideas can be traced through the Pyramid Texts and the Coffin Texts to the Book of the Dead – the fullest development of this genre.

The Book of the Dead was a book of magic – a collection of spells to empower, protect and guide the dead on their perilous journey. Those who knew these spells, or had them written on a papyrus roll or inscribed on their coffin, believed that they could escape the clutches of death and reach eternal paradise. By entering this blessed state a man was released from the inert rigidity of death, and freed to move in spirit form out of the darkness of the tomb and into the sunlight. This desire underlies the ancient Egyptian name for these texts, the 'spells for coming forth by day'. The Book of the Dead arose from a complex system of religious belief, the supernatural world of gods in which the Egyptians believed, but it was not a statement of doctrine, a creed. Though it contains many allusions to myths, it was not a synthesis of those myths; rather it was a way of applying mythological knowledge for personal ends. Nonetheless it preserves for us a great deal that is not expressed so fully anywhere else, revealing much about what was thought to happen to the dead.

The Book of the Dead has come down to us through a variety of different media, including texts and images on the walls of tombs and the surfaces of coffins. But the main source is the papyrus rolls; thousands of examples have survived, many of them vividly illustrated. The term 'book' is perhaps misleading: this was not a consistent composition with a fixed sequence of canonical texts. When writing a roll a scribe would make a selection from a repertoire of around 200 spells, so each manuscript is individual: no two are identical.

This great collection of writings was first translated and studied in the early nineteenth century. Some of the earliest researchers interpreted it as the 'script' of a ritual for restoring the dead to life, while others have seen it as the 'road map' for a personal journey to paradise. More recent study has shown that an individual Book of the Dead manuscript cannot be interpreted in those ways.[1] Over the centuries the contents varied much in their arrangement, making it difficult for a modern reader to detect a pattern or meaning in the whole. The linear, or narrative, structure which we today naturally expect to find was not a strong feature of the Book of the Dead. The spells do, however, fall into categories which reflect specific situations which a man would face between death and arrival in the hereafter. It was these encounters for which they looked to the Book of the Dead for help. In arranging this catalogue I have focused on these themes in an attempt to make the Book of the Dead accessible to a modern audience. With this in mind a narrative sequence has been adopted here, one which it is hoped is not inconsistent with the thought processes of the ancient Egyptians.

John H. Taylor

CROSSING
BOUNDARIES

I

1 Life and Afterlife in the Ancient Egyptian Cosmos

John H. Taylor

The Egyptian universe

By the time the Book of the Dead emerged in the seventeenth century BC, settled society in Egypt was already thousands of years old, and a complex system of religious beliefs was set in place. The ancient Egyptians' interpretation of their universe was conditioned strongly by the environment and their experience of life. For them the earthly existence was short. Most ancient Egyptians began to produce children in their teens and were dead by the age of thirty-five. This compression of the lifespan and the rapid succession of generations emphasized the changeable nature of human life and gave weight to the Egyptians' view of it as a series of transformations: birth, growing up, parenthood, old age, death, followed by rebirth. Their cyclical view of life was supported by the recurring patterns of natural phenomena which they observed – the motions of the sun, moon and stars, the annual flooding of the Nile and the growth of vegetation. These cycles were seemingly repeated for ever and hence it could be supposed that beyond the threshold of death, human existence, as part of the cosmos, would also go on eternally. Death was regarded in various different ways – as the disintegration of the person (both physically and figuratively), as isolation from one's social context, as an enemy to be fought[1] – but the Egyptians devised strategies to counter all of these situations. Death could thus also be viewed more optimistically as a transition, one more in a sequence of changes, the entering of a new phase of being. One of the oldest mortuary liturgies from Egypt contains the assurance to the dead man 'You have not departed dead, you have departed alive',[2] and many texts emphasize that the dead were expected to enter a new and eternal existence.

Human life was therefore perceived as an integral part of nature, and the Egyptians' explanation of natural phenomena was codified in myths. Some of these myths described how the universe was created out of a formless and infinite watery chaos. In some versions the creator is the god Atum, in others the sun-god Ra. Earth and sky are first brought into existence and then peopled, initially with gods and then with men. The supernatural and natural worlds were thought to be closely intertwined. Each was dependent on the other, with a reciprocal relationship governing life throughout the cosmos. The Egyptian king, on behalf of his subjects, made offerings to the gods in their temples to sustain and satisfy them, while the gods in turn gave life to men. The same principle made possible the survival of the dead, as expressed through the opening words of the commonest ritual formula found in tombs: 'An offering which the king gives to Osiris ... so that he might give bread, beer, meat, fowl [etc.] to the *ka* [spirit] of the deceased ...'. Hence offerings were made to the gods so that they would provide for the dead. For those in the world of the living, then, there were recognized procedures for gaining access to both the gods and the dead. Boundaries existed, but they could be crossed. Magic and ritual were used to deal with the supernatural, both in life and death. Although the king was nominally the intermediary between these realms, in practice the challenges of life and death were met by the use of magical approaches which opened a more direct channel of communication with the divine.

Many societies, ancient and modern, have conceived of the person as comprising body and spirit (or 'soul'). The view of the ancient Egyptians was more complex. For them, the individual was a composite of different aspects, which they called *kheperu*, or modes of existence. Prominent among these were the physical body and its most important organ, the heart. The heart – rather than the brain – was regarded as the functional centre of the person's being and also the site of the mind or intelligence. The name and the shadow were also important, as each embodied the individual essence of the person. Everyone also possessed spirit aspects called the *ka* and the *ba*. Both of these concepts are challenging to interpret. They have no precise equivalents in modern thought, and since their characters evolved through time the Egyptians' own understanding of them changed. The *ka* is often equated with the life-force. It was passed on from parent to child down the generations, but it was also personal to every individual, a kind of 'double', which is often represented in art as an exact copy of the owner. After death the *ka* remained at the tomb, where it was nourished by food offerings. The *ba* was the nearest equivalent to the modern notion of the 'soul'. To a greater extent than the *ka*, the *ba* represented the personality. It remained with its owner during life, but after death it acquired special importance. It had the ability to move freely and independently of the body, and hence could leave the tomb by day. Probably on account of this characteristic the *ba* was regularly depicted as a human-headed bird. This form also emphasized the *ba*'s ability to transform itself into different shapes, particularly various kinds of birds (see pp. 180–83). The freedom of movement of the *ba* is a constant theme of the Book of the Dead, many spells asserting that the deceased would go forth from the tomb as a living *ba* (fig. 1). It was required, however, to return each night to be reunited with the mummy.

The destiny of the dead

At death the connection between all these aspects of the self was temporarily severed. Only by means of proper rituals and magical spells could they be reconnected and the person reanimated.[3] The dead had therefore to be physically transformed through mummification, their material needs had to be supplied, and they had to be endowed with supernatural attributes, like those of the gods, before they could set off on a passage to another realm. If all the ritual and magical processes were correctly performed the individual became *akh*, a 'transfigured spirit'. The *akhu* (plural), the 'blessed dead', were endowed with creative magical powers and were enabled to dwell among the gods.

The more practical necessities were taken care of by preserving the corpse, interring it in a tomb, and providing the *ka* with food and other supplies (see also pp. 163–4). All of these actions were carried out within the context of rituals, which would elevate the deceased to the blessed state of *akh*. By this

Fig. 1 Ani 'comes forth' from his tomb with his *ba* flying above holding a *shen*-ring, symbolizing eternity. Vignette of spell 92. Papyrus of Ani, 19th Dynasty, *c.* 1275 BC. EA 10470/18.

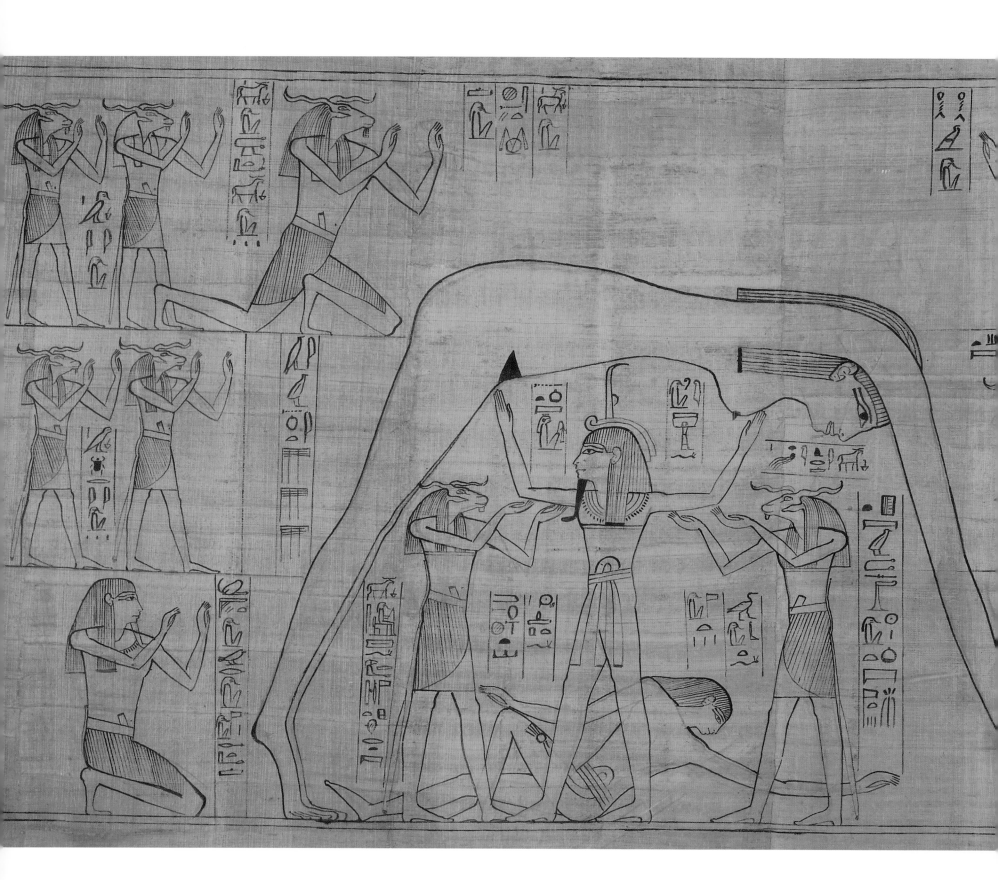

means the dead would also be assimilated to specific gods who were specifically connected with creation and rebirth. One of these was Ra, the sun-god, who in one major myth was the creator of the world and of all living things. As he travelled across the sky by day he brought life to the inhabitants of earth. At sunset he was thought to experience a symbolic death, after which he journeyed through the Netherworld during the night, retracing his path from west back to east to re-emerge from the horizon at dawn. At this morning reappearance Ra took the form of a scarab beetle or a newborn child, the latter emphasizing that during the night he had undergone rejuvenation. The Egyptians sought to take part in this endless cycle of recurring life, and much of their funerary literature concerns praise of the sun-god and the desire to gain admittance to his company.

The other great guarantor of immortality was the god Osiris. The mythology relates that he, his brother Seth and sisters Isis and Nephthys, were among the earliest gods, children of Geb (earth) and Nut (sky; fig. 2). Osiris ruled on earth as king, but was treacherously murdered by Seth, who took his place. Isis, Osiris's wife as well as his sister, had his body mummified and he was restored to life. His son Horus fought against Seth and avenged Osiris, becoming king in his father's place. Osiris, though alive again, did not return to earth but became the eternal ruler of the realm of the dead. The dead wished to experience renewal of life just as Osiris had, and for this reason the mortuary rituals inducted them into a special relationship with Osiris, placing them among a divine community of those who followed or worshipped the god. It became standard practice to indicate this exalted status by writing the name 'Osiris' before that of the deceased, who thus became 'the Osiris of X' (written with or without the genitive 'of').[4] Yet although the dead sought to be like Osiris, they were not fully integrated into his being, since they retained their earthly identities even in the god's Netherworld realm.

Fig. 2 Image representing the creation of the world: Nut, goddess of the sky, is raised by Shu above the prone earth-god Geb. Papyrus of Nesitanebisheru, late 21st or early 22nd Dynasty, c. 950–930 BC. EA 10554/87.

Having reached the afterlife an individual might expect to enter into community with the sun-god or Osiris, or both (fig. 3). But as time passed the two myths were woven together. Osiris and Ra came to be regarded as simultaneously opposite and complementary parts of a single divine entity.[5] Ra was visible every day in the sky, while Osiris was hidden from sight in his Netherworld realm. During the sun's nocturnal journey through the Netherworld he met Osiris. The two 'embraced' or merged momentarily, and this joining rejuvenated them both, enabling the life cycle to continue (figs 4–5). The notion of the two gods as counterparts is referred to several times in the Book of the Dead, for example in spell 17: 'I know yesterday. I know tomorrow. "What does that mean?" "Yesterday" is Osiris. "Tomorrow" is Ra.' It is clear that at this moment of union Ra represented the *ba* and Osiris the body of the single divine being whom they formed; it was the model for the uniting of the *ba* with the mummy, the event which would bring new life to mortals.

The dead transformed

It was believed that the dead should take on a new appearance, which was achieved through mummification. The decay of the corpse was repellent to the Egyptians, and they believed that it was necessary to transform the body, purging it of the foul-smelling fluids of corruption and refashioning it to make an eternal image called a *sah* (see cat. no. 1). This was the name given to the familiar form of the mummy with limbs confined in linen wrappings and adorned with a gilded headpiece or mask (see cat. no. 3). The *sah* shape expressed the divine qualities of the deceased and assimilated him to Osiris (the mythological prototype of the mummy). Although the dead are often depicted in *sah* form, this was only a temporary state of existence. The tight wrappings had ambivalent meaning. They served to preserve the integrity of the corpse and played an essential part in the process of regeneration by forming a kind of cocoon from which new life could emerge. But at the same time they confined the deceased in a state of rigid immobility. To break free from this restraint was an important aim, as was repeatedly expressed even in the earliest funerary literature, the Pyramid Texts, in which the dead king is urged to loosen and throw off his confining bandages. Many depictions of the dead as active spirits in the afterlife show them not as mummies but as *ba*s or men and women enjoying the full use of their bodily faculties and dressed in the clothes of the living. The ultimate desire was to be embodied as a perfect version of the earthly form. This does not of course mean that the body was expected to arise physically from its coffin and walk. Although freedom to move and escape the tomb was one of the chief goals of the dead, such movement would take place in the guise of the *ba* or in one of the other shapes into which the deceased could be transformed.

Where did the dead go? A very early notion was that the realm of the dead was situated in the west, the place where the sun set. Graves and tombs were often located on the west bank of the Nile. Throughout Egyptian history the realm of the dead was often called the West or the Beautiful West. Here the 'Goddess of the West' welcomed and nurtured the dead, and Osiris himself was frequently described as the 'Foremost of the Westerners'. But the realm of the dead was not a part of the physical world which the living could reach. The tombs there were a point of access to that realm. Ideas of where the afterlife actually took

Fig. 3 The sun-god Ra-Horakhty ('Ra-Horus of the Horizon') (left) and Sokar-Osiris (right), a fusion of the king of the Netherworld and Sokar, a funerary god of Memphis. Papyrus of Nodjmet, early 21st Dynasty, c. 1050 BC. EA 10541.

place varied through time. In the Old Kingdom the dead king ascended from his pyramid to the sky, at first to the circumpolar stars and later to the boat of the sun-god; so at this time the afterlife was located in the sky. The funerary inscriptions of non-royal persons place more emphasis on dwelling with Osiris beneath the earth. The idea developed that only the body rested in the tomb, while the spirit – *ba* or *akh* – could leave it and travel to other places. It might revisit the world of the living, it might travel with the sun-god, or it might enter the Duat (the Netherworld), ruled over by Osiris.

Since the boundaries between the natural and supernatural were permeable, the dead remained accessible even though they had passed into another world. One of the most striking differences between ancient Egyptian religion and modern monotheistic religions is in their attitudes towards the dead: according to the modern view, contact with the dead is usually regarded as taboo; to the ancient Egyptians it was an accepted part of the world.[6] Family ties remained active; indeed, a man depended on his relatives to arrange for his burial and to support his spirit via the mortuary cult, visiting the tomb periodically to make offerings. The nature of the treatment of the dead by the living could have serious consequences, for the dead could both help the living and cause them harm. Letters written to dead persons by their relatives were placed in the tomb, on pottery bowls or papyri, asking for their help to deal with troubles such as sickness or persecution. Sometimes the problem was attributed to the dead person himself. The most troublesome dead were the *mutu*, 'the damned'. They could be persons who had been executed as enemies of the state or the unrighteous who had suffered condemnation to the 'second death' in the hereafter; this was meant to put an end to their existence but there seems to have been a popular belief that they could still harm the living. Many spells used by the living were aimed at warding off the evil influence of the dead, who could bring bad dreams, illness, and threats to mothers and infants. The *akhu*, the transfigured spirits of the dead, were generally less malevolent. Their cult was sometimes maintained in the home or at the tomb, focusing on sculpted busts or stelae which depicted these ancestors. But even *akhu* could be troublesome, as a passage from the wisdom text known as the *Instruction of Ani* makes clear:

> Satisfy the *akh*; do what he wishes, keep yourself clear of what he abominates,
> that you may remain unscathed by his many hurts. Beware of every sort of
> damage. The cow in the field was stolen? It is he who does the like. As for any
> loss from the threshing floor in the field, 'It is an *akh*!' they say.[7]

Trouble attributed to *akhu* usually seems to indicate that these spirits were restless either because their tombs had fallen into ruin or because they had not received the proper offerings from their relatives.[8] Since it was in everyone's interest to ensure that the dead reached the blessed state, preparations for that crucial transition were held to be of supreme importance. For the wealthy, tombs, coffins and other funerary equipment were made in advance of death, or resources were set aside to pay for them when the time came. Among the most highly valued of these magical aids was the Book of the Dead.

Fig. 5 The gods Ra and Osiris meet in the form of birds. The two *djed* pillars denote the name of Mendes, the place at which they meet according to spell 17 of the Book of the Dead. Papyrus of Ani, 19th Dynasty, *c.* 1275 BC. EA 10470/9.

Fig. 4 Ra and Osiris united and represented as a single mummiform ram-headed deity, protected by the goddesses Isis and Nephthys. Tomb of Queen Nefertary, Valley of the Queens, 19th Dynasty, *c.* 1250 BC.

1 The appearance of the dead: Ipay as a *sah*

Limestone
H 108.0 cm; W 34.0 cm; D 26.0 cm
18th Dynasty, reign of Amenhotep III, *c.* 1390–1352 BC
Saqqara
Leiden, Rijksmuseum van Oudheden, Inv. AST 14

Mummification transformed the corpse into a new and perfect form called a *sah*. This term, which was related to a word meaning 'noble', denoted a body which had been purged of its perishable parts and refashioned into a divine image using magical materials (see p. 20). Some early Egyptian mummies were made to look like a living person, with each part of the body separately modelled in plaster or resin-soaked linen, but from the First Intermediate Period onwards it was usual to confine the limbs within a shroud, with only the head, and sometimes the hands, depicted as being uncovered. The enveloping of the body in a covering signified the gestation process from which it was thought that the dead would emerge into a new phase of existence. It also symbolically linked the dead person with Osiris, whose wrappings restored the integrity of his dismembered corpse and helped to restore him to life.

This is a rare example of a large statue depicting the dead person in this form. It represents the Chantress of Amun, Nurse of the King, Praised One of Hathor and Lady of the House Ipay. She was the wife of Tjenuro, mayor of Memphis. She is depicted wearing a collar and holding a folded cloth. Once the dead had entered the afterlife they would be released from their confining bandages and for this reason they are more usually depicted either as living beings, clothed in the garments of daily life, or as *ba* spirits (see cat. no. 2).

Schneider 1999, 126, no. 194; Ziegler 2008, 292, 294, no. 109.

2 **The *ba* embracing the body: the shabti of Sunero**

Steatite
H 22.0 cm; W 8.0 cm
19th Dynasty, *c.* 1295–1186 BC
Provenance unknown
London, British Museum, EA 65206

The regular reuniting of the *ba*-spirit with the body was thought to be
crucial to a person's survival beyond death (p. 17). Depicting this union
was thought to ensure by magic that it would always take place, and
this event was represented not only in papyrus vignettes (see pp. 90–91)
but on three-dimensional objects as well. This shabti figure, made for
the Master of Horse Sunero, was primarily intended to act as a substitute
worker for its owner in the afterlife, and it bears the appropriate text, spell
6 from the Book of the Dead, carved around the sides and back (see p.245).
Additionally, the figure shows the *ba* of Sunero, in its usual form as a
human-headed bird, pressed against his chest. In a mutual embrace the
dead man clasps the *ba* in his arms, while the spirit in turn enfolds him in
its wings, renewing the life-force of the individual. The high status of the
subject is conveyed through his rich dress: a pleated gown, sandals, a bead
collar and an elaborately curled wig.

Andrews 1998, 212–13, no. 65.

3 The dead transfigured: the mummy mask of Satdjehuty

Gilded and painted cartonnage
H 61.0 cm
18th Dynasty, c. 1500 BC
Thebes
London, British Museum, EA 29770

The divine qualities which the dead acquired through mummification were manifested in the masks that were placed over the head of the corpse (see p. 109). This example, made for Satdjehuty, a woman of high rank, is typical. It has been modelled in cartonnage (layers of linen and plaster). The gold leaf which covers the face shows that Satdjehuty has become like the gods, whose flesh was said to have been made of gold. The colouring of the hair is also symbolic. A headpiece of lapis lazuli was the ideal because the hair of gods was supposed to be made of this exotic blue mineral. Here the colour is imitated in paint. The winged headdress was a standard feature of anthropoid coffins and masks during the Second Intermediate Period, perhaps suggesting the avian character of the *ba* or the wings of protective goddesses. A short double inscription below the amuletic collar requests funerary offerings from Osiris and Anubis. Such masks came into fashion at the end of the Old Kingdom and were provided mainly for the burials of persons of high status. The identity of the owner of this example was established from several large pieces of fine linen which were buried with her (see fig. 6). These bear inscriptions in ink, giving her name and the information that she was 'a praised one' of Queen Ahmose-Nefertary, the wife of King Ahmose I. Satdjehuty was perhaps a favoured member of the queen's entourage and through this association may have received the privilege of an exceptionally well-appointed burial.

Taylor 1995; Taylor 1996; Russmann 2001, 204–6, no. 106; Strudwick 2006, 122–3, 343.

Fig. 6 Fringed linen sheet with a red ink inscription giving the name of Satdjehuty, 'praised one' of Queen Ahmose-Nefertary. 18th Dynasty, c. 1500 BC. EA 37104.

2 Preparing for the Afterlife

John H. Taylor

If a man speaks this spell when he is in a state of purity, it means going forth after death into the day and assuming whatever shape he desires. As for anyone who shall read it daily for his own benefit, it means being hale on earth; he shall come forth from every fire and nothing evil shall reach him. It is a matter a million times true; I have seen and it has indeed come to pass through me. (Spell 17)

Fig. 8 Prince Khaemwaset, son of Ramesses II. He was renowned in later tradition as a magician and as the discoverer of some spells which were incorporated into the Book of the Dead. Conglomerate statue, probably originally from Abydos, H. 138 cm. 19th Dynasty, c. 1250 BC. EA 947.

Fig. 7 A lector-priest reads from a book-roll at the head of the funeral procession. The other men make gestures of mourning. Papyrus of Hunefer, 19th Dynasty, c. 1280 BC. EA 9901/4.

IN order to reach the afterlife the ancient Egyptians evolved a range of practices which have left conspicuous traces in the archaeological record. The corpse was subjected to special treatments, including the use of preservatives, wrapping and adornment; the body was disposed of in a formal place of burial – a simple grave-pit or a monumental tomb, depending on status; and the dead were provisioned with material goods (food, drink, clothing, etc.), and with magical objects or writings to give them knowledge and power.

As in almost all societies, ancient and modern, ritual played a strong role in the passage through death (fig. 7). Ritual may be loosely defined as the pronouncing of words and the performance of actions according to prescribed patterns in order to bring about results beyond those that were possible by ordinary means. For these words and acts to be effective some supernatural power had to be activated. The usual name which the Egyptians gave to this power was *heka*, which may be translated as 'magic'. The gods possessed *heka* power. It was used by the creator when making the universe, and it safeguarded Maat, the cosmic order, though it could be a destructive influence as well. *Heka* could also be used by mortals, both living and dead, provided that they had the requisite knowledge (fig. 8). Another term for magical power was *akhu*. This was particularly associated with the deities who dwelt in the realm of the dead; the blessed dead, who were themselves called *akhu*, also wielded this power.

For the Egyptians magic was an integral part of religion. In modern societies religion and magic are often differentiated. Religion is generally viewed in a positive light as providing a moral code for its followers and benefiting society as a whole; magic tends to be regarded more negatively as 'unorthodox and subversive',[1] and as directed primarily to furthering an individual's own personal desires. But this distinction did not apply in ancient Egypt. *Heka* magic could be used by priests in temples for the benefit of all, just as it could be used by individuals in the context of everyday life. It was a way of gaining direct personal access to the divine, in which the king usually did not have to act as the intermediary.

The natural and supernatural were closely interwoven. Magic was just one of a range of approaches, all regarded as legitimate, which could be adopted to deal with the challenges posed by everyday life such as childbirth, sickness and snakebites, and also those of death – reconnecting the components of the self, nourishing the dead, protecting them from danger. So a sick person could be treated both by herbal remedies and incantations, while a dead man could be transferred to the afterlife through the chemical treatment of his corpse and the use of spells. Egyptian magic was both remedial and prophylactic. It could provide a response to a problem (whether disease or death) and it could also help to prevent a crisis by creating a defensive situation, such as protecting the home from snakes or a dead person from hostile demons in the next world.

Magic for the dead

The magical texts used to benefit the dead were of two main types. One important category was that of the mortuary liturgies or recitation texts. These were the actual words of rituals, pronounced by the living for the benefit of the dead during mummification, burial and the performance of the mortuary cult. It was at those times that the words were chiefly effective, but since the living could not be relied upon to care for the dead forever, the texts were often included in the tomb to perpetuate the effects of the ritual acts without the need for human agency. The second category was that of funerary texts proper, such as the Book of the Dead – collections of individual spells primarily, for the personal use of the dead (fig. 9).[2] The dead were thus provided with *heka* power so that they could act as magicians in their own right. The Book of the Dead was a large collection of these spells for use in different situations. It was part of a long tradition of providing funerary literature for the dead which had begun with the Pyramid Texts and evolved via the Coffin Texts. Many of the Book of the Dead spells had antecedents in the Coffin Texts.

The spells in the Book of the Dead were of a wide range of types: hymns and prayers to the gods; spells to protect from harm and to repel enemies; spells to empower (to have control over natural forces, the elements of one's personality and divine powers); 'guides to the hereafter' (spells demonstrating knowledge); and spells to gain access or permission to pass in safety.

Fundamental to the working of all Egyptian magic was a belief in the power of the spoken and written word. The most frequently used word which we translate as 'spell' literally means 'utterance'; another common expression was *djed medu*, literally 'words to be

Fig. 9 Spell 30B of the Book of the Dead written in vertical columns. The second column from the right reads 'Spell for [written in red] the heart of the Osiris the Royal Scribe Hunefer, true-of-voice'. The signs drawn in red in the adjacent column read 'He says:' and introduce the actual words of the spell. Papyrus of Hunefer, 19th Dynasty, *c.* 1280 BC. EA 9901/3.

Fig. 10 The god Thoth depicted with the head of an ibis. He holds a group of hieroglyphic signs denoting the expression 'All life and dominion'. Papyrus of Hunefer, 19th Dynasty, *c.* 1280 BC. EA 9901/2.

spoken'. Speaking prescribed words aloud, in a ritual context, was a process of creation, as exemplified by the very common funerary formula in which a god is asked to provide for the dead (see p. 16). The offerings requested are called *peret em kheru*, literally 'that which comes forth through the voice': the act of pronouncing the words itself was believed to call up the food, drink and other goods that were required. The written word was scarcely less powerful. The hieroglyphic script, known as the 'god's words', was supposed to have been invented by the god Thoth, and the hieroglyphic signs themselves were believed to contain great power (fig. 10). Having access to the written word endowed one with the power that those words conveyed. Writing spells on a papyrus roll or coffin transferred the power of the words to that object and would be of direct benefit to its owner.

Above all, the name of a thing was held to be of great importance. Saying something's name brought it into existence, as in the text known as the Memphite theology of creation, in which the god Ptah conceives things in his mind, and then brings them into existence by speaking their names. The name contained the essence or identity of that being, and knowledge of a name gave control over its possessor, even if that individual were a god. Thus in the late story of the 'Cunning of Isis' the goddess obtains great power by means of a stratagem to compel the sun-god Ra to reveal to her his secret name. A simple type of spell used in daily life would drive away snakes by first addressing them and then commanding them to depart, and since snakes were also expected to pose a threat to the dead, the Book of the Dead contains spells of exactly the same type (see pp. 186, 192, 194–5). In the afterlife the individual expected to encounter many gods and demons, so knowing their names would equip him with power to negotiate his passage. The words 'I know you and I know your names' occur repeatedly in spells in the Book of the Dead.

Many spells are more than just simple commands. They worked by means of the power contained within the words. Puns and wordplay are frequent as they provided the key to unlock different levels of meaning. It is evident from this that a transference of magical power between similar-sounding words was believed possible, and this applied especially to names. Often the speaker identifies himself with a god, and by this means he acquires the power of that god or ensures that he will share in his experiences. This kind of identification could be done directly, as in spell 43: 'I am put together, just and young, for I indeed am Osiris, the Lord of Eternity.' In many passages, however, the identification is phrased indirectly by making an allusion to the role of a particular god in a myth. Spell 9 illustrates this:

> Words spoken by Ani: 'O you Soul [*ba*], greatly majestic, behold, I have come
> that I may see you; I open the Netherworld that I may see my father Osiris and
> drive away darkness, for I am beloved of him. I have come that I may see my father
> Osiris and that I may cut out the heart of Seth who has harmed my father Osiris.
> I have opened up every path which is in the sky and on earth, for I am the well-
> beloved son of my father Osiris. I am noble, I am a spirit [*akh*], I am equipped;
> O all you gods and all you spirits [*akhu*], prepare a path for me.'

Here Ani takes on the role of the god Horus, the son of Osiris (see cat. no. 5). The words of this and other spells allude to various aspects of myths, chiefly those of Osiris, Ra and Atum. They do not recount the myth narratives, but mention many names and epithets of gods and sacred places. Often the wording makes allusion to situations or incidents in myths where right triumphs over wrong, or right is affirmed. In the spell just quoted, Seth's murder of Osiris is alluded to but any possible danger that might accrue from the reference to this negative incident is coun- teracted by the clear statement that Seth will be defeated and that Horus (with whom Ani is identified) will perform beneficial acts for his father Osiris.

Such statements reaffirmed that right would be victorious over evil. The situation for which the spell is needed is transferred to the divine sphere: just as right (Maat) is triumphant among the gods, so all will go well for the deceased. The words confirm the correct order of the cosmos in which (among other good things) the dead are eternally reborn.

The anatomy of Book of the Dead spells

In Book of the Dead papyri the spells are laid out with the title clearly distinguished, usually in red ink. The main text follows, in black ink, though red (and occasionally white) is used to emphasize special words (see p. 270). When spells are written on the walls of tombs or on coffins, blue is the preferred colour for the signs. In papyri, there is often a colophon, a short

Fig. 11 Four baboons and flaming torches surrounding a pool called the 'Lake of Fire', a feature of the Netherworld which is illustrated in spell 126. This small image, painted on the coffin of Inpehefnakht (see cat. no. 92), could have served as a condensed version of the complete spell. 21st Dynasty, *c.* 1000 BC. EA 29591.

concluding note, which may give instructions for the correct use of the spell or provide a recommendation for its efficacy. Sometimes double lines separate one spell from the next, but they may run on without a clear indication of where one ends and the next begins. Sometimes, as in the Pyramid Texts, each spell has at one end a small rectangle, so that the enclosed space of the text resembles the hieroglyphic sign (*ḥwt*) that means 'house', defining the words within as a distinct and sacred text (see p. 75). Despite the importance of individual words, spells and their illustrations could be abbreviated – often the scribe abandoned a spell before the end if he ran out of space, but this did not weaken its effectiveness. A small extract of a spell (especially the opening words) was believed to be as efficacious as the whole text (fig. 11; see p. 58).

The spells were written in Middle Egyptian. This 'classic' phase of the language was becoming increasingly archaic as the New Kingdom advanced – Late Egyptian being the stage of the language that was used in everyday life – so the vocabulary and grammatical constructions in the Book of the Dead would have had an archaic feel to its users. This flavour of great antiquity and mystique may well have contributed to the perceived authority of the texts. It is a situation comparable to the widespread use until recent times of sixteenth- to seventeenth-century English translations of the Bible and editions of the Book of Common Prayer.

In the New Kingdom a special script was used on papyri and sometimes on tomb walls. Known as 'Book of the Dead cursive' it was halfway between hieroglyphic and hieratic. The spells in this script are written in vertical columns in a distinctive orientation; the text usually runs from the left to the right edge of the roll, and the individual hieroglyphic signs faced away from the direction in which the columns were read, contrary to the usual practice.[3] Later true hieratic was used in horizontal lines arranged in broad columns resembling modern 'pages'.

One of the most strikingly original features of the Book of the Dead is the inclusion of the many illustrations which Egyptologists conventionally call 'vignettes'. The Pyramid Texts had no illustrations, and the Coffin Texts very few, but during the New Kingdom images grew steadily more numerous in copies of the Book of the Dead and were regularly attached to many spells. They were often enclosed within frames next to the words but could also occupy spaces with the text written around them; in the Late Period the vignettes were often arranged in a series running along the top of the roll above the texts. Many of these pictures expressed the content or meaning of the text in a concise way, but in a few cases the image carried as much weight as the words. Certain very important spells had vignettes which covered the full height of the roll – such as the sunrise scene, the judgement and the Field of Reeds. Because of the power inherent in an image, the vignette could stand in place of the text, representing the whole spell pictorially.

How the spells were used

For a spell to work effectively special conditions had to be observed. Sometimes the text was accompanied by instructions (the 'rubric') for correct performance, which might specify the appropriate time of day and particular actions which ought to be carried out. These could involve encircling (*pekher*, 'encircling', was another Egyptian term for a spell) or facing in a particular direction – some spells were to be repeated four times, which probably implies facing the cardinal points from which danger might approach. The colophon to spell 144 states: 'To be recited and erased, item by item, after reciting these directions, four hours of the day having passed, and taking great care as to the position [of the sun] in the sky.' This passage continues: 'You shall recite this book without letting anyone see it', and other spells emphasize the secret nature of the knowledge contained in them and the importance of restricting access to that knowledge. Spell 190 opens impressively with the statement: '[It contains] secrets of the Netherworld, mysteries of the god's domain: [how] to cleave mountains and penetrate valleys. [It contains] secrets wholly unknown ... This roll is a very real secret. The rabble, of all people, must never see [it].'[4]

Sometimes the spell was to be recited in connection with certain objects – bowls, cloths, figurines or other images – which had to be made from particular materials. The words were sometimes directed to be written using special ink or spoken 'over' an object such as an amulet, so that magical power would be transferred into it. If the amulet was then placed on the body it gave power or protection to its possessor. The notion that power, and even life, could be transferred into a man-made image was a fundamental tenet of Egyptian magical practice. Spells sometimes involved fashioning something which could then be controlled. In a story a magician makes a wax crocodile which becomes real at his command, and in the 'Cunning of Isis' the goddess makes a serpent of mud, which comes to life and bites the sun-god, enabling Isis to obtain the god's name in return for curing his pain. Since hieroglyphic signs were based on images, care was needed in using them. In the Second Intermediate Period signs representing snakes, birds or other potentially dangerous creatures were often depicted mutilated or incomplete when written on coffins or other objects destined for the tomb, to avert the possibility of these tiny images venting harm on the dead person (see p. 226).

The spells in the Book of the Dead are generally cast as speeches in the first person by the owner of the papyrus. It is unclear whether he was supposed to speak them aloud or whether the mere presence of the power-charged written words in his tomb would suffice. Some spells certainly indicate that the words needed only to be in close proximity to the owner: 'As for him who knows this book on earth, or it is put in writing on the coffin, it is my word that he shall go out into the day in any shape that he desires ...'.

As noted above, some Book of the Dead spells belong to types which were commonly used in everyday life. Although no examples of the Book of the Dead have been found in domestic contexts, several of the spells contain indications that they were read by the living as well as being provided for the dead. A note at the end of spell 135 assures that it will benefit the dead, and that 'as for him who knows it on earth, he will be like Thoth, he will be worshipped by the living, he will not fall to the power of the king or the hot rage of Bastet, and he will proceed to a very happy old age'. And spell 70 carries the note: 'As for him who knows this book on earth, he shall come out into the day, he shall walk on earth among the living, and his name shall not perish for ever.' Some spells were certainly used by the living in non-funerary contexts, such as in temple ritual, and later incorporated into the Book of the Dead, such as those for entering the sun-god's barque (see p. 48).

Authority

The spells of the Book of the Dead were not all composed at one time. They were collected together from various sources, such as documents kept in temple archives or libraries, and seem to have been used to benefit the dead for many centuries. A large number of the spells can be found, in earlier versions, among the Coffin Texts and some occur even earlier in the Pyramid Texts. There is no reliable account of who composed them, but notes appended to some of them record traditions about their alleged discovery in a temple or on the burial of a king:

> Found by a Supervisor of Wall-builders under Semty [Den?] 'in the foundations of the One-who-is-in-the-Henu-barque' [i.e. under the temple of Sokar].
>
> (Spell 64)

> This spell was found in Hermopolis, under the feet of this god. It was written on a block of mineral of Upper Egypt in the writing of the god himself, and was discovered in the time of ... [King] Menkaure. It was the king's son Hordjedef who found it while he was going around making an inspection of the temples.   (Spell 30B)

Prince Hordjedef was a famous wise man of the 4th Dynasty who featured in several traditions but spell 30B is actually first attested in the Second Intermediate Period. Another Book of the Dead text said to have been found by him was spell 137A. This document, also written 'in the god's hand', was stated to have been discovered in a secret chest in the temple of the hare-goddess Wenut at Hermopolis.

While some of these miraculous discoveries were set in the remote past, others were reported to have been of more recent occurrence. Spell 167 was allegedly found by Prince Khaemwaset, the son of Ramesses II (see fig. 8), at Saqqara (an alternative tradition attributes its composition to the sage Amenhotep, son of Hapu), while spell 166 was 'found at the neck of the mummy of King Usermaatre in the necropolis'. The king referred to may have been Ramesses II or III, and since the mummies of those rulers were rewrapped and restored by Theban priests in the 21st Dynasty it is quite possible that a papyrus inscribed with a spell was found on one of them at that time.

Statements of this kind occur in other classes of Egyptian texts which contain sacred knowledge, such as books of healing or magic. Hence some of the remedies in the Ebers medical papyrus (c. 1535 BC) were said to have been found beneath the feet of a statue of Anubis in the reign of King Den (c. 2950 BC). Obviously such statements were thought to lend authority to the spell, whereas the effectiveness of others was the proof of their worth. Several spells have colophons, recommending them as efficacious. One such has been quoted at the beginning of this chapter. Another example occurs at the end of spell 71:

> As for him who shall recite this spell, it means prosperity on earth with
> Ra and a goodly burial with Osiris; it will go very well with a man in
> the realm of the dead, and there shall be given to him the loaves which
> are issued daily in the Presence. A matter a million times true.

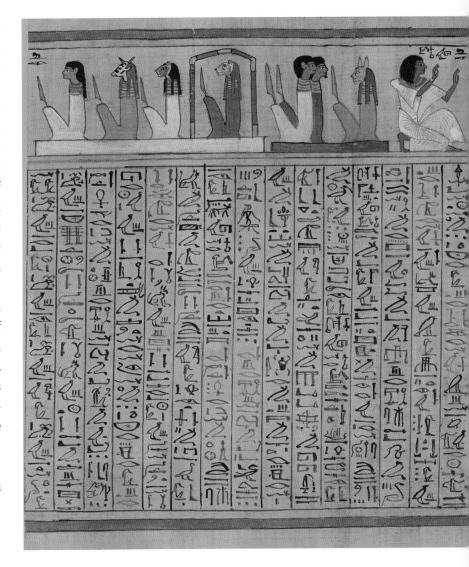

Fig. 12 Part of the long vignette and text of spell 17 of the Book of the Dead. The words written in red introduce alternative passages and commentaries on the mythological content of the spell. Papyrus of Hunefer, 19th Dynasty, c. 1280 BC. EA 9901/8.

Because the Book of the Dead was compiled from different sources there was duplication and variation among its spells. Several of them performed essentially the same task, and this was indicated in the titles, such as 'another spell …'. Since many spells from the earlier Coffin Texts were omitted from the Book of the Dead corpus, the reasons for including near-duplicates can only be speculated on. Perhaps, like healing remedies, different spells acquired a reputation for efficacy and were therefore considered indispensable. More rarely there are in-text comments or glosses which explain some of the names, epithets and obscurities in the more arcane spells, with citations of alternative passages. These seem to indicate that learned experts studied, compared and made commentaries on some of the spells. The best-known examples occur in spell 17, one of the longest and most frequently included Book of the Dead texts (fig. 12; see also cat. no. 19). This complex text about the nature of the creator-god can be traced back to the Coffin Texts (as spell 335). Some of these Middle Kingdom versions lack the commentaries but in others of the same period they are already present, perhaps indicating that the glosses quickly became established as essential parts of the canonical text.

4 **A classic Book of the Dead: the papyrus of Ani**

Painted papyrus
Total L 23.5 m; average H 42.0 cm
19th Dynasty, *c*. 1275 BC
Thebes
London, British Museum, EA 10470/19

The papyrus of Ani is one of the longest and most famous manuscripts of the Book of the Dead from the New Kingdom. It contains over sixty spells, many of which are accompanied by lavishly coloured illustrations. Ani's titles show that he was a member of the extensive and highly organized bureaucracy of Egypt in the prosperous days of the Ramesside rulers. He was a 'true scribe of the king, his beloved', a 'scribe reckoning divine offerings of all the gods' and 'overseer of the double granary of the lord of Tawer'. He is depicted several times in his papyrus, dressed in fine linen garments and jewellery, and accompanied by his wife Tutu. She was a Chantress of Amun and is represented holding the sistrum, a rattling percussion instrument which ladies of rank shook to provide a musical background to the temple rituals. The length of the papyrus and its richly coloured decoration suggest that it was probably an expensive item of burial equipment, yet it was not made specifically for Ani. His name was inserted into spaces left blank in the text, and the complete roll was assembled from several prefabricated sections (see p. 286). The papyrus was acquired in Egypt by E.A. Wallis Budge in 1887–8. He stated that it was found in a niche in the burial chamber of Ani, but this cannot be proven as the location of the tomb is now unknown. Several items which entered the collections of the British Museum around the same time as the papyrus are reputed to have come from Ani's tomb, including a wooden cosmetic box complete with jars of ointment (fig. 13) and toilet articles that may have belonged to Tutu.

British Museum 1890, pl. 19;
Budge 1895; Budge 1913;
Munro 1988, 296, b.1;
Quirke 1993, 32, no. 24.

Fig. 13 Wooden box containing cosmetic objects, stated to have been found in the tomb of Ani at Thebes, H. 35.5 cm. 19th Dynasty, *c*. 1275 BC. EA 24708.

5 **A spell for the dead: spell 9 from the papyrus of Ani**

Painted papyrus
H 42.0 cm
19th Dynasty, *c.* 1275 BC
Thebes
London, British Museum, EA 10470/18

The papyrus of Ani provides a typical example of the manner in which individual Book of the Dead spells were laid out in the manuscripts of the New Kingdom. The vignette, and sometimes the text as well, is surrounded by a yellow border, as here. Each spell begins with a title, usually written in red ink (see p. 270). In this case the title is 'spell for coming forth by day after opening the tomb'. The text follows in black ink. This particular spell (translated on p. 31) relies for its power on the repeated declaration that Ani is the son of Osiris (i.e. he assumes the role of the god Horus) and has the ability to destroy Seth. Its chief aim is to give Ani freedom to leave the tomb and to move freely through the afterlife, and although he declares that he has the power to do this he also calls on the gods to 'prepare a path' for him. The vignette shows Ani adoring the 'soul' mentioned in the text, which takes the form of a ram standing on a plinth, with an incense burner in front of it. The choice of this image was influenced by the Egyptians' belief in the power of wordplay: the words for 'soul' and 'ram' were phonetically similar (*ba*).

British Museum 1890, pl. 18; British Museum 1894, pl. 18; Budge 1895; Budge 1913; Faulkner 1985, 39.

6 An ivory 'wand' (apotropaion) with protective deities

L 37.0 cm
Late 12th Dynasty, *c.* 1850 BC
Thebes
London, British Museum, EA 18175

'Wands' made from hippopotamus ivory were used around 2000–1600 BC in rituals to protect mothers and newborn children. They were either placed on the child's body or used to draw a protective circle on the ground, as well as being put into tombs to bring about the rebirth of the dead. Their magical power derived in part from the images carved on their surfaces: usually a series of deities called 'protectors' (*sau*) or just 'gods' (*netjeru*), who included the dwarf-like deity Aha, a hippopotamus-goddess and various snakes and other creatures, often holding knives. As well as protecting the living, these divine beings appear as denizens of the Netherworld in the Book of the Dead, where they guard gateways and shield the dead from danger.

This apotropaion, in its pronounced symmetrical curvature (suggesting the horizon) and the arrangement of its decoration, also hints at the association of the newborn child (and/or the deceased) with the sun-god. The lions at each end may be an early version of the double-lion motif which appears later in the Book of the Dead. The central grouping of double-headed sphinx and scarab beetle, with a ram's head to the left, may allude to the sun-god's nocturnal rejuvenation, which was to become a crucial motif of funerary iconography in the New Kingdom.

Altenmüller 1965, II, 50–52; Pinch 2006, 40, fig. 19; Roberson 2009, 438–42.

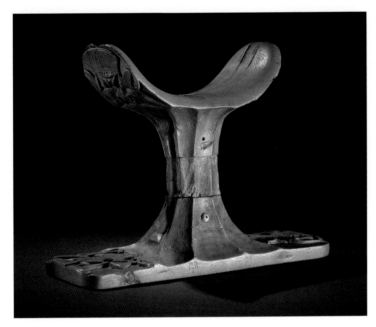

7 **A headrest with protective figures**

Wood and ivory
H 22.5 cm; w 29.3 cm
Late 18th or early 19th Dynasty, *c.* 1350–1250 BC
Provenance unrecorded
London, British Museum, EA 51806

Headrests in the form of a curved support, resting on a plinth
and flat base, were widely used in ancient Egypt. Many examples
have been found both in domestic contexts and in tombs. Sleep
was regarded as a state similar to death. Both a sleeping person
and a dead person were thought to be vulnerable to attack by
supernatural forces (for the sleeper this could be manifested
through nightmares). To keep enemies away at night, protective
images were often carved on the headboards and legs of beds,
and also on headrests. These were usually the favoured gods of
domestic safety – the lion-faced, dwarf-like Aha or Bes and the
hippopotamus Taweret or Ipet, who also watched over women
and children. On this headrest, made in three parts, the face of
the Bes-like deity is carved on the underside of the support, while
his full form is depicted in high relief on the base, flourishing
the protective symbols of the *sa*-loop and the Eye of Horus.

Szpakowska 2003, 171–4.

8 Bronze serpent staff

L 164.0 cm
Early 18th Dynasty, c. 1500 BC
Thebes, Birabi tomb 37
London, British Museum, EA 52831

Snakes feature prominently in Egyptian mythology as both positive and negative forces. Several deities were depicted in snake form, such as Wadjit, Weret-hekau and Meretseger, but snakes were also perceived as enemies. They were believed to attack both the living and the dead: the great serpent Apep was the most formidable foe of the sun-god during his journey through the night. Having control over a snake neutralized its hostile force and enabled the controller to use its magical powers protectively or offensively. For this reason protector-gods were frequently depicted grasping serpents (see cat. nos 94 and 101).

The concept of the snake as a symbol of magical power probably explains the form of this staff, which was found in the coffin of its owner, a man named Mentuhotep. Its cobra shape may be connected with the snake-goddess Weret-hekau, whose name means 'the Great of Magic'. Snake-shaped wands or rods were employed by magic-users in the same contexts as ivory wands (see cat. no. 6). The Old Testament Bible story in which the pharaoh's magicians transform their staffs into living snakes perhaps also reflects a tradition of such staffs being used in Egyptian magic.

Reeves and Taylor 1992, 97; Pinch 2006, 10–11, fig. 3.

9 **A decree to keep its owner safe from dangers**

Ink on papyrus
L 50.0 cm; W 5.5 cm
Third Intermediate Period, *c.* 1069–664 BC
Provenance unrecorded
London, British Museum, EA 10321

From the 21st and 22nd Dynasties comes a series of narrow strips of papyrus, densely covered with hieratic texts which were designed to protect the owner against a wide range of threats and misfortunes. The documents are oracular decrees by deities such as Amun, Mut and Khons, and are thought to have been procured from temples by parents on behalf of young children. The decrees promise protection from a wide range of misfortunes.

In this example the composite god Montu-Ra-Horakhty promises to keep Paditwerisheru healthy in every part of his body, and to protect him from various demons, from every kind of 'evil magic', from the bites of snakes and scorpions and from illnesses of every kind. These charms were thought to work by containing the words of the god in writing. The documents were rolled up tightly, secured with a cord and placed inside hollow cylindrical containers of gold, wood or leather. These would be worn around the neck as amulets. Though the fears which they address are mainly those encountered in life, other examples of this genre of text were incorporated into the Book of the Dead in the Late Period (see cat. no. 14).

Edwards 1960, 29–33, pls X–XIA.

10 **A healing stela (*cippus*)**

Steatite
H 19.5 cm; W 13.0 cm
Sixth–third centuries BC
Provenance unrecorded
London, British Museum, EA 36250

The principles of Egyptian protective magic were essentially the same whether used on behalf of the living or the dead. This *cippus*, or healing stela, bears a sculpted image of the child-deity Horus-Shed, whose protective and healing powers are explained by his pose: standing on crocodiles, and grasping snakes and scorpions in his hands, he is triumphant over the dangers with which those creatures menace the living. Other deities, including Heka, the personification of magic (third register, second from left), are depicted at each side, many of them also armed with serpents. Such stelae were set up in temple courtyards and other public places, where people could approach them directly to obtain divine aid to heal the bites of snakes and scorpions. Water poured over the stela was believed to acquire curative powers. Deities holding snakes also appear frequently in the Book of the Dead as guardians of gateways and protectors of the deceased.

Robins 1997, 244, fig. 293; Pinch 2006, 20, fig. 7.

11 An amulet with its spell from the Book of the Dead

Carnelian
H 4.6 cm; W 2.0 cm
18th Dynasty, *c.* 1400 BC
Provenance unrecorded
London, British Museum, EA 20624

Several spells in the Book of the Dead conveyed magical power to amulets. Spell 156 relates to the *tit*, or knot of Isis, a representation of the tie of a sash which placed its owner under the protection of the goddess. This example is incised with part of the text of the spell. The spell was often accompanied by detailed instructions for its use and a recommendation of its virtue:

> To be said over a knot amulet of red jasper, moistened with juice of the 'life-is-in-it' fruit and embellished with sycamore-bast and placed on the neck of the deceased on the day of interment. As for him for whom this is done, the power of Isis will be the protection of his body, and Horus son of Isis will rejoice over him when he sees him; no path will be hidden from him, and one side of him will be towards the sky and the other towards the earth. A true matter; you shall not let anyone see it in your hand, for there is nothing equal to it.

Spell for a knot amulet of red jasper:

You have your blood, O Isis; you have your power, O Isis; you have your magic, O Isis. The amulet is a protection for this Great One, which will drive away whoever would commit a crime against him.

(Spell 156)

12 A funerary statuette (shabti) with its spell from the Book of the Dead

Painted and gilded wood
H 22.5 cm
19th Dynasty, c. 1280 BC
Provenance unrecorded (probably Thebes)
London, British Museum, EA 34113

The figurines called shabtis acted as substitutes for their owners to work on their behalf in the afterlife (see p. 245). Spell 6 of the Book of the Dead activated these figures. The earliest version of the text (in spell 472 of the Coffin Texts) includes instructions for its use: 'To be spoken over an image of the owner as he was on earth, made of tamarisk or zizyphus wood and placed [in] the chapel of the deceased.' This figure, made for Pashed, is typical in representing the deceased in mummy form, holding hoes to perform his agricultural tasks (see p. 245). The text of the shabti spell is carved on the body.

Spell for causing a shabti to do work for a man in the realm of the dead:

O shabti, allotted to me, if I be summoned or if I be detailed to do any work which has to be done in the realm of the dead; if indeed obstacles are implanted for you therewith as a man at his duties, you shall detail yourself for me on every occasion of making arable the fields, of flooding the banks or of conveying sand from east to west; 'Here I am', you shall say.

(Spell 6)

13 **A heart-scarab amulet with its spell from the Book of the Dead**

Basalt and gold
L of scarab 6.5 cm; max. D of ring 11.8 cm
18th–19th Dynasties, *c.* 1400–1200 BC
Provenance unrecorded
London, British Museum, EA 29626

Spell 30B prevented the owner's heart from testifying against him at the judgement of the dead (see p. 209). The words were usually inscribed on a scarab-shaped amulet, and the instructions for the spell explain how the amulet was to be made and used: 'To be inscribed on a scarab made from *nemehef*, mounted in fine gold, with a ring of silver, and placed at the throat of the deceased.' The prescribed material, *nemehef*, was an unidentified green stone. Heart scarabs were actually made from a variety of dark-coloured stones. On this example the abbreviated text of the spell is carved on the base, with a blank space left for the name of the owner, which was never inserted. Hence it was made in advance and purchased from stock. Gold foil has been applied to the surround and the suspension loop. The rigid neck-band is made of gold foil over a core of some other material; it takes the form of a snake and, when closed, would appear to be eating its tail – a symbol of eternity.

Andrews 2000, 126–7.

O my heart of my mother! O my heart of my mother! O my heart of my different forms! Do not stand up as a witness against me, do not be opposed to me in the tribunal, do not be hostile to me in the presence of the Keeper of the Balance, for you are my ka *which was in my body, the protector who made my members hale. Go forth to the happy place whereto we speed; do not make my name stink to the Entourage who make men. Do not tell lies about me in the presence of the god. It is indeed well that you should hear!*

(Spell 30B)[5]

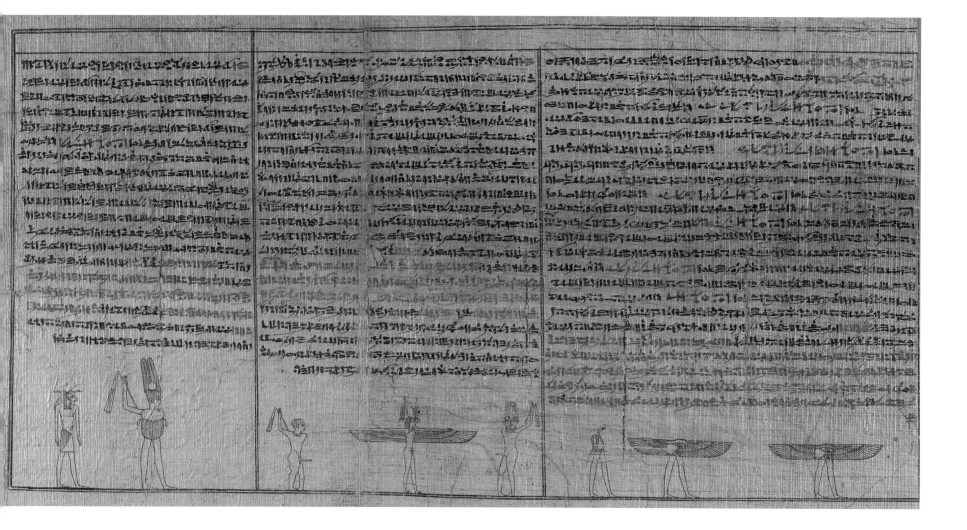

14 Treating death as an illness: spells 163–5 in the Book of the Dead of Ankhwahibra

Ink on papyrus
Average H 27.0 cm
Late 26th Dynasty, 550–525 BC
Provenance unrecorded (probably Memphite necropolis)
London, British Museum, EA 10558/28

Spells for the living and the dead were not always rigidly distinguished. Some straddle these categories, as illustrated by the three spells 163–5, which were added to the Book of the Dead in the Late Period 'from another papyrus, as additions to coming forth by day'. This source document is stated to have come from the Delta city of Tanis. Though the spells protected the body and ensured admittance to the afterlife, the colophon of spell 163 states that the text could be used 'upon earth' to preserve the person from injury and death, and from being condemned in the tribunal. Other features of these spells hint at their origins in the context of magic for the living. The wording and the illustrations recall those of healing spells of the Ramesside period. The gods invoked, such as Amun and Mut, were not funerary deities, but were among those who provided oracular protection for the living (see cat. no. 9). The vignettes depict them as strange composite beings, drawn according to very precise instructions which are cited in the colophons to the spells. To increase the impression that the spells were mysterious, some of the words were written in a manner which suggested that they were of foreign origin. By including such spells in the Book of the Dead, the scribes of the Late Period acknowledged an ancient approach to death as analogous to an illness which could be treated with healing remedies.

Mosher 1992, 155–6; Quirke 1993, 32, no. 23; Bohleke 1997, 162–3; Munro 2010.

15 A single spell from the Book of the Dead used as a charm

Ink on papyrus
H 41.0 cm; W 62.0 cm
19th Dynasty, *c.* 1250 BC
Thebes
Reading Museum Service, REDMG: 1998.29.1

While most manuscripts of the Book of the Dead contained a selection of spells – sometimes more than a hundred – there are also examples of papyri on which only one spell was written, such as this specimen from the burial of Henutmehyt (see cat. nos 38, 46, 48–51, 54, 134 and 135). It is said to have been found wrapped around the mummy in the coffin. The cursive hieroglyphic text contains spell 100 for 'going aboard the barque of Ra', and has an illustration of the god's boat. The text was first inscribed in red ink and then overwritten using a white pigment made from magnesium silicate (see p. 270). The name of the serpent Apep was left in red. By using a special ink on a new piece of papyrus, and by placing the sheet over the body, those who prepared Henutmehyt's burial were closely following the prescription in the rubric for this spell. This stated that it should be 'written on a clean blank roll with powder of green glaze mixed with water of myrrh. To be placed on the breast of the blessed dead ...'. In this it parallels the practice of writing a text on a separate sheet as an amulet or charm for use by the living (see cat. no.9).

Taylor 1999, 63–4, col. pl. XVI; Illés 2006, 123, 125, 127–9.

16 **A text for use at a religious festival: spell 134 from the papyrus of Nebseny**

Ink on papyrus
H 35.8 cm
18th Dynasty, c. 1400 BC
Memphite necropolis
London, British Museum, EA 9900/6

There is a group of spells in the Book of the Dead for use by the living that were to be pronounced on the days when religious festivals were held at the temples of the gods. An example is spell 134. Its title is 'for making a spirit worthy' and its purpose as a funerary text was to ensure that the deceased triumphed over his enemies. The ritual context in which it was first used is described in the last four columns of the spell as it appears in the papyrus of Nebseny:

To be spoken over a falcon standing with the White Crown on his head; Atum, Shu and Tefnut, Geb and Nut, Osiris and Isis, Seth and Nephthys being drawn in ochre [sic] on a new bowl placed in the sacred barque, together with an image of this spirit (ba) whom you wish to be made worthy, it being anointed with oil. Offer to them incense on the fire and roasted ducks, and worship Ra. It means that he for whom this is done will voyage and be with Ra every day in every place he desires to travel, and it means that the enemies of Ra will be driven off in very deed. A matter a million times true.

The vignette shows Nebseny and his daughter Tentmennefer before a barque in which stands a row of gods and goddesses corresponding closely, but not exactly, to those in the spell.

Lapp 2004, pl. 16; Eaton 2005–2006.

17 Pottery bowls used in association with spells

Clay with ink and pigment
D 28.5 cm (EA 5137), 28.6 cm (EA 5138), 32.3 cm (EA 5141)
Late New Kingdom or Third Intermediate Period, c. 1150–750 BC
Probably from Abydos
London, British Museum, EA 5137, 5138, 5141

Evidence for the correct performance of rituals such as that described in spell 134 of the Book of the Dead includes redware pottery bowls on which images of gods have been drawn. The first of these (EA 5137) shows the deities who are specified in the papyrus of Nebseny (see cat. no. 16). Others have a single figure of Osiris or another god, perhaps relating to different spells. Bowls of this kind have been found at temple sites, notably at Abydos, the cult centre of Osiris.

Eaton 2005–2006.

18 The Perovski Stone: an unusual Book of the Dead document (replica)

H of original 14.5 cm; W 16.5 cm; D 2.0 cm
26th Dynasty, c. 650–630 BC
Original perhaps from the tomb of Padiamenope, Asasif, Thebes
London, British Museum, EA 29553

This is a facsimile of a slab of dark green stone (perhaps serpentine) with parts of spells 26, 30 and 64 of the Book of the Dead inscribed on both sides and around its edge. The original was once in the possession of a Russian army officer named Perovski and is now in the Hermitage Museum in St Petersburg (Inv. 1101). The main inscription on the stone is spell 64 of the Book of the Dead, a special text which enabled the owner to know all the spells for coming forth by day. Some copies of this spell include an account of its alleged discovery in the reign of King Den (1st Dynasty, c. 2950 BC) on a brick in the foundations of a temple of the god Sokar. The strange irregular shape of the stone, unique among Book of the Dead documents, provokes speculation: could it have been created as an exact copy of the brick on which the text of spell 64 was reputedly discovered, or is the dark green material the *nemehef* stone, which was prescribed in spell 30 for the making of amulets (see cat. no. 13)? It is perhaps no coincidence that the object also bears the name of the Chief Lector Priest Padiamenope (c. 650–630 BC?), whose enormous tomb on the Theban west bank contained very full and accurate copies of many important funerary texts. He has been tentatively suggested as one of the key figures in the revival of the Book of the Dead tradition in the seventh century BC, and might then have had an interest in owning copies of source documents of some of the spells.

Landa and Lapis 1974, no. 118; Säve-Söderbergh 1993.

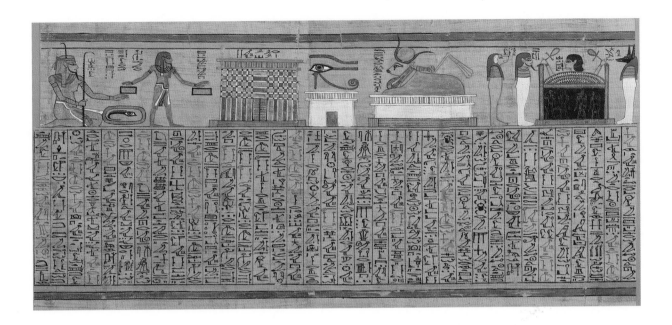

19 The importance of knowledge: spell 17 in the Book of the Dead of Ani

Painted papyrus
H 42.0 cm
19th Dynasty, c. 1275 BC
Thebes
London, British Museum, EA 10470/8

Many of the spells in the Book of the Dead 'worked' by means of the deceased assuming the persona of a god or making references to myths, deities and sacred places so as to demonstrate his knowledge of religious matters. Spell 17 was one of the most important texts in the Book of the Dead (see p. 35). It had a long history, and occurs among the Coffin Texts as spell 335. In the New Kingdom it was given special prominence, and is often found near to the beginning of papyri. The spell has sometimes been described as the quintessence of the Book of the Dead, summarizing the main purposes of the entire corpus. Much of the text consists of a series of statements about the creator-god Atum, with many allusions to episodes in myths. The long series of illustrations which runs above the words expounds different parts of the text in pictorial form.

Spell 17 is a particularly obscure text and many passages were open to different interpretations. Included within the body of the text are glosses (indicated by some words in red) – alternative versions of phrases, and explanations of the symbolic meaning of names and expressions (see overleaf).

Since these glosses appear in some of the earliest Coffin Text versions of the spell their function may have been less to clarify obscurities than to allow a wider range of possibilities for interpretation.

The section illustrated shows, at the left, the two fecundity deities who are mentioned in the passage quoted overleaf. The kneeling figure with watery body is Heh, god of Eternity, and the standing figure is named as 'Great Green' (the Egyptian term for 'sea'). With their hands they protect two miniature bodies of water, the 'Lake of Natron' and the 'Lake of Maat', places of purification and rebirth. Next to these is an elaborate panelled doorway, named as Rosetjau (a term which denoted the Netherworld realm of Osiris), the *wedjat* (Eye of Horus), the celestial cow Mehet-weret, and a coffin-shaped chest from which a human head emerges, the Sons of Horus standing around it in protection.

British Museum 1890, pl. 8; British Museum 1894, pl. 8; Munro 1988, 296 (b. 1); Quirke 1993, 32 (no. 24).

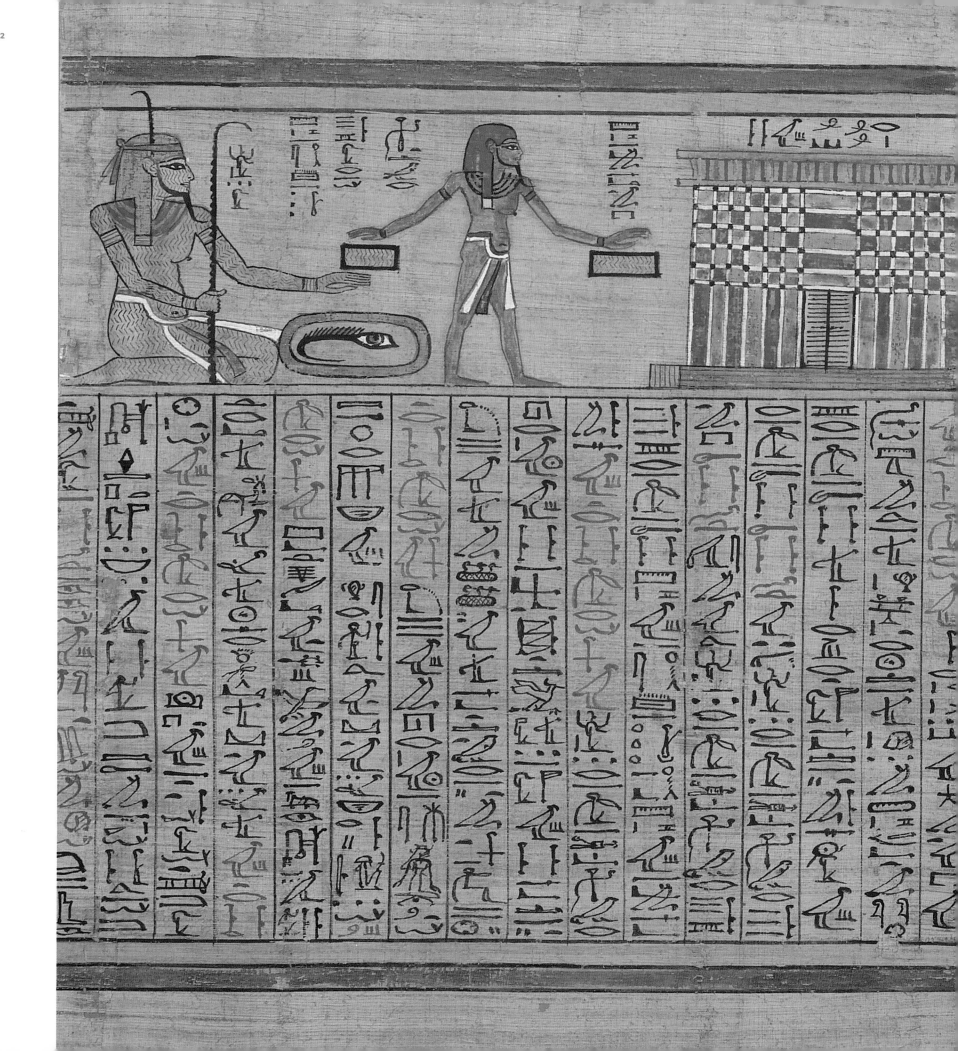

*All the evil which was on me has
been removed.*
What does that mean? *It means
that I was cleansed on the day
of my birth in the two great
and noble marshes which are in
Heracleopolis on the day when
the common folk make offerings
to the Great God who is therein.*
What are they? *'Eternity' is
the name of one; 'Sea' is the name
of the other. They are the Lake
of Natron and the Lake of Maat.
Otherwise said: 'Eternity governs'
is the name of one; 'Sea' is the
name of the other.
Otherwise said: 'Seed of Eternity'
is the name of one; 'Sea' is the
name of the other. As for that
Great God who is therein, he is
Ra himself.* (Spell 17)

3 The Evolution of the Book of the Dead

Irmtraut Munro

THE Book of the Dead was the most popular and longest-lasting collection of funerary texts created by the ancient Egyptians for the protection and guidance of the deceased. It came into use before the beginning of the New Kingdom (*c.* 1550 BC) and remained widespread for more than a millennium and a half.

The Pyramid Texts and Coffin Texts

The Pyramid Texts are the oldest collection of religious writings from Egypt. They first appeared at the end of the 5th Dynasty on the internal walls of the burial chamber and adjoining rooms of the pyramid of King Unas (fig. 14). All the texts reflect the importance that was attached to securing the king's existence in the afterlife and enabling him to become part of the cosmic order. At this early period the Netherworld was thought to be located in the sky and ruled by the sun-god Ra, the pharaoh's heavenly father, to whose barque the dead king had to ascend in order to join him (see p.23).

Besides hymns, prayers, litanies and magical spells for warding off dangerous animals, compositions such as ritual spells predominated. No illustrations or headings yet accompanied the texts, which were written in a very special orthography: many of the hieroglyphs of human beings or animals were incomplete or mutilated by knives so that they could not cause any harm to the dead king (see p. 34).[1] In the 6th Dynasty these exclusively royal funerary texts were also made available to queens. Later, coinciding with the decline of centralized power and the breakdown of the Old Kingdom, local governors and high-ranking officials started to decorate their tombs and coffins with these royal funerary texts. They also adopted the royal privilege of identifying themselves with Osiris, god of the Netherworld, who had according to myth triumphed over death and therefore embodied the hope of resurrection (see p. 19).

Although Pyramid Texts continued to be used on coffins in the Middle Kingdom, a new text corpus was created, the so-called Coffin Texts, which predominated in the cemeteries of Middle Egypt. They were mainly written on the inner surfaces of wooden coffins (see cat. no. 20), but sometimes also occurred on tomb walls or papyri. Three surviving papyri, one of them in the British Museum, most probably functioned as master copies.[2] We find spells based on the Pyramid Texts together with newly composed spells, now in a 'modernized' grammar (in other words an updated contemporary language). In contrast to the Pyramid Texts the editors now added headings to the spells and included some illustrations, although these were still rare. The Pyramid Texts and the Coffin Texts continued to be an important source for funerary inscriptions in later centuries after the emergence of the Book of the Dead.[3]

Both of these genres of religious texts derive their names from their location in royal pyramids and on coffins respectively. The Book of the Dead differed in that it was in most cases a papyrus roll. Its modern name, first coined by the Egyptologist Richard Lepsius (see pp. 289–90),

Fig. 14 Burial chamber of the pyramid of King Unas. Saqqara, *c.* 2345 BC.

was probably taken from the term used by Egyptian workers on excavations when they found such manuscripts. However, today this term does not denote a single Book of the Dead roll but is conventionally used to mean the whole text corpus of the Book of the Dead. The ancient Egyptians themselves called this funerary composition the 'book of coming forth by day'.

The emergence of the Book of the Dead

It was at Thebes, the centre of the redaction of the text, where the creation of the new text corpus took place at the beginning of the Second Intermediate Period (*c.* 1700 BC). Many of the nearly 200 spells which comprised this collection were based on the Coffin Texts, but completely new spells were also compiled. The earliest occurrence of Book of the Dead spells is found on the coffin of Queen Mentuhotep, which according to the latest research should be dated to the 13th Dynasty.[4] This highly important documentary source was found at Thebes and was fortunately copied by the Egyptologist J.G. Wilkinson before it was lost. The inscriptions consist both of Coffin Texts and new Book of the Dead spells which had no precursors among the Coffin Texts. Another document from the same period as the 'lost' coffin of Mentuhotep is a fragmentary coffin belonging to Prince Herunefer, and illustrates the beginning of the use of Book of the Dead texts for members of the royal family.[5] It appears that in its initial phase the Book of the Dead underwent a lengthy process of composition and was not yet fully developed. The range of spells was limited and the spell sequences differed considerably from the later sources of the 17th Dynasty and the beginning of the New Kingdom. By that time the new Book of the Dead texts had been ordered more systematically in a pattern which was in common use and is attested on many Book of the Dead documents for members of the royal families, courtiers and non-royal officials.[6]

Although the texts are once attested on an anthropoid coffin of Queen Satdjehuty, they were mostly inscribed on linen shrouds, which were wrapped tightly around the bodies of the deceased. An important reason for doing this was to place the powerful magical spells at the deceased's disposal whenever they might be needed. Besides such shrouds, only a few examples of these texts on papyrus are known from the beginning of the 18th Dynasty. This practice changed a few generations later in the joint reign of Hatshepsut and Thutmose III.

Spells and vignettes in the New Kingdom

At the beginning of the New Kingdom an innovation in funerary customs took place in the replacement of rectangular sarcophagi with anthropoid coffins. These coffins lacked sufficient space on their surfaces to inscribe the new collection of funerary spells, a development which may have influenced the emergence and wide acceptance of papyrus rolls as the usual medium for the texts. Papyri of any length, with a variable number of spells, could be rolled up and put inside the coffin to be on hand if needed. By this time the range of spells known throughout the 18th Dynasty had been fully developed. But there existed no binding canon and order which an ideal Book of the Dead roll had to follow, no obligatory sequence of spells: almost every manuscript was unique and contained its own selection and arrangement. We know of complete surviving manuscripts measuring between nearly 20 metres (such as the Papyrus of Nu: see cat. nos 64, 66, 88 and 102) and about 6 metres (such as the Papyrus of Nebqed, cat. no. 41). The individual

Fig. 15 The Book of the Dead owner Tjenena and his wife in adoration before Osiris. 18th Dynasty. Musée du Louvre, N 3074.

Fig. 16 *Ba*-bird hovering above the corpse from the Book of the Dead of Tjenena. 18th Dynasty. Musée du Louvre, N 3074.

selection from the range of spells was made at the special request of the customer and was also influenced by his financial capacities.

Nonetheless, the ideal 18th Dynasty Book of the Dead roll addressed certain key themes which were considered essential for the deceased's existence in the afterlife. The most frequent themes, or main spells, were as follows. After an elaborate introductory adoration scene (fig. 15) we often find spell 1 (see cat. no. 33), which is an allusion to the deceased's arrival in the Netherworld. One of the most lengthy and complex spells is number 17, which refers to the various characteristics of the creator-god Atum and the deceased's identification with him (see cat. no. 19). There are spells for securing essential abilities (21–5), heart spells (26–30), spells against potentially dangerous animals (31–40; see cat. nos 89–91), groups of spells for providing air to breathe or water to drink in the necropolis (38, 54–6 and 57–63). There are also transformation spells, which refer to the deceased's transformation into different forms, such as a living *ba* (see p. 17), a lotus as a symbol of rebirth, a snake, a crocodile or even the creator-god Ptah (spells 76–88; see cat nos 87–8). Spell 89 was intended to ensure the unification of the *ba*-bird with the body through the *ba*'s ability to move freely on earth and to return regularly by night to the corpse (fig. 16) through the tomb shaft (cat. no. 41). The ferryboat spells refer to the journey through the Netherworld, where the deceased has to pass an inquiry about the names of the various parts of ships (spells 98–9). Another important group of spells (100–2 and 130–6) focuses on the journey of the deceased in the sun barque. This daily course across the sky in the company of the sun-god Ra and his divine passengers guarantees his participation in the god's daily rebirth and in being part of the everlasting cyclical system (see p. 19). Extensive space is reserved for the gate spells, which provide knowledge of the names of the gates and their demon-like guardians (see pp. 136–7). Likewise, knowledge and information about mysterious regions, the fourteen mounds of the Netherworld, were supplied by spell 149/150 (see pp. 137–8). The idea of a judgement on the moral conduct of the deceased before Osiris and a divine tribunal is expressed in spell 125, where the dead man has to make a declaration of his innocence (see pp. 207–9). This spell seems to form the core of each roll, although it is first found in the joint reign of Hatshepsut and Thutmose III in the 18th Dynasty, which was generally a time of great activity in the production and spread of Book of the Dead manuscripts.

Illustrations or vignettes, which only occur exceptionally in the early manuscripts, now accompany the text more frequently. Most of the vignettes are closely linked thematically to their corresponding spells. The motifs were meant to be the visualization of the spell's essential idea and evoked as much magic power as the written word (see p. 33). In some cases the depiction, such as that of a striding human figure, occasionally with a staff, seems to be a rather neutral motif without any obvious link to the text. Yet this figure was considered to be the complete embodiment of the deceased, equipped with his staff of authority and fully active, whom no enemy could harm (fig. 17). During the New Kingdom the vignettes varied in number and manner of colouring, but in the 19th Dynasty there is a tendency towards more glamorous and elaborately designed vignettes, which sometimes led to lack of care in the writing of the text.[7]

The Amarna period at the end of the 18th Dynasty marked a major hiatus in the production of Book of the Dead rolls, since the traditional view of the afterlife was temporarily repudiated. So far no document has been preserved from this period, although, in the years which immediately followed, Tutankhamun himself was provided with amulets and funerary objects related to Book of the Dead vignettes or decorated with Book of the Dead spells, such as the well-known gilded shrines found in his tomb. It is obvious that the emphasis on the sun-god in the religion of this period created stimuli for incorporating new spells and various illustrated solar and other hymns into the Book of the Dead repertoire (see cat. no. 129). For the first time the long spell 17 found its corresponding vignette (see cat. no. 19).

Fig. 17 Striding figure of the Book of the Dead owner Amenemhat. 18th Dynasty. Private collection.

Developments in the Third Intermediate Period
While Book of the Dead papyri in a cursive form of hieroglyphic writing followed the old tradition and types, manuscripts in hieratic script (a swifter style of handwriting) occurred with no illustration other than a full-size introductory vignette. Most of these papyri were limited to half of the traditional height (i.e. 18 cm) and contained fewer Book of the Dead spells, so they

must have been much cheaper in price. However, they were considered to be just as protective as the long rolls due to the *pars pro toto* principle (whereby a part of a text or vignette could magically function as effectively as the complete version). Many owners now had a second funerary papyrus of another book of the Netherworld, the Amduat (previously a royal prerogative), either a shortened version or one which showed the sun's journey for the last four hours of the night, or only the twelfth hour depicting the rebirth of the sun-god. The influential priestly class of the Theban State of Amun adopted this exclusively royal funerary literature for their own benefit (see cat. nos 28 and 106). The two funerary papyri of different genres were considered complementary.[8] In some cases yet a third type of funerary composition complemented the ensemble, the so-called mythological papyri: manuscripts full of mysterious illustrations of the Netherworld and magical figures, partly interwoven with vignettes alluding to the Book of the Dead, which reflected the creative and rich religious imagery of their time.

The Saite recension

Throughout the long tradition of Book of the Dead production, many revisions of its text can be observed, owing to the corruptions which resulted from the transmission of the text from one master copy or manuscript to another. But no revision was more fundamental than the 'Saite recension', so called because this new version came into widespread use in the 26th (Saite) Dynasty. The anonymous authors of the Saite recension canonized the contents of the Book of the Dead, and defined its sequence and vignettes more rigidly.[9] Systematic research and investigation must have taken place during the 25th Dynasty, leading to the copying of monuments and documents from the past, a characteristic of the general archaism of this time.[10] Thebes, which had developed as a religious centre since the beginning of the composition of Book of the Dead texts and had remained the focus of the tradition during the Third Intermediate Period and later, was probably the source of this comprehensive revision. At the end of the 25th Dynasty the highest-ranking Theban individuals had access to archives and were able to equip their tombs with a collection of Book of the Dead texts and other religious compositions.[11] Moreover, most of the manuscripts of the 26th Dynasty, the period after the recension, derive from Thebes. In their layout they recall Theban manuscripts of the joint reign of Hatshepsut and Thutmose III in the 18th Dynasty. This period was regarded by later generations as one of Egypt's most prosperous 'golden ages', which they wanted to revive.[12] The Saite recension not only reworked the text and supplemented it with compositions of Theban origin (spells 162–5),[13] but also codified the range and spell sequence of the entire corpus, as known from the standard edition, based on the Turin papyrus of Iuefankh (see p. 288, fig. 83).[14] The edition established a consecutive numbering of the spells, which became the standardized order in manuscripts of the Late and Ptolemaic Periods.

Developments in the Late and Ptolemaic Periods

A full canonized version of the Book of the Dead roll with the ideal complement of 165 spells might be considered a standard handbook from which the deceased could be supplied a selection of spells, but in reality such rolls survive in much smaller numbers than abbreviated manuscripts. Even by the Late Period there was no obligatory rule as to the extent of a proper

Fig. 18 The deceased receives liquid from a tree goddess (spell 59). Detail from a shroud, second/third century AD. Hildesheim, Pelizaeaus-Museum, LH 3l.

Book of the Dead document. The scribes would simply copy a selection of spells from a standardized full version for the benefit of the deceased. The same procedure also applied to the inscribed mummy wrappings. They occur from the fourth century BC onwards, and had their main centre in the northern necropoleis (see cat. no. 32). Because of the limited height of the strips many metres of linen were required to copy the contents of the 'canonical' text. In some cases a complete set was formed of successive strips with a consecutive numbering, measuring about 50 metres in length.[15]

In the 26th Dynasty (seventh century BC) all the attested papyri were written in hieratic (see fig. 20), whereas in the following epochs both hieratic and hieroglyphic scripts were used. In the second half of the Ptolemaic Period there was a significant decline in Book of the Dead manuscripts, manifested in severely shortened texts and carelessly executed vignettes.[16] This demise was probably linked to the rise in production of other funerary compositions – the various 'Documents of Breathing' and the 'Book of Traversing Eternity' – which were now becoming very popular at Thebes.[17] Occasionally traditional Book of the Dead spells were interwoven with these new mortuary compositions, which would also ensure the afterlife: the wish for breathing air and for water, or the justification by Osiris demonstrated in the full-size judgement scene (see cat. no. 111) remained important. The reasons for this rapid decline cannot be fully explained. There may have been a lack of literate scribes who possessed the necessary understanding of the now 'old-fashioned' Book of the Dead spells, which had been composed in a language that was spoken more than a thousand years earlier. The purchasers also perhaps preferred their Netherworld guides to be written in the more easily understandable contemporary demotic language, the successor of the hieroglyphic and hieratic scripts.

In the first century BC, after a long tradition lasting more than a millennium and a half, the Book of the Dead as a corpus of funerary literature finally came to its end,[18] although Book of the Dead motifs on large shrouds survived into Roman times (fig. 18).

The Book of the Dead in different media

Besides inscribed shrouds, which were in use from the very early stage of Book of the Dead production until the reign of Amenhotep II – one of the latest shrouds discovered is that of Thutmose III (produced on order by his son Amenhotep II; see p. 66) – and in rare cases leather rolls with Book of the Dead spells, the papyrus roll became the most frequent medium for these texts. Book of the Dead spells are also attested on coffins as early as the end of the 13th Dynasty and the beginning of the 18th Dynasty, but in the following generations they rarely appear on coffins except for royal sarcophagi and a few Book of the Dead vignettes on Ramesside coffins. It was during the Third Intermediate Period and the 25th Dynasty that the custom of copying the spells or vignettes onto coffins came into vogue, remaining popular during the 26th Dynasty and throughout the Ptolemaic era (see cat. no. 29).

While the kings had their tomb chambers decorated with different Books of the Netherworld (fig. 19), which were at first exclusively royal compositions, some high-ranking Egyptians in the joint reign of Hatshepsut and Thutmose III covered their tomb chambers with spells from the Book of the Dead. However, this practice remained an exception until the Ramesside period,[19] when Book of the Dead spells also found their way into royal tombs. Some Book of the

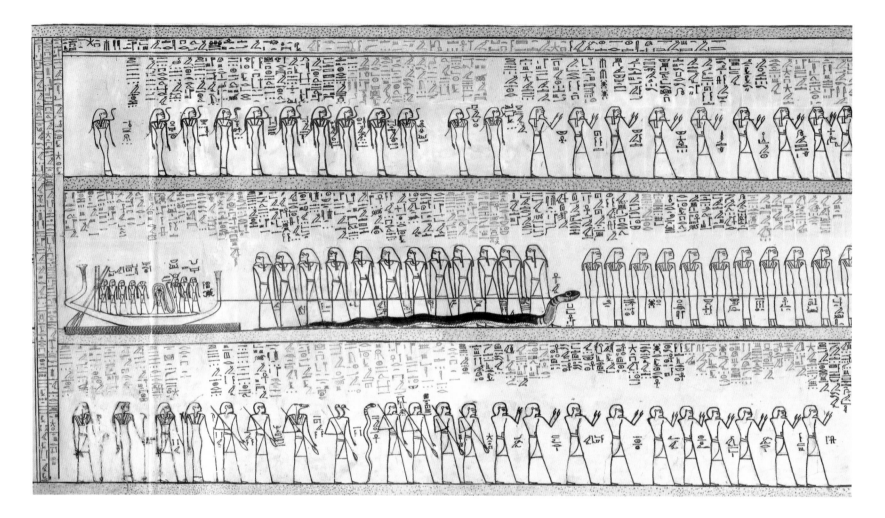

Fig. 19 12th hour of Amduat in the burial chamber of the tomb of Thutmose III. Valley of the Kings, *c.* 1425 BC.

Dead vignettes also appeared on temple walls, as attested at Medinet Habu, the mortuary temple of Ramesses III. During the Amarna period, when the traditional concept of the Netherworld was abandoned, the Book of the Dead was not used, but this short phase with its predominantly solar emphasis did influence the occurrence of sun hymns, which became especially popular on stelae of the following Ramesside period.

Single Book of the Dead spells were written on various objects of funerary equipment. Shabti figurines usually bear spell 6 for avoiding labour in the Netherworld, for example in the Field of Reed (see cat. nos 134–6), by activating the statuette as a substitute for the deceased (see pp. 244–5). Heart scarabs carry spell 30B to command the heart not to testify against its owner at the tribunal (see cat. nos 117–20). Some headrests have abbreviations of spell 166 for securing the head (see cat. no. 83).[20] Even small amulets, such as a snake, a swallow or a heron found inside the mummy wrappings of Tutankhamun, are clear allusions to the corresponding Book of the Dead vignette and its spell, and were enough to confer their entire protective power on the owner.[21] In the Late Period golden amulets such as the *djed* pillar, the symbol for stability and endurance, were provided, with reference to spell 155 (see cat. no. 59); the *djed* also had a role as one of the amulets of the four magic bricks (see cat. nos 48–51). It was not before the Late Period that the custom of producing mummy wrappings with Book of the Dead texts came into vogue. The majority of these consisted of narrow strips of linen filled with a few lines of text and the accompanying vignette (cat. no. 32). In contrast to the early shrouds, the strips were wrapped around each limb of the corpse and enclosed the whole body like an amulet case.[22] Disc-shaped objects known as hypocephali also came into use in the Late Period as bearers of spell 162 (see cat. no. 61). They were placed under the deceased's head for protection and to evoke warmth and light as expressed in the corresponding spell.

The placement of the rolls and mummy wrappings in the tomb

Only Book of the Dead papyri which derive from controlled excavations or from intact burials can give us information about the position of their storage. It appears that there was no exact instruction as to where a Book of the Dead roll should be positioned, either outside or inside the coffin. It might be placed on the upper part of the body, under the arms, between the thighs or under the head, like the roll of Iahtesnakht (fig. 20). In any case, the roll had to be in close contact with the deceased to enable him to activate personal empowerment, knowledge, provisions or divine helpers. Dark spots caused by the liquids used in the mummification process, which appear regularly on the inscribed mummy wrappings, make it quite clear that they were placed directly on the body, but there are also cases in which linen rolls were placed on the body without being wrapped around it. The same applies to some large shrouds which were folded tightly and stored near the corpse.[23] In Ptolemaic times we know of a few cases where even papyrus sheets were placed around the deceased, a custom practised at Akhmim and at Thebes,[24] apparently a reversion to an old custom from the beginning of the production of the Book of the Dead (fig. 21). But there is one distinctive funerary object which is closely connected

Fig. 20 Book of the Dead of Iahtesnakht, 25th/26th Dynasty. Universität zu Köln, Aeg 10207/20.

Fig. 21 Mummy of Nes-shu covered with a Book of the Dead papyrus. Ptolemaic Period, 305–30 BC. Musée d'Yverdon et région.

Fig. 22 A self-made copy of a Book of the Dead papyrus on the shroud of Siaa. Cairo, J.E. 33984.

with the storage of funerary papyri inside the tomb: the Ptah-Sokar-Osiris statuette (see cat. no. 25). The oldest known example of the practice is the 19th Dynasty papyrus of Hunefer (cat. nos 34–5 and 160), which was found inside a statue representing the god Ptah-Sokar-Osiris. The base or the body of the figure contained a cavity, in which the papyrus roll lay under the protection of the god. Ptah-Sokar-Osiris statues were in frequent use during the Third Intermediate Period, such as that which contained the papyrus of Anhai (cat. no. 26).[25]

The owners of Book of the Dead rolls

The majority of Egyptians could afford neither effective mummification nor a Book of the Dead roll, much less a tomb. They had to be content with some pottery for offerings, a linen cloth to be wrapped in and burial in the arid desert sand. A minority of less than 10 per cent of the population had the necessary financial resources to buy a Book of the Dead roll as funerary equipment. We only have a rough idea about the price of a roll: one *deben* of silver, which had an equivalent value of about three asses.[26] Papyrus itself was not cheap – we know enough cases of papyrus sheets that were erased and reused – and the coloured pigments for the decoration were extremely expensive. Furthermore, the cost of an illustrated Book of the Dead roll depended a great deal on the artistic abilities of the draughtsmen. Even in the tombs of Deir el-Medina, the village of the kings' tomb-builders, where we might expect a considerable in-house production, we fail to find many Book of the Dead manuscripts. The artisans – not of elite status – who were occupied with the manufacture of various funerary objects, were not skilled enough to craft a decorated copy of the Book of the Dead for themselves. So they had to purchase one or obtain it by exchange, which did not happen very often, perhaps because of the high price involved.[27] We do not know for certain of any individual of poor status who made his own Book of the Dead manuscript, except for the shroud of a certain Siaa: the crude and clumsy handwriting on this item is far below the standard of a skilled scribe, its text full of repetitions and errors (fig. 22).[28]

The social status of the owners of Books of the Dead has not yet been the subject of in-depth research. Nevertheless it is clear that most owners came from the upper strata of society, though the practice clearly changed over time. The coffins and linen shrouds which bore the first attestations of the Book of the Dead belonged to members of the royal family, females as well as males, who were certainly the highest-ranking people in society, followed at the beginning of the 18th Dynasty by members of the royal court and high officials of non-royal blood – one of them an immigrant of Asiatic name.[29] We know of some influential officials such as the vizier Useramun (also with parents of foreign origin), who owned two tombs and a Book of the Dead papyrus; or Sennefer, the mayor of Thebes, who could afford not only an elaborate tomb but also had a shroud and three different Book of the Dead rolls. The owners of many papyri held high administrative titles, such as overseer of all works, as one of the various scribes in secular and temple administration, or as priests of different kinds. But in many cases the papyri give no title at all, although their quality and sumptuous paintings can only suggest an owner who was a member of the social elite or of an elite family. Is it too speculative to assume that some of these papyri were crafted for beloved sons of rich families, who failed to achieve a conspicuous career because of their early deaths?

In the 18th and 19th Dynasties the majority of copies of the Book of the Dead (the

Fig. 23 The sumptuous gilding of the papyrus of Amenemhat. Ptolemaic Period, *c.* 320 BC. Royal Ontario Museum, Toronto.

proportion is about 10:1) were produced for men. Since the vignettes in most cases included a depiction of the owner's wife, a separate copy for her was perhaps considered unnecessary (see fig. 15).[30] Therefore, distinct copies written for women are relatively rare (see cat. no. 26). The proportion changed dramatically in the Third Intermediate Period, when a high percentage of copies were produced for women (about 68 per cent, archiving date 2009). Some of these women were of the highest social status, such as Nesitanebisheru (see cat. nos 93, 152 and 161) and other female members of the High Priest of Amun's family, who themselves held important religious titles in addition to their interrelations and marriages with the highest representatives of the state (see cat. no. 123 and p. 271). But a great number of female owners held no high-ranking titles linked with the cult of Amun at Thebes.

One of the two manuscripts known from the 25th Dynasty belonged to a woman who had a high official and a vizier as ancestors, and who was married to a member of one of the noblest families of the time.[31] In the Late and Ptolemaic Periods the proportion of female owners of Theban papyri, mostly of moderate length in hieratic script, and of mummy wrappings (the majority of which come from northern Egypt) is about a third of all known sources. However, their titles were not high-ranking – they were either housewives or sistrum-shakers. The male owners mostly held titles belonging to the middle and high clergy; some were also specified as a general, chief of the royal fleet or courtier of the pharaoh. Sometimes, however, only the costly and sumptuous draughtsmanship of a papyrus, or the voluminously applied gilding of the decoration can provide a clue as to the wealth and status of the owner (fig. 23).

20 A precursor of the Book of the Dead: Coffin Texts on the inner coffin of Seni

Painted cedar wood
L 215.5 cm; H 62.5 cm; W 61.0 cm
12th Dynasty, c. 1850 BC
From El-Bersha, probably Tomb 11
London, British Museum, EA 30842

Before the New Kingdom, the most important texts for the dead were inscribed on the surfaces of rectangular wooden coffins. The inscriptions on the exterior were often taken from mortuary liturgies: the words of the gods or the priests who played their parts in the rituals to resurrect the dead. The texts placed on the interior were chiefly to empower, protect and guide the deceased. This repertoire of spells had been derived from the Pyramid Texts, with many adaptations and additions. Known today as the Coffin Texts, they were the direct precursors of the Book of the Dead.

The Coffin Texts were generally inscribed in long columns on the inner walls of the coffin so as to be directly accessible by the deceased. They run continuously from column to column, but the phrase *djed medu*, 'words to be spoken', appears at the head of each column, emphasizing the nature of the texts as incantations. The Coffin Texts very rarely included illustrations, but above them there was often a pictorial frieze depicting clothing, jewellery, tools, weapons, writing equipment and other objects for the use of the occupant. This coffin was made for Seni, the chief physician of the governor of the Hare province in Upper Egypt. Although hundreds of such coffins have survived, only a small proportion of them contain Coffin Texts, which were evidently available only to the elite members of society.

Davies 1995, 147.

21 **The Book of the Dead on the shroud of King Thutmose III**

Ink on linen
H 63.5 cm; W 111.0 cm
18th Dynasty, *c.* 1425 BC
Royal Cache, Deir el-Bahri
Boston, Museum of Fine Arts, gift of Horace L. Mayer, 60.1472

During the late 17th and early 18th Dynasties spells from the Book of the Dead were inscribed in ink on the linen mummy shrouds of members of the royal family. Some of these shrouds have been found in the tombs of princes and princesses in the Valley of the Queens. The texts are written in cursive hieroglyphs without vignettes.

The mummy of King Thutmose III, found in the 'Royal Cache' at Deir el-Bahri, was also wrapped in an inscribed shroud, originally over 5 metres long. A dedication text records that it was made for him by his son and successor Amenhotep II. A portion of the shroud, now in the Egyptian Museum, Cairo, joins the left edge of the Boston fragment. The Cairo piece is covered with texts from the Litany of Ra, an address to the seventy-five different forms of the sun-god, and this and the Boston fragment also include spells from the Book of the Dead (numbers 1, 21–4, 90, 125, 154, 17, 18, 68, 69, 70, 75, 83–6, 88, 105) as well as short passages from the Pyramid Texts. The selection of texts on the shroud was evidently made according to a careful programme that related this item of the mummy's trappings to other elements of the king's burial arrangements. Thus, the sections of the Litany of Ra that appear on the shroud complemented other parts of that composition which were inscribed on the pillars in the antechamber of the king's tomb. This may suggest that, in its original state, Thutmose III's burial included further extracts from the Book of the Dead.

Dunham 1931; Nagel 1949; Ziegler 2002, 478, no. 238.

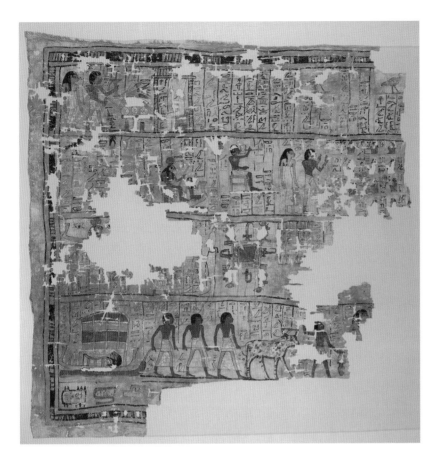

22 Mummy shroud with texts and vignettes from the Book of the Dead

Ink and paint on linen
H 134.5 cm; W 130.0 cm
Early 18th Dynasty, c. 1450 BC
Provenance unrecorded
London, British Museum, EA 73808

During the reign of Thutmose III the Book of the Dead began to appear on papyrus rolls and on the mummy shrouds of private individuals. This shroud illustrates the importance that was attached to the vignettes, which occupy at least as much space as the texts. The first three registers include words and illustrations from transformation spells, and spells for breathing air and knowing the gates of the Netherworld. In the fourth register is the scene of the transport of the mummy to the tomb, and below this (only partly preserved) some of the mound diagrams from spell 150 (see cat. nos 66–7) – here marking the end of the document, as often on papyri of the same period.

The texts contain spaces for the insertion of the names of the owner and his wife. These were not filled in, but what appear to be names have been inserted in a small hand in front of the faces of several of the figures. Thus the man at top left appears to be called Ka and a woman in the funeral procession is apparently Taperet (?).

23 **Rolled papyrus**

L 29.2 cm; D 6.5 cm
Third Intermediate Period (c. 1069–664 BC) or later?
Thebes
London, British Museum, EA 10748

24 **Rolled papyrus with clay seals**

L 18.6 cm
Third Intermediate Period (c. 1069–664 BC) or later?
Provenance unknown
London, British Museum, EA 36831

Books of the Dead on papyrus were usually tightly rolled. They were sometimes placed inside the coffin or within the wrappings of the mummy (see p. 61). In the late New Kingdom and Third Intermediate Period, one roll was often secreted inside the body or base of a wooden statuette of Osiris (see cat. no. 25). Some rolled documents were bound with narrow papyrus tapes, to which clay seals were affixed to ensure that the contents were not tampered with. The tapes that survive on the smaller roll recall the bindings which are depicted on the hieroglyphic sign for a book-roll. Since neither of these documents has been opened in modern times, their contents and date are unknown. The resin staining of the larger roll, however, suggests that it had been in contact with a mummified body, and hence it is likely to contain funerary texts.

Parkinson and Quirke 1995, 16, fig. 6 (EA 10748).

25 A statue of Osiris: the container for Anhai's Book of the Dead

Painted wood
H 63.5 cm
20th Dynasty, *c.* 1100 BC
Probably from Thebes
London, British Museum, EA 20868

During the 19th and 20th Dynasties, Book of the Dead papyrus rolls were sometimes placed inside a wooden statuette of the god Osiris, which was stored in the tomb. This example contained the Book of the Dead of the woman Anhai (see cat. no. 26). The wooden figure stands on a plinth shaped like the hieroglyphic sign for *maa* which was used in writing the word *Maat* ('order', 'justice, 'truth'). Osiris is depicted wearing the feathered *atef* crown and grasping the royal crook and flail sceptres. His upper body is clad in a patterned garment, while a stylized feathered motif covers his legs and feet. His skin is painted green, the colour of vegetation, which symbolized his power to renew life. In the 21st and 22nd Dynasties these statuettes, usually coloured black to symbolize regeneration, became more frequent as receptacles for one of the two papyri which were then standard elements of elite burial assemblages.

Andrews 1998, 74, fig. 77; Strudwick 2006, 236.

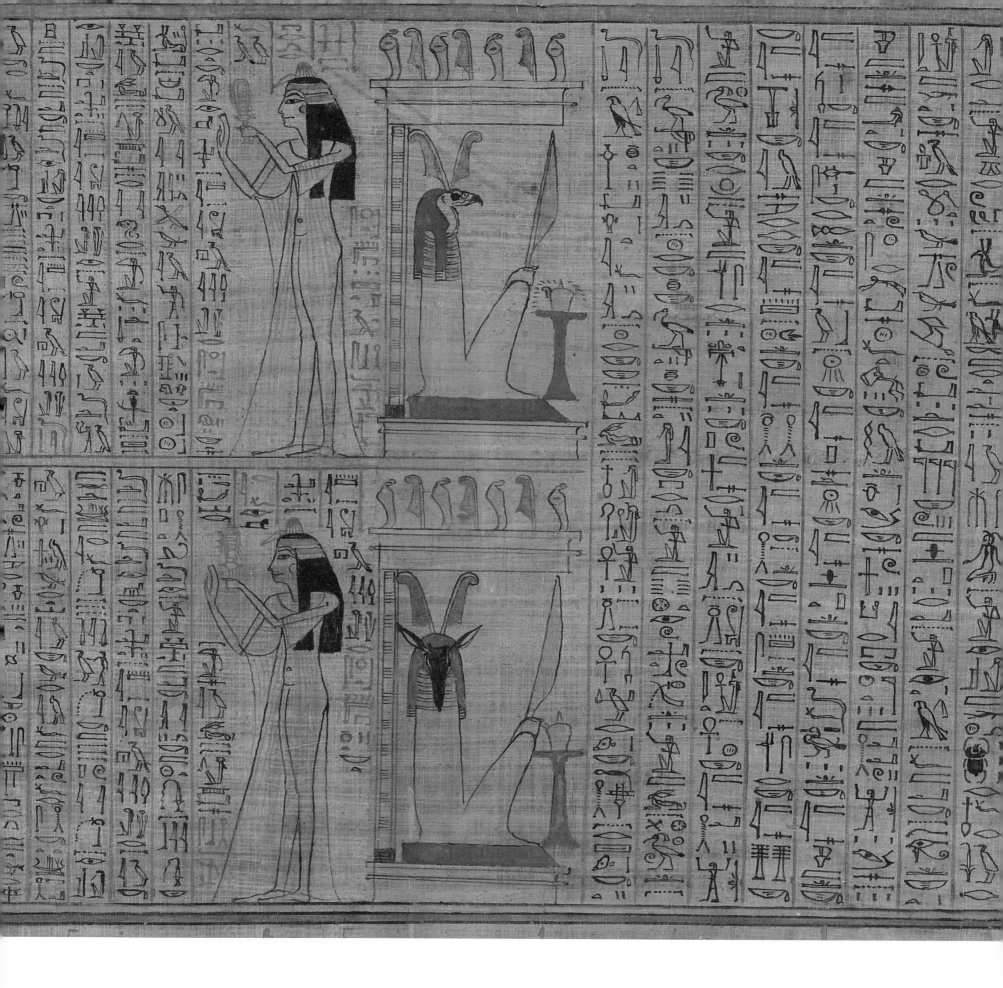

26 A woman's Book of the Dead of the late New Kingdom: the papyrus of Anhai

Ink and paint on papyrus
H 46.0 CM
20th Dynasty, c. 1100 BC
Probably from Thebes
London, British Museum, EA 10472/2

During the 18th and 19th Dynasties the majority of funerary papyri were made for men. Sometimes the wife is depicted in the vignettes alongside her husband, but he alone is named in the text of the spells. At the end of the New Kingdom it became more common for women to have papyri of their own (see pp. 62–3). One of the finest Book of the Dead papyri of the late New Kingdom is that of Anhai (see also cat. nos 121, 124 and 132). It contains a small selection of important spells (numbers 15, 125, 146, 110, 82 and 79) illustrated with exceptionally fine vignettes, and ends with two unusual regeneration scenes – one drawn from the Book of Gates, the other a unique depiction of the mummy supported by a stepped platform.

Anhai was a woman of high status. Beside her common title Chantress of Amun, she was the Chief of the Musicians of two cults, that of Osiris at Abydos and that of Khnum and his consort Nebtu at Esna. Holders of such titles were usually members of the most important priestly families. Anhai's high rank is reflected in the unusual features of her papyrus, notably its large size and the rare use of gold leaf to embellish a vignette (see p. 246). The date of the papyrus is uncertain, but several features indicate that it belongs in the 20th Dynasty. The style of drawing is paralleled by vignettes in the Great Harris Papyrus of the reign of Ramesses IV, while Anhai's husband Nebsumenu holds the typically Ramesside title Stablemaster of the Residence; he may have been related to persons named in the inscriptions of the 20th-Dynasty tomb 148 at Thebes, although absolute proof is lacking.

In this section Anhai is led forward by Horus, at the right, and approaches some of the gates of the Netherworld at the left. Two of the guardians of these gates are depicted, one of whom has the head of a vulture, while the other, a jackal-headed figure, is unusually depicted turning to face the onlooker.

Budge 1899, pls 1–8; Andrews 1978; Quirke and Forman 1996, 132–4.

27 A short version of the Book of the Dead in hieratic script

Ink and paint on papyrus
H 25.5 cm
Late 21st or early 22nd Dynasty, c. 950–900 BC
Probably from Thebes
London, British Museum, EA 10063

In the 21st Dynasty and the first half of the 22nd Dynasty a new tradition of funerary manuscripts predominated at Thebes. Elite burials now included a pair of papyrus rolls, one a short version of the Book of the Dead, often comprising only a few spells, the other a document containing extracts from the Books of the Netherworld, texts which had previously been the prerogative of kings (see pp. 57–8). One scroll was placed inside a wooden figure of Osiris (see cat. no. 25), the other deposited in the coffin.

This papyrus of Padiamenet, chief baker of the domain of Amun, is a typical example of the shorter Books of the Dead from the later part of this period. It is approximately half the height of the New Kingdom rolls and has only a single coloured vignette to open the document, a scene of the deceased offering food and burning incense before the enthroned Osiris. To the left is the actual text from the Book of the Dead, consisting only of spells 23–8, and written not in the traditional hieroglyphic script but in hieratic, the script of daily life. In contrast to the Books of the Dead of the New Kingdom, these late manuscripts read from right to left.

The creation of these new manuscripts was part of a revision of funerary texts during this period. This process involved careful editing of the sources; it has been noted that the hieratic funerary papyri of this period contain fewer errors and corruptions than their hieroglyphic precursors of the New Kingdom.

Quirke and Spencer 1992, 220, fig. 170; Quirke 1993, 55, no. 154; Niwinski 1989, 333–4.

28 Pictorial extracts from the Book of the Dead: the papyrus of Tameni

Ink and paint on papyrus
H 32.9 cm
21st Dynasty, c. 1069–945 BC
Thebes
London, British Museum, EA 10002/2–3

Some members of the Theban elite in the 21st Dynasty possessed funerary papyrus rolls which were predominantly pictorial. These documents often begin with a scene of adoration of Osiris or Ra-Horakhty (see p. 72) and then proceed with a complex arrangement of pictorial extracts from the vignettes of different spells of the Book of the Dead or sections from the Books of the Netherworld. Sometimes the elements of different compositions were mixed together. By the principle known as *pars pro toto* (a part standing in place of the whole) each image could convey the magical efficacy of the complete spell, condensed into a small space.

This papyrus of Tameni begins with an adoration scene (not illustrated) and includes pictorial elements of spell 125 (birth brick and squatting deceased), 126 (Lake of Fire), 149 (crocodile), 81A (lotus), 87 (*Sata* serpent), and 59 (the goddess Nut in a tree feeding Tameni and her *ba*). The figures of knife-bearing guardian gods at the upper left may have been taken from one of several spells which are illustrated with such images. Tameni's second papyrus (cat. no. 106) contained both pictorial and textual extracts from the Book of the Dead, together with images from other sources.

Quirke 1993, 64, no. 242; Niwinski 1989, 326.

29 The Book of the Dead on a coffin

Inner coffin of Besenmut, priest of Montu
Painted wood
H 190.0 cm
Late 25th to early 26th Dynasties, *c.* 650 BC
Deir el-Bahri
London, British Museum, EA 22940

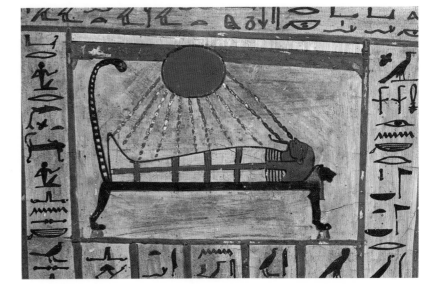

During the 25th and 26th Dynasties a number of wooden coffins were covered with lengthy extracts from the Book of the Dead, painted or written in ink both on the exterior and interior surfaces. In this way the texts surrounded the mummified body, where they not only provided a protective 'armoury' through the inherent power of the written word, but were also directly accessible to be read by the deceased for his personal use (see pp. 29–30).

In the centre of the lid of Besenmut's coffin is spell 154, the important text for not letting the corpse perish. It is inscribed in vertical lines, with a small rectangular compartment containing the appropriate vignette, which shows the mummy lying on a bier under the rejuvenating rays of the sun. Some spells chosen for inclusion on this coffin include general wishes that the deceased should 'come forth by day' equipped with special powers (spells 68 and 71, on the back). Others are more specific, and the location of several of these on the surfaces has a direct link with their content. So spell 19, to enable Besenmut to wear a 'wreath of vindication', is written inside the lid at the head, while spell 23, for opening the mouth, is close by, also at the head. The all-important spell 89, which allowed the *ba*-spirit to rejoin the body, is written on the inside of the lid over the abdomen, and spell 43, to prevent decapitation in the hereafter, appears at the back of the head. Among the other spells written on this coffin is an important group which empowers the deceased to avoid the attacks of undesirable creatures such as crocodiles, snakes and beetles (spells 31, 32, 34–6). These texts are located on the inside of the coffin base, i.e. close to the ground, from which such threats were most likely to emerge (see pp. 184–8).

The placing of the inscriptions on Besenmut's coffin shows great care, and this is also manifested in the accuracy with which the scribes copied the passages of the Book of the Dead, written here without the many errors which occur on other coffins of the same period. Unusually, the beginnings and ends of spells are marked with the *hwt*-sign (see p. 32) (visible at lower right, central column).

Legrain 1893, 11–16; Quirke and Spencer 1992, 107, fig. 84.

30 **A move towards standardization: the papyrus of Ankhwahibra**

Ink on papyrus
H 27.0 cm
Late 26th Dynasty, 550–525 BC
Provenance unrecorded (probably Memphite necropolis)
London, British Museum, EA 10558/10

Following a hiatus in its use during the eighth century BC, the Book of the Dead underwent a major revision, now known as the 'Saite recension' (see p. 58). One feature of this revision was a tendency for the spells to be arranged in a standard sequence, in place of the much more fluid ordering found in earlier manuscripts. A papyrus with this new sequence, that of Iuefankh in Turin, was used by Richard Lepsius in 1842 as the basis for the modern numbering of the spells (see pp. 289–90). In many manuscripts, such as that of Ankhwahibra, the spells are written in hieratic script inside rectangular compartments, with the title and vignette, also enclosed in boxes, arranged in a horizontal line at the top of the roll. Even here, however, variations occur in the order of the spells and in the linking of vignettes to texts: although the layout of individual spells in this papyrus reflects innovations, their sequence does not correspond to the Saite recension.

The standardization process also resulted in a more consistent style in the drawing of vignettes. During the New Kingdom there had been considerable freedom of invention on the part of the artists who drew these illustrations, leading to numerous variants. In the Late Period the vignettes were based more closely on the texts of the spells, often reflecting the interpretation of particular passages – an approach which lent them enhanced power as substitutes for the actual words of the spells (see p. 33).

Quirke 1993, 32, 71, no. 23; Munro 2010.

31 An alternative style of layout: the papyrus of Tentameniy

Ink and paint on papyrus
H 48.5 cm
Ptolemaic Period, 305–30 BC
Provenance unrecorded
London, British Museum, EA 10086/4

There were several different ways of laying out and inscribing spells in the papyri of the Late Period. One style dispensed with framelines for the columns of text, and located the vignettes above or within the words of the relevant spell. Several spells could occupy a single column, and sometimes the text ran continuously from one column to the next. This method required less careful planning than the more formal style used in the papyrus of Ankhwahibra (see p. 76) and perhaps cost less to produce.

Quirke 1993, 65–6, no. 258.

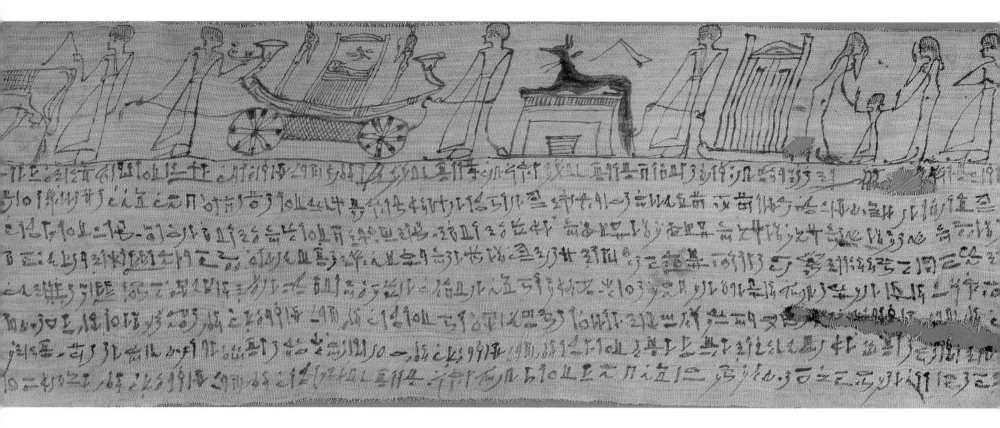

32 The Book of the Dead written on linen bandages

Ink on linen
H 16.2–17.7 cm; L 242.0 cm
Ptolemaic Period, late third or first half of second century BC
Memphite necropolis
London, British Museum, EA 10265

During the Ptolemaic Period a new medium for the provision of the Book of the Dead was introduced. The spells, sometimes with vignettes, were inscribed in ink on the linen bandages which formed part of the wrappings of the mummy (see pp. 60–61). The strips varied in length and some were numbered so the spells could be arranged in the correct canonical sequence.

This strip is the first of a long sequence of bandages which were wrapped around the body of Hor, a priest of Ptah. Known as the 'Memphis Mummy', it was unwrapped in London in 1837 by the celebrated 'unroller' of Egyptian mummies, Thomas Pettigrew (1791–1865). The inscribed bandages were subsequently dispersed and are now in museums in London and Berlin, as well as in the Pierpont Morgan Library, New York.

Containing 117 spells (originally perhaps 120), written accurately and with great care, the bandages of Hor constitute the best-preserved and most complete linen Book of the Dead known. In addition to the inscribed portions, there was also a series of linen amulets – pieces of cloth on which figures of different deities had been drawn.

This portion contains the beginning of the series of Book of the Dead spells, and bears the number '1' at the right-hand edge to assist the embalmer in the correct arrangement of the strips. At right is the introductory vignette in which Hor adores the enthroned Osiris. The figure of the ibis-headed Thoth, who acts as the guide to the dead man, is exceptional in this type of scene. To the left is spell 1, for the day of burial. Above the hieratic text is a long vignette showing the procession to the tomb. This includes many traditional features (cf pp. 92–4) such as the transport of the mummy under a canopy mounted on a boat, the canopic chest with a jackal figure representing Anubis, and the male and female mourners. However, the mummy's boat is mounted not on a sledge but on a wheeled cart, an unusual depiction which is found on a few other linen Books of the Dead and papyri of the Ptolemaic Period.

Kockelmann 2008, I, 1 Photo-Taf. 2–3.

FROM ONE WORLD
TO THE NEXT

II

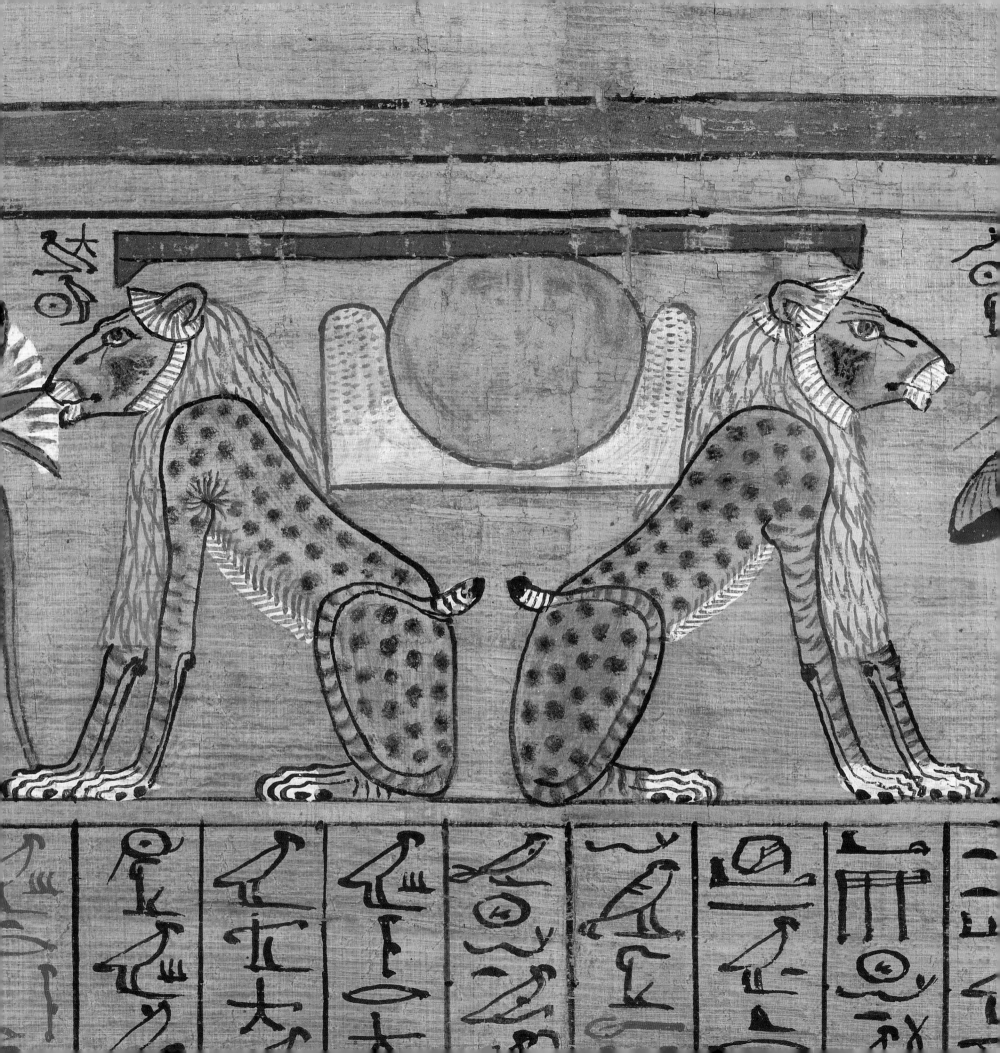

4 The Day of Burial

John H. Taylor

Hail to you, my father Osiris! You shall possess your body; you shall not become corrupt, you shall not have worms, you shall not be distended, you shall not stink, you shall not become putrid, you shall not become worms.

(Spell 154, 'for not letting the corpse perish')

Here begin the spells of coming forth by day, the praises and recitations for going to and fro in the realm of the dead which are beneficial in the beautiful West, and which are to be spoken on the day of burial and of going in after coming forth.

(Title of spell 1)

DEATH was a constant presence in ancient Egypt. Life expectancy was low, infant mortality high, disease and danger never far away. The Egyptians had an ambivalent attitude towards death; while they hated it for depriving them of the joys of life, they accepted that it was a threshold which had to be crossed if the eternal afterlife was to be reached. It was not, however, considered a fitting subject for representation in art, nor was it described at length in writing, except as a punishment for Egypt's enemies or those who had offended the gods. Apart from in these situations, death was usually referred to obliquely or by euphemisms, such as 'reaching the mooring post' or 'being weary'. Even the death of the god Osiris, which is the crux of his myth, is not explicitly mentioned in Egyptian texts; instead, he is termed 'the weary one' or 'the one who has fallen on his side'.

Nonetheless, death provoked a strong expression of grief among the living. The Greek historian Herodotus describes the immediate reaction to a death in an Egyptian community:

> In the case of people in whose houses there perishes a man of some consequence, all the females from these houses smear their heads with dust, and sometimes also the face, and then they leave the corpse in the house and themselves wander through the town and beat their breasts, with garments girt up and revealing their breasts, and with them all his female relatives. And the males beat their breasts separately, these too with their garments girt up. And when they have done this, so do they carry forth the corpse to be mummified.

Fig. 24 Female mourners at the burial of Hunefer gathering dust from the ground and casting it on their heads. The woman at the back beats her arms in a traditional gesture of lamentation. Behind them a servant carries a chair, a staff and a mat to the tomb. Papyrus of Hunefer, 19th Dynasty, *c.* 1280 BC. EA 9901/4.

This was written in the fifth century BC, but the customs Herodotus mentions had long been established; many depictions on the walls of tombs and on papyri show these acts of mourning (fig. 24). They are a manifestation of a universal response to death; in terms of the psychology of bereavement, it is the 'separation stage', the initial reaction of the living to their loss.[1]

Mummification

The public display of grief served to announce the death to the dead person's community. It also the marked the beginning of the ritualized process of transmitting the deceased from the world of the living to that of the dead. First the corpse was taken from the house to a place of embalming. This was usually done without delay because in the hot Egyptian climate the body would begin to decay immediately. Traditionally mummification took place on the western side of the Nile. In formal 'funeral scenes' in tombs the dead person is first conveyed across the river by boat to the west bank, a representation of the journey to the place of embalming which also symbolized the transition from death to the afterlife realm of the gods.[2]

The actual embalming was performed out of sight, in an isolated structure, perhaps a tent. The procedures involved were not depicted and were rarely described except by curious 'outsiders' such as Herodotus. The process involved the use of magic (*heka*) and it is very likely that incantations were spoken as the body was embalmed, but these words are not among the texts that were usually put into the tomb. The Book of the Dead does not dwell at length on mummification; it contains only occasional references, such as spell 154 (quoted at

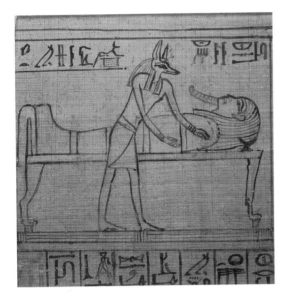

Formal depictions of mummification.
Fig. 25 (above) Anubis lays his hands on the mummy. Papyrus of Nebseny, 18th Dynasty *c.* 1400 BC. EA 9900.

Fig. 26 (above right) A similar scene on the interior wall of the coffin of Inpehefnakht (see cat. no. 92). Here the mummy's crown identifies it clearly with Osiris. 21st Dynasty, *c.* 1000 BC. EA 29591.

the beginning of this chapter), where the horrors of decomposition are mentioned only to emphasize that the dead person would escape them. The aim of mummification was to purge the corpse of the fluids of corruption and rebuild it into a perfect and eternal body, raised to divine status and similar to the body of Osiris (figs 25–6). It was sometimes called a *tut*, 'image', and like a statue it would serve as a receptacle for the spirit aspects of the person after death. The purification and perfection which embalming aimed to effect are reflected in another common Egyptian term for a mummy, *sah*, which is etymologically linked to a word meaning 'noble' (see p. 20). The ideological model for mummification was the reconstitution and preservation of the corpse of Osiris, which is supposed to have been carried out by Anubis. It is this god who appears, as a jackal-headed figure, presiding over the mummification of the deceased in Book of the Dead spell 151 (see p. 106–7). Among his most prominent titles are 'He

Fig. 27 A set of calcite canopic jars made for Neskhons, wife of the high priest of Amun Pinedjem II. The painted wooden lids represent the four Sons of Horus. 21st Dynasty, *c.* 1000 BC. EA 59197–59200.

who is in the embalming place' and 'the foremost of the god's booth' (another allusion to the place of mummification). By invoking Anubis in this context the same resurrection which Osiris experienced could be effected for the dead person (see p. 19).

From the study of human remains found in tombs and from limited written sources we know that Egyptian mummification consisted essentially of extracting the most perishable organs, drying the body using natron (a naturally occurring compound of sodium salts), anointing it with oils and resins, packing the cavities and 'beautifying' the features. After these operations the body was wrapped in layers of linen and fashioned into the correct shape (see cat. nos 1 and 3). In the most elaborate versions of embalming the internal organs were also preserved: they were wrapped in bundles and placed in four containers known to Egyptologists as canopic jars (see fig. 27 and cat. no. 54).

Herodotus mentions three styles of mummification, varying as to cost and quality, and examination of the mummies themselves confirms that different techniques were used. The cheaper process probably required less time than the most elaborate, which occupied seventy days – a time-span which had religious connotations. At the end of the process the body was wrapped in the *sah*-shape and adorned with a mask (if the family could afford one). Since the mummy was basically an eternal image of the deceased, its external appearance was of great importance. Often this seems to have taken priority over the care expended on the preservation process, since many mummies which were elaborately wrapped and masked have been found to contain poorly embalmed bodies, sometimes with the bones of the skeleton in disorder.

The day of burial

At the end of the mummification period the body was returned to the relatives. The transfiguration process reached its climax with the rituals that were enacted on the day of burial, when the mummy was taken from the place of embalming to the tomb. This was a formal and conspicuous occasion, analogous to a religious festival, with the mummy taking the place of the image of a god. The ideal funeral is described in the Tale of Sinuhe (*c.* 1900 BC):

> Think of the day of burial, the passing to the state of reverence, when a night is
> assigned to you of ointments and wrappings from the hands of Tayit [a reference
> to mummification; Tayit was a goddess of weaving] and a funeral procession is
> made for you on the day of burial, the mummy case being of gold, its head of lapis
> lazuli, and a canopy being over you as you lie in the hearse, oxen drawing you and
> musicians being before you, and the dance of the *muu* is performed at the door
> of your tomb, and the offering-list is read for you, and sacrifice is made at your
> offering-stone ...

These elements of the good funeral were heavily traditional and are depicted in tombs at other periods. The procession to the tomb comprised a number of key features. The focal point was the coffin-sledge, pulled by men and oxen, and followed by lamenting women or an escort of relatives, also mourning. Behind came a shrine containing the canopic jars, and in the New Kingdom the scenes often show the dragging of the *tekenu*, an amorphous bundle wrapped in

Fig. 28 Male mourners following the mummy in the funeral procession of Ani. At the head of the group is a man whose white hair denotes his advanced age – he is perhaps a senior member of the deceased's family. Papyrus of Ani, 19th Dynasty, *c.* 1275 BC. EA 10470/5.

Fig. 29 The final farewell. Ani's widow, Tutu, kneels, clasping his mummified body and weeping, as Anubis (or a priest playing the part of the god) receives him into the Netherworld at the entrance to the tomb. Papyrus of Ani, 19th Dynasty, *c.* 1275 BC. EA 10470/6.

an animal skin, perhaps containing the parts of the body which were not incorporated into the mummy.[3] Servants are also shown bringing goods for the tomb, including domestic furniture and magical objects such as shabti figures. Whereas funeral scenes in older tombs include much idealized – and no doubt archaic – detail, those of the Ramesside period reflect the reality of the occasion more faithfully in terms of the clothes worn, the participants and the acts performed, and this is true of the Book of the Dead vignettes of the same period.[4]

The expression of lamentation for the dead followed traditional patterns and is graphically depicted in scenes on papyri (fig. 28). The women mourn dramatically – weeping, with hair dishevelled and dusty, and breasts exposed – all as Herodotus reports. They raise their hands or beat them against their breasts. For men the expression of grief shows more restraint: a hand supports the face or they squat with heads bent low.

The procession ended at the entrance to the tomb (fig. 29). In the New Kingdom a nobleman's tomb usually comprised a forecourt with a stone facade, often with a small pyramid on top, and one or more stelae set up outside, their inscriptions identifying the owner and containing prayers on his behalf. Here the mummy was taken from its catafalque and, as tomb inscriptions state, placed upright in front of the stela, facing south and bathed in the life-giving rays of the sun. Great importance was attached to setting up the mummy 'before Ra' and these

Fig. 30 The Keeper of the Balance touches the mouth of the deceased. Vignette of spell 22 of the Book of the Dead. Papyrus of Nebseny, 18th Dynasty, *c.* 1400 BC, EA 9900/5.

Fig. 31 A priest wearing a leopard skin touches the face of Nebqed's mummy with an adze, a key episode in the Opening of the Mouth ritual. 18th Dynasty, *c.* 1400–1370 BC. Musée du Louvre, N 3068.

directions may indicate that the rituals took place at midday.[5] Here a group called the *muu* performed a ritual dance, and the family members expressed their grief: 'may the children of your children all be assembled and wail with loving heart'.[6] In psychological terms this is the 'recovery stage'; the public nature of the event perhaps helped 'the reintegration of the deceased' into his social group, foremost his family, but also the wider community.[7]

The rituals for the day of burial form a prominent part of the Book of the Dead. Spells 1 and 1B are specified as recitations for that occasion, and spell 1 often has an elaborate vignette showing the procession to the tomb and the rites performed there. The most important of these formalities was the 'Opening of the Mouth', a ritual of animation, which conferred the ability to support life on any object – a statue, a mummy, a coffin, or even an entire building such as a temple. To perform it on a mummy a priest would touch the face-mask with a series of implements, accompanied by offerings and incantations (fig. 30). In this way the mouth, eyes, ears and nostrils were symbolically unstopped and the corpse regained its faculties. The ritual changed over time and the range of objects used in it grew. It is thought to have originated in a series of ritual acts to enable a newborn child to take in nourishment. In the Old Kingdom, the most important implements in the funerary Opening of the Mouth ritual were the *pesesh-kef*, a forked knife perhaps originally used to cut the umbilical cord, and two blades of meteoric iron called *netjerwy* which represented the little fingers of the priest or midwife (who would clear mucus from the baby's mouth). The ritual was also performed on statues to enable them to receive the spirit of the person represented, and craftsmen's tools – especially the woodcarver's adze – were added to the repertoire of ritual implements with which the mouth was touched (see fig. 31; see also cat. nos 39–40). The New Kingdom depictions of the ritual place emphasis on the adze, the chisel and on a rod with a ram's head.[8]

Another important part of the ritual was the sacrifice of a calf. While the animal was still alive its foreleg was cut off and its heart cut out, a scene which is depicted clearly in the papyrus of Hunefer (see pp. 94–5). Here the mother cow stands nearby with raised head and open mouth, making a mournful cry, which symbolized lamentation for the dead person. The heart and the foreleg of the calf were taken by priests and immediately presented to the mummy. By this means the life force in the still-pulsating limb was transferred to the dead person – another expression of the ritual's function of renewing life.[9]

The actual words of the Opening of the Mouth are not included in the Book of the Dead, but spells 21–3 ensured that the ritual was performed. The description in spell 23 represents a different tradition of the ritual from that traceable back to the Pyramid Texts of the Old Kingdom,[10] but the use of an iron blade, as a tool of great magical power, is prominent in both versions. In spell 23 the deceased says: 'My mouth is opened, my mouth is split open by Shu with that iron harpoon of his with which he split open the mouths of the gods.' The Book of the Dead also emphasizes that the Opening of the Mouth is not merely the reconstitution of the person; it is a prerequisite for the deceased's successful passage to the beyond – for he must use his mouth to pronounce the names of door-guardians and answer their questions, and he must speak at the judgement to prove himself worthy to enter the afterlife. This connection between the Opening of the Mouth and the judgement is demonstrated in spell 22, the words of which include 'my mouth has been given to me that I may speak with it in the presence of the Great

God'; the vignette (at least in the papyrus of Nebseny) shows the 'Keeper of the Balance' touching the mouth of the deceased to enable him to speak (see fig. 30).

After the completion of the rituals the mummy was placed in the tomb, together with the canopic jars and the other burial goods. The typical Egyptian tomb comprised two parts – the burial chamber, usually subterranean and inaccessible after the interment, and the cult place or chapel, which remained open so that relatives could periodically make offerings to the deceased there. Through the Opening of the Mouth the connection between the different components of the person was restored. Henceforth they experienced a new relationship. The mummy would remain in the tomb, and there also the *ka* would dwell, passing from the burial chamber to the chapel to receive offerings when they were presented. The *ba* would enjoy greater freedom, having the capacity to rejoin and leave not only the mummy, but even the tomb. This freedom was the root of the expression 'coming forth by day', the core concept of the Book of the Dead. In the papyrus of Nebqed there is a unique depiction of the *ba* descending the tomb shaft to the burial chamber where the mummy lies surrounded by burial goods (see p. 100). This is the preliminary to the uniting of *ba* and mummy, the crucial act of rejuvenation which would ensure the eternal survival of the deceased. Spell 89 of the Book of the Dead, 'for letting a soul rejoin its corpse', made sure that no obstacle prevented this from taking place:

> Come for my soul, O you wardens of the sky! If you delay letting my soul see my
> corpse, you will find the eye of Horus standing up thus against you … The sacred
> barque will be joyful and the great god will proceed in peace when you allow this
> soul of mine to ascend vindicated to the gods … May it see my corpse, may it rest
> on my mummy, which will never be destroyed or perish.

This text, together with its eloquent vignette (see p. 90), was included in many papyri, and in the Late Period was a favourite element of the decoration of coffin lids.

It was on the day of burial that the deceased's now closer relationship with the gods Osiris and Ra was made manifest. Praises of both gods would have formed part of the burial rites. Hymns to them feature prominently on stelae and doorways at the tomb, and they also occur in the Book of the Dead, often at the beginnings of papyrus rolls. It is common for the opening vignette to show the deceased worshipping Osiris, often with a prayer and request for offerings. On papyri of the Late Period the group of spells which deals with the procession to the tomb and the rituals there (1–14) is often framed by a homage to Osiris and a homage to Ra. The latter consists of a hymn to the sun-god (spell 15), which is often accompanied by a large vignette of the sunrise, conventionally numbered 'spell 16', although it has no text. 'Spell 15' is not a standard text: the term is used simply to denote the presence of a solar hymn, of which many different examples have been recorded, not only on Book of the Dead papyri but also in tombs and on stelae. The diverse vignettes which are classed as 'spell 16' are among the few which occupy the full height of papyrus rolls. They are not merely expressions of praise to the sun-god but encapsulate in one scene the cyclical path on which Ra and Osiris were thought to be rejuvenated. It is an image both of the beginning of the deceased's journey and also of its goal (see pp. 246–9).

Fig. 32 The *ba* descends to embrace the mummy. Vignette of spell 89. Papyrus of Astemakhbit, 21st Dynasty, *c.* 1069–945 BC. EA 9904/2.

33 **The funeral procession from the papyrus of Ani**

Painted papyrus
Average H 39.2 cm
19th Dynasty, *c.* 1275 BC
Thebes
London, British Museum, EA 10470/5–6

Ani's papyrus offers one of the classic examples of the funeral scene from spell 1 of the Book of the Dead. The long vignette incorporates both the procession and the rituals at the tomb in one image. The focal element of the procession is the mummy itself, drawn along on a sledge pulled by two pairs of oxen and four men, while a priest clad in a panther skin burns incense and pours a libation, and another man sprinkles milk from a jar. The catafalque is shaped like a shrine to emphasize the divine character of the dead person. The mummy also lies on a model boat, recalling the barques in which the gods were believed to sail. Figures of

the goddesses Isis and Nephthys are positioned at the prow and stern, alluding to Ani's assimilation with Osiris. A more personal note is struck by the figure of his widow kneeling by the side of the mummy and lamenting with tears. A group of women stand at the point where the procession reaches the tomb, dressed in bluish garments which reveal their breasts; they are making a public demonstration of grief by weeping and enacting mourning gestures. Eight men, probably relatives of Ani, walk behind the catafalque, also lamenting. At the front and rear of the procession, men bring goods for the tomb – boxes, household furniture and the canopic chest, surmounted by a figure of Anubis and dragged on a sledge. At the right, Ani's mummy is supported at the entrance to his tomb, while Tutu mourns and priests perform the Opening of the Mouth. A calf is sacrificed and large piles of foodstuffs are offered to the deceased.

British Museum 1890, pls 5–6; British Museum 1894, pls 5–6; Faulkner 1985, 38; Barthelmess 1992, 158.

34 The funeral procession from the papyrus of Hunefer

Painted papyrus
H 39.0 cm
19th Dynasty, *c.* 1280 BC
Thebes
London, British Museum, EA 9901/4

The depiction of the procession in Hunefer's papyrus is shorter and more simplified than that of Ani (see p. 92). The procession is headed by three men, one of whom reads the words of the liturgy from a papyrus roll. They are followed by a group of women performing traditional gestures of mourning. The transport of the grave goods is here reduced to a single figure of a servant carrying a chair, a pen-case and a staff. Next comes the catafalque on its sledge pulled by four oxen, with a driver and four men. A priest walking directly in front of the sledge burns incense and pours libations. The catafalque is adorned with bouquets of flowers and a small jackal figure. The mummy is clearly visible within, resting on a lion-shaped bier with four bags beneath it, perhaps containing natron to symbolise the process of mummification which Hunefer has undergone. The procession ends with the canopic chest, also bedecked with flowers, which is drawn on a sledge by four men. The text written in columns beneath the image consists of spell 1 of the Book of the Dead and is followed directly by the short spell 22 (see pp. 88–9).

Budge 1895; Budge 1899, 1–18, pls. 1–11; Budge 1913; Barthelmess 1992, 158–9.

35 The Opening of the Mouth from the papyrus of Hunefer

Painted papyrus
H 39.0 cm
19th Dynasty, *c.* 1280 BC
Thebes
London, British Museum, EA 9901/5

The funeral procession is followed in the papyrus of Hunefer by a full-height image of the rituals at the tomb. In front of the facade of the chapel, with its steeply angled pyramid, stands a stela depicted in unusual detail, with an offering prayer to Osiris and an address to Anubis. The mummy is supported on a heap of clean sand by a jackal-headed figure. This may represent Anubis himself, although since the burial scenes of the 19th Dynasty tend to closely reflect the reality of the events depicted, the artist may have intended this to be a priest wearing a mask to impersonate the god. Hunefer is mourned by his wife Nasha and another female figure, perhaps meant to represent his daughter. Facing the mummy, two priests hold implements and vessels used in the Opening of the Mouth (see p. 88). Behind them another priest burns incense and consecrates a heap of offerings with water poured from a spouted vessel. The sub-scene shows the sacrifice of the calf in the presence of the mother cow, who gives vent to a mournful bellow, while attendants carry the calf's heart and foreleg, still pulsating with life, to be presented to the mummy. To the right stands a table on which are arranged the implements to be used in the ritual and the panther skin which the chief officiant would wear.

Budge 1895; Budge 1899, 1–18, pls 1–11; Budge 1913; Assmann 2005, 310.

36 The Opening of the Mouth from the stela of Neferabu

Limestone
H 63.0 cm; W 42.0 cm
19th Dynasty, probably reign of Ramesses II, c. 1279–1213 BC
Probably from tomb TT 5 at Deir el-Medina
London, British Museum, EA 305

Neferabu was a member of the community of specialized craftsmen who built the royal tombs in the Valley of the Kings. These men and their families lived in the village of Deir el-Medina and were buried in tombs which overlooked their homes. This stela was probably part of the fittings of Neferabu's tomb. The scene at the top depicts the ceremonies at the burial, where the Opening of the Mouth (see p. 88) is performed on four mummies: those of Neferabu himself, his wife Taiset, his mother Mahy and probably that of his father Neferrenpet. The rites are carried out by members of the family, who are named in the inscriptions. In the middle register Anubis embalms a mummy which lies on a bier – probably again that of Neferrenpet, as the relatives depicted at the right include his sons and grandson. The hieroglyphic inscription at the bottom of the stela contains extracts from spell 1 of the Book of the Dead, which includes a note that it had been provided for Neferrenpet by his son Neferabu 'to make his name live'. The Deir el-Medina craftsmen seem to have developed their own special version of the Book of the Dead, which can be identified by distinctive features of the text and vignettes occurring on certain papyri and also in some of the tombs at the site. This stela includes peculiarities which reflect this local tradition.

James 1970, 36–7, pl. XXXII; Kitchen 2000, 516–17; Strudwick and Taylor 2005, 148–9; Lüscher forthcoming.

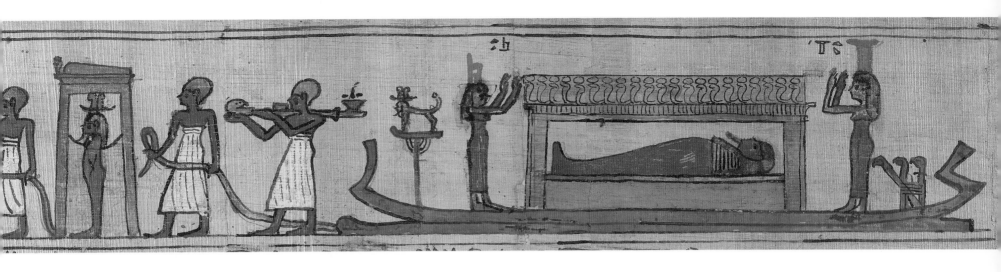

37 The funeral procession and Opening of the Mouth from the papyrus of Kerasher

Painted papyrus
H 23.5 cm
Reign of Augustus, late first century BC
Thebes
London, British Museum, EA 9995/3

The papyrus of Kerasher is a Book of Breathing, a funerary text which was often used instead of the Book of the Dead at Thebes in the Roman period. However, it includes vignettes from the Book of the Dead tradition (see cat. no. 111), providing one of the latest depictions of the rites on the day of burial. The mummy, lying in its catafalque, is drawn on a sledge, which is now pulled by just one man. A priest carries a censer on his shoulder, the incense cup facing towards the mummy. The small figures of Isis and Nephthys from the New Kingdom vignettes of spell 1 (see cat. no. 33) have now become lifesize images, and were perhaps intended to represent the goddesses themselves, rather than statues. To the left, a man hauls a rope attached to a shrine in which stands a divine figure wearing a plumed headdress. This may be a statue of the deceased in divine form or possibly a reinterpretation of the canopic chest, which is not otherwise present in this scene. Three men carrying divine standards (not illustrated) lead the procession. The Opening of the Mouth ritual is depicted in simplified form (see p. 88). A lector priest with feathers in his headband reads from a papyrus roll before a shrine or container. The elaborate New Kingdom depiction of the tomb and its environs is replaced by a pair of obelisks. The mummy is supported by Anubis to receive a libation poured by a priest, while the widow of the deceased laments at a respectful distance.

Budge 1899, pl. 3; Quirke and Spencer 1992, 54–5, fig. 37; Quirke 1993, 43, no. 102; Herbin 2008, 37–45, pls 15–24.

38 Inner coffin of Henutmehyt

Painted and gilded wood; eyes inlaid
H 193.0 cm; W 50.0 cm
19th Dynasty, *c.* 1250 BC
Thebes
London, British Museum, EA 48001

In depictions of the Opening of the Mouth from the New Kingdom the
ritual is shown being performed on a mummy or on an anthropoid coffin.
As a *sah*-image (see p. 20) the coffin, like the mummy itself, needed to
be given the means to receive the spiritual manifestation of its occupant,
and hence it underwent the animation ritual.

The Chantress of Amun Henutmehyt was a woman of high status who
possessed a rich burial assemblage, comprising two anthropoid coffins and
an inner mummy cover (see also cat. nos 15, 46, 48–51, 54 and 134–5). The
smaller of the two coffins, made of tamarisk wood, is covered extensively
with gold leaf as an indication of Henutmehyt's elevation to divine status.
She is represented with her hands crossed, and dressed in an elaborate
wig, collar and pectoral pendant. An interlinking arrangement of inscribed
bands recalls the linen binding tapes which secured the mummy
wrappings (see p. 118). The raised-relief inscriptions on these bands include
an address to the mother-goddess Nut, who is depicted on the abdomen,
and speeches by Anubis, the Sons of Horus and other gods whose figures
are represented in the intervening spaces on both the lid and the case.
These texts and images are drawn chiefly from spells 151 and 161 of the
Book of the Dead, and served to establish a magically protective
environment around the mummy (see p. 117).

Taylor 1999, 61–2, col. pls XI–XII; Cooney 2007, 400–2, fig. 2, 10–15.

39 Set of model implements for the Opening of the Mouth ritual

Limestone, rock crystal and obsidian
L 17.2 cm; W 12.1 cm
6th Dynasty, *c.* 2300 BC
Abydos, tomb of Idy
London, British Museum, EA 5526

In tombs of the late Old Kingdom small sets of model implements for the Opening of the Mouth were included (see p. 88). These comprised the bifurcate *pesesh-kef*, two curved blades called *netjerwy* and miniature vessels, all set into a stone slab. It has been suggested that during this period the implements were based on items used in the rituals of birth – the *pesesh-kef* to cut the umbilical cord, and the blades representing the little fingers of the midwife which would be used to clear mucus from the baby's mouth so that it could begin to feed. Ideally the blades were supposed to be made of meteoric iron, which was supposed to have magical significance, but in practice blades of stone are substituted in these models.

Taylor 2001, 191, fig. 134, left.

40 Adze

Wood and copper alloy with leather binding
L 34.3 cm
18th Dynasty, reign of Hatshepsut, *c.* 1473–1458 BC
Deir el-Bahri, temple of Hatshepsut
London, British Museum, EA 26279

In the New Kingdom the main implement used in the Opening of the Mouth was the adze, a carpenter's tool. This was originally used when the ritual was performed on statues in order to render them capable of receiving the spirit of the owner (see p. 88). The adze may have been transferred from this context to the version of the ritual which was enacted on the mummy. This adze formed part of a votive deposit of tools buried in the foundations of a temple; models of such implements were sometimes placed in the tomb to perpetuate the effectiveness of the Opening of the Mouth ritual for eternity.

41 **The *ba* rejoins the mummy: the papyrus of Nebqed**

Ink and paint on papyrus
H 31.0 cm
18th Dynasty, reign of Tuthmosis IV or Amenhotep III, *c.* 1400–1370 BC
Thebes
Paris, Musée du Louvre, N 3068

The effect of the Opening of the Mouth was to restore the human faculties to the deceased, reuniting the elements of his existence which had been dispersed during the transitional phase between death and burial (see p. 88). The most important consequence of this reanimation was the establishing of a new relationship between the *ba* and the mummy. While the mummy remained in the burial chamber, the deceased in *ba* form gained the freedom to leave the tomb and visit the sunlit world above, returning at night to rejoin the corpse (see p. 17). The papyrus of Nebqed illustrates this in an unusually graphic way. It shows not just the ritual at the tomb facade, but also what is happening below ground. Directly beneath the tomb chapel is the vertical shaft, by which the *ba* is seen descending to the subterranean burial apartments. In its human hands the *ba* carries a loaf and a jar of water to sustain the deceased. The hidden space underground is divided into three chambers, each with a separate door. Two contain burial goods, and in the third lies the mummy, with which the *ba* is about to be reunited. Nebqed as a living person is also shown rising from the burial chamber under the shining sun, with the legend 'Coming forth by day by the scribe Nebqed'. The scene encapsulates the whole cycle of eternal life which the spells of the Book of the Dead were intended to guarantee.

Ziegler 1982, 288–9, no. 244; Munro 1988, 281–2; Forman and Quirke 1996, 122–3.

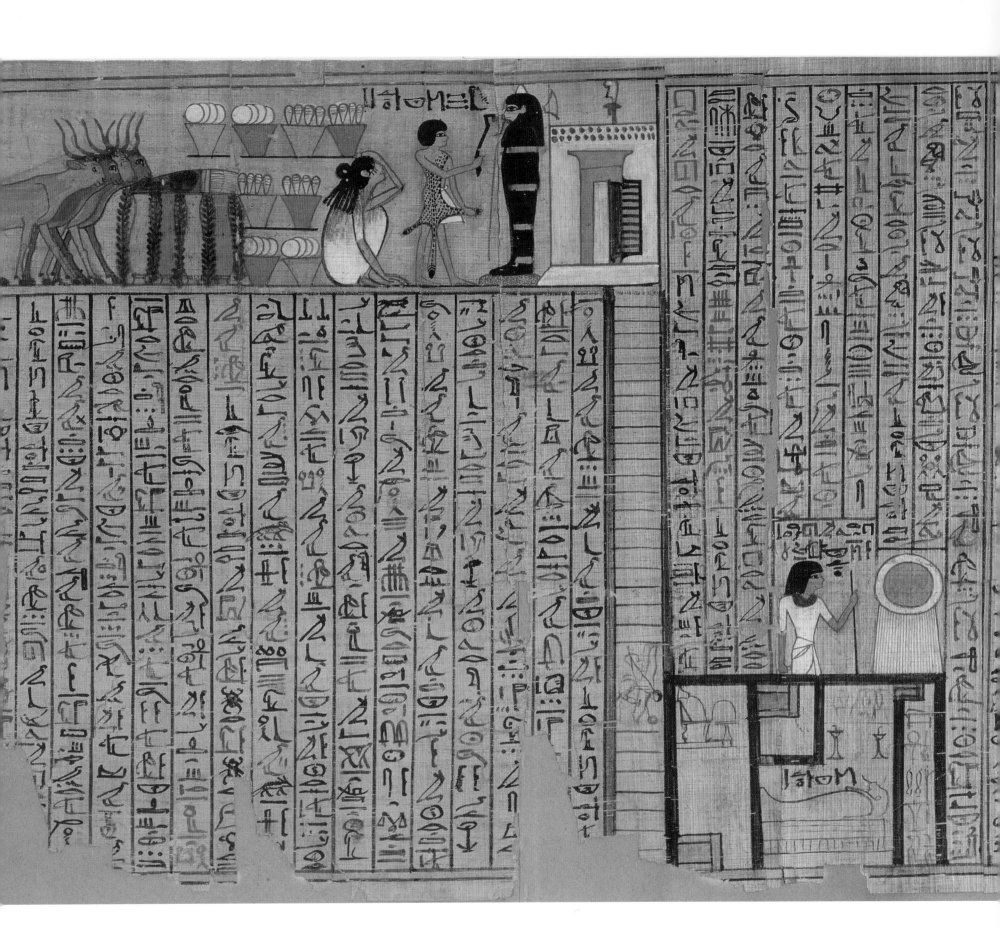

42 Approaching the dead: the ancestral bust of Muteminet

Limestone
H 51.0 cm; W 26.0 cm
19th Dynasty, c. 1250 BC
Probably from Thebes
London, British Museum, EA 1198

It was believed that contact with members of one's family could be maintained even after they had died. Letters to dead relatives, written on papyrus or on pottery bowls, were left in tombs; these often reveal that the writer was suffering from some bodily or mental affliction and that the dead were being petitioned to alleviate it. Household shrines sometimes contained small sculptured busts depicting ancestors. These probably acted as the focus of domestic cults, in which the ancestors were again invoked to use their influence in the Netherworld in order to help their still-living relatives.

The majority of the busts have no inscriptions and were perhaps meant only to act as generic images of unspecified forebears. Some, however, are inscribed with the name of the person represented, as in this example, which is also one of the largest and most elaborate busts of this kind so far known. The central inscription identifies it as an image of Muteminet, the sistrum-player of Amun, Mut and Khons, the divine 'family' of Thebes. Muteminet was the mother of Amenmose, owner of tomb 373 in the Theban necropolis, and it is possible that the bust was originally located in this tomb, rather than in a household shrine.

Habachi 1976, 85–6, 96, fig. 21; Seyfried 1990, 296, 299, fig. 187.

5 The Mummy in the Tomb

John H. Taylor

THE burial of the corpse, which took place on the 'day of joining the earth', marked the beginning of a new phase of existence. The components of the person had been reunited by means of mummification and the Opening of the Mouth (see p. 88), and the individual had been restored to life. The different aspects of his makeup would henceforth be maintained in a new way, with the tomb as the physical setting.

The living were expected to bring offerings to the tomb to nourish their dead relatives by means of a mortuary cult. Both real and symbolic foodstuffs were offered, and the deceased, having been reanimated at the Opening of the Mouth, was able to partake of nourishment just like a newborn child.[1] This feeding – the 'maintenance stage' in the psychology of bereavement[2] – was for the benefit of the *ka*, which remained in the tomb, close to the body (see p. 17). However, the deceased person now possessed the capacity for free movement, which enabled

Fig. 33 (below) A typical nobleman's tomb of the 19th–20th Dynasties, comprising a courtyard open to the sun, a chapel with a small pyramid, and a shaft leading to the subterranean burial apartments.

Fig. 34 (far right) Stylized depiction of a tomb of the type illustrated opposite. The chapel with its open door is represented at the top. Below this the *ba* descends the shaft to the burial chamber containing the mummy and other funerary goods. Papyrus of Nebqed, 18th Dynasty, *c.* 1400–1370 BC. Musée du Louvre, N 3068.

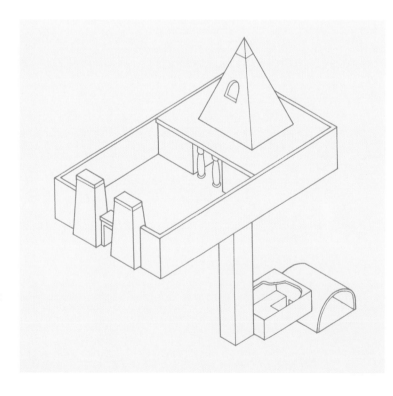

him or her to leave the confinement of the tomb and to travel to the world above, where he could revisit the habitations of the living, journey in the sun-god's boat or follow the paths to the realm of Osiris. This liberation took place in the guise of the *ba*, and in this form the person could not only receive the life-renewing rays of the sun but also enjoy the earthly pleasures of food and drink, and even have sexual relations. This ability to leave the tomb at will was referred to by the Egyptians as 'coming forth by day'. In the New Kingdom it became the single most important concept which influenced preparations for the afterlife. Many of the spells in the Book of the Dead were designed with this specific aim in mind, and indeed it became the collective title for the whole work.

However, the *ba* could not exist independently for ever. At the close of each day its visit to the sunlit world ended, and it had to return to the tomb to be reunited with the corpse in the burial chamber. The union between Ra and Osiris every night made possible the eternal life of both gods and the continuation of human existence on earth (see p. 20). It was essential for every deceased person to undergo a similar union. Hence the preservation of the body was of crucial importance; it had to remain intact and undisturbed in the burial chamber so that the *ba* could find it and re-enter it. Spell 89 of the Book of the Dead ensured that this would happen (see p. 89).

Since the mummy's role was crucial, the Egyptians were greatly concerned for its safety. Although after death the body had been cleansed of corruption and fashioned into a divine image, it remained vulnerable not only to decay and the depredations of animals and thieves but to magical attack by the forces of Seth. Protection could be provided in a practical way by massive architecture and by locating the burial in an underground chamber which would be sealed and blocked after the funeral (figs 33–5). For those who could afford it, a heavy stone coffin gave added protection. But most of all, the protection was to be effected by magic.

The magical processes which would safeguard the body began to be implemented as soon as the corpse arrived in the embalmers' workshop, with ritual washing to remove impurities, and incantations to place protection around the body and keep all possible harm at bay. Some of these spells and rituals reflected aspects of the myth of Osiris (see p. 19). The murdered god's body had been dismembered and scattered by his enemy Seth, and to prevent any similar violation of a corpse magic was employed. Diodorus Siculus recorded a strange tradition that the embalmer who made the first incision in the body, to extract the viscera, was pelted with stones and cursed by his colleagues – probably a symbolic act to avert any evil consequences which might arise from this necessary violation. There may have been other rituals, but the best-documented is the 'Stundenwache', a vigil that was maintained around the mummy on the night before the burial to ward off the threats of evil beings. In this nocturnal watch the deceased was supposed to be surrounded by deities. These protective measures also involved the placing of objects of power (such as the mask and amulets, see pp. 108–10) on the body itself.

Some of these protective devices would be transferred to the tomb by placing the words of spells and images there in order to perpetuate the protective magic eternally and to equip the deceased with the means to activate it himself. Much of this magic was incorporated into the Book of the Dead. Following the interment, the burial chamber of the tomb became the

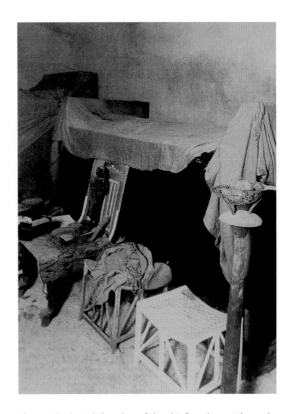

Fig. 35 The burial chamber of the chief workman Kha and his wife Meryt at Deir el-Medina. The tomb of this couple, who died about 1380 BC, remained undisturbed until its discovery in 1906. The original sheets are still draped over the rectangular coffins. A chair, tall lamp and stools stand in front of them.

focal point for the ritual protection of the body. This chamber was a most sacred spot. Usually located deep in the earth and hidden from sight, it was symbolically the resting place of Osiris, and also the womb of Nut, the sky-goddess – the mother of Osiris and thus the eternal mother of the dead person. Here the protection made for Osiris was recreated for the benefit of the deceased. In addition there were magical safeguards which derived from a different sphere. The deceased, about to enter a new life, was vulnerable just as a newborn baby is vulnerable. The Egyptians had long since developed an armoury of magical defences for the perilous time of childbirth, and some of these rituals were transferred to the situation of the reborn deceased. The protective magic from these differing, yet interrelated, realms was also focused into several important spells of the Book of the Dead.

Protection in the tomb: spell 151

In contrast to the highly decorated cult chapel, the burial chamber of an Egyptian tomb rarely had inscriptions or images on its walls, but the objects that were placed inside it played a crucial role in the safeguarding of the deceased, and great importance was attached to their positioning. Spell 151 of the Book of the Dead focused on the role of the burial chamber and its equipping. The spell is unusual in that it consists of an exceptionally large illustration, usually occupying the full height of the papyrus roll, which incorporates a number of smaller images with accompanying texts (see cat. nos 43–4).

The illustration resembles a 'net', an exploded diagram of a three-dimensional space. At its centre is the image of the mummy, recumbent on a lion-shaped bed which stands on the floor of the burial chamber. The *ba*-bird is close by, and all around the mummy are divine

Fig. 36 The goddess Isis in her station at the foot of the mummy, as prescribed in spell 151. Granodiorite inner coffin of the Viceroy of Nubia, Merymose. 18th Dynasty, *c.* 1370 BC. EA 1001.

entities, stationed to provide protection. Closest to the mummy stands Anubis, placing his hands on the body in a symbolic representation of the embalming of the corpse. At the head and foot ends of the bier kneel the goddesses Nephthys and Isis, who make speeches in which they promise their protection (see fig. 36). On the walls are four amulets mounted on mud bricks, which served to repel hostile forces (see cat. nos 48–51), and at the corners the four Sons of Horus. Each figure or amulet provides magical protection and each is accompanied by a text:

> Words spoken by Isis: 'I have come as your protection, O Osiris, with the north wind which issued from Atum. I have let your throat breathe, I have caused you to be a god, and I have placed your enemies under your sandals.'

> Words spoken by Hapy [one of the Sons of Horus]: 'I have come that I may be your protection, O [deceased]: I have joined together your head and your members, I have smitten your enemies beneath you, and I have given you your head for ever.'

All of these formulae existed independently among the Coffin Texts of the Middle Kingdom, but it was not until the New Kingdom that they were collected together and functioned as commentaries to the illustrations. Spell 151 is often interpreted as a kind of inventory of the sepulchral chamber, a list of the magical aids which were required for a proper burial. Although this is a reasonable view, the function of the spell was more far-reaching; it acted rather to perpetuate the protective rituals which would keep the dead person safe.[3] Although the words and images would be effective simply by being present on the papyrus roll in the tomb, in the case of this spell a further effort was made to install the protectors around the mummy in a more concrete form. So some of the images and texts were regularly painted or carved on the surfaces of the coffins – particularly in the 18th and 19th Dynasties, from which period the fullest examples of the spell 151 vignette on papyri come. Isis and Nephthys are depicted at the foot and the head of the coffin respectively, sometimes standing but often kneeling exactly as they are shown on the papyri. Anubis is depicted twice, once on each side of the coffin, as though he were standing by the side of the mummy, and the Sons of Horus are represented, two on each side and hence approximately at the corners, as in the vignette (see cat. no. 46).

The four 'magic bricks' and their amulets were not usually depicted on the coffin. In the tombs of royal and elite individuals they were placed in niches cut into the walls. Each consisted of a small brick of unbaked mud, which served as the plinth for an image: a mummiform figure, a *djed* pillar, a jackal and a torch (see cat. nos 48–51). The texts which accompanied these images were either incised into the bricks or written in ink on their upper surface. The words explain that the emblems on the bricks were to ward off harmful forces which might enter the burial chamber from the four cardinal points:

> The torch: 'I am he who catches the sand to choke the hidden place [burial chamber], I drive off him who would oppose himself to the torch of the necropolis. I have fired the necropolis, I have confused the path, for I am [deceased's] protection.'

Magic bricks have been found in tombs dating from the New Kingdom to the Late Period. It is striking that, in spite of the precise indications given in the spells for the form of the amulets and their positioning, there were in practice numerous variations in the objects mounted on the bricks and in their location within the burial chamber.[4]

A great deal of magical significance was attached to mud bricks in ancient Egypt. The mud from which they were made was the medium for the growth of plants, and hence they symbolized the emergence of new life. Traditionally, mothers were positioned on mud bricks at childbirth (a custom which persists today in some areas). Immediately after birth, it was thought that the destiny of the child was determined by the gods, and the newborn infant was placed on bricks while this episode occurred.[5] The placing of bricks in the tomb therefore recalled the individual's birth and helped magically to assert that the burial chamber was itself a place where new life was to emerge. The notion of the completion of a cycle was strongly emphasized: the 'birth bricks', which were associated with the goddess Meskhenet, are sometimes depicted at the judgement of the dead, at which the destiny decreed for the person at birth was finally fulfilled (see pp. 215, 221, 231).

The diagram of spell 151 also includes two human-headed birds in the corners, *ba* spirits, which worshipped the sun-god as he rose into the sky. A shabti figure also appears in the burial chamber, together with its text (spell 6), perhaps reflecting the importance that these images had acquired by the New Kingdom as essential elements of a properly equipped burial (see cat. no. 55).

On the coffins the three-dimensional rendering of the burial chamber is often completed with four figures of the god Thoth holding the hieroglyphic sign for the sky on a pole. These relate to another text from the Book of the Dead, spell 161, 'for breaking an opening into the sky'. Its purpose and its connection with the coffin are shown in the rubric:

> As for any noble dead for whom this ritual is performed over his coffin, there shall
> be opened for him four openings in the sky, one for the north wind – that is Osiris;
> another for the south wind – that is Ra; another for the west wind – that is Isis;
> another for the east wind – that is Nephthys. As for each one of these winds which
> is in its opening, its task is to enter into his nose.

The winds therefore provided the breath of life for the dead; ensuring air to breathe is a concern which appears elsewhere in the Book of the Dead (see Chapter 7).

Power and protection for the mummy: the mask and amulets

The whole process of mummification, at its most elaborate, was carried out in a context of ritual. The salts, oils and resins that were used, in addition to their preservative qualities, were held to magically purify and regenerate the dead, and to make them like gods. The wrappings also had divine associations: the linen cloth which was used was ideally supposed to have been woven by the goddess Tayet or the weavers of the goddess Neith. These connections are mentioned in the Pyramid Texts, where the wrappings are also stated to have been fashioned from the protective eye of Horus.[6] The external appearance of the mummy was of great importance: the *sah* shape was the visible indication that the person had been transformed into a divine being.

Most crucial to establishing this godlike status was the mask which was placed over the head of the mummy (see cat. nos 3 and 57–8). This mask was called the *tep en seshta*, 'head of mystery' (or 'mysterious head'); the 'mystery' here means the mummified corpse. The mask's purpose is mentioned in a liturgy, where the dead person is said to be 'one who sees with the head of a god'.[7] The role of the mask is described more fully in spell 151 of the Book of the Dead:

> Anubis speaks, the embalmer, lord of the divine hall, when he has placed his hands on the coffin of [the deceased] and equipped him with what [he] needs: 'Hail, O beautiful of face, lord of vision, whom Ptah-Sokar has gathered together and whom Anubis has upraised, to whom Shu gave support, O beautiful of face among the gods!'

> 'Your right eye is the night barque, your left eye is the day barque, your eyebrows are the Ennead. The crown of your head is Anubis, the back of your head is Horus. Your fingers are Thoth, your lock of hair Ptah-Sokar. You [the mask] are in front of [the deceased], he sees by means of you. [You] lead him to the goodly ways, you repel Seth's band for him and cast his enemies under his feet for him in front of the Ennead in the great House of the Noble in Heliopolis. You take the goodly way to the presence of Horus, the lord of the nobles.'[8]

These words were for the Egyptians probably the most important part of spell 151, which is actually entitled the 'spell for the head of mystery'. The text makes two points clear: that the mask enabled the deceased to see and that it drove away his enemies. The spell is found in the Coffin Texts of the Middle Kingdom and it was sometimes inscribed on the helmet-like masks that began to be used at that period. It even appears – in its Book of the Dead version – on the back of the gold mask of Tutankhamun (see fig. 38) and it recurred on the cartonnage masks of the Ptolemaic Period (see p. 127). Finally the spell emphasizes that through mummification by Anubis the deceased had become wholly divine, a transformation which is expressed through the equation of all parts of the head with those of deities or with divine barques.

The materials from which the mask was made were also indications of divinity. The golden skin and the blue-coloured hair suggest the gold and lapis lazuli of which the flesh and hair of the gods was supposed to consist. For the very highest elite, such as the pharaoh, a mummy mask of solid gold would be provided (see fig. 38); for people of lower status, gold leaf or just yellow paint for the face, and blue paint for the wig sufficed, but by magical transference these would obtain the qualities of the real materials they imitated.

The mummy was also protected and empowered by means of amulets (fig. 37). These small images could enshrine and convey magical power, both for the purpose of protection and to endow the owner with special qualities. Common Egyptian words for amulet relate to notions of 'protecting' and of being sound or whole. They were used extensively by the living and were often incorporated into jewellery, as well as being provided for the dead.

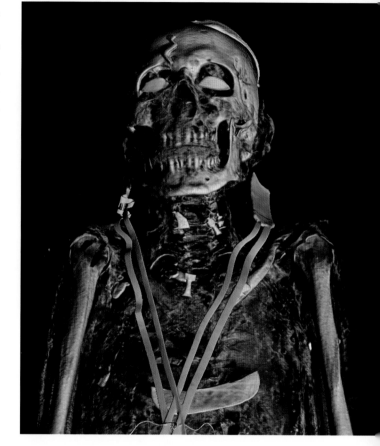

Fig. 37 CT scan image of the fully wrapped mummy of the priest of Khons, Nesperennub, showing amulets on the upper body, including a *djed* pillar, vulture and winged sun disc, and a serpent above the right eye. 22nd Dynasty, *c.* 800 BC. EA 30720.

Fig. 38 The gold mummy mask of Tutankhamun. On the rear surface is the text relating to the mask from spell 151 of the Book of the Dead. Late 18th Dynasty, *c.* 1327 BC. Cairo, J 60672.

Amulets go back to the beginnings of Egyptian culture. The range of types began to develop in the Old Kingdom, and by the Late Period they had become numerous and varied. Spells for some of the most important amulets were incorporated into the Book of the Dead, particularly the *djed* pillar and Isis knot, the heart scarab, heart, headrest, and papyrus column – all of which are found frequently on mummies (see cat. nos 59, 60 and 62). Various ornamental collars also carried amuletic qualities. The power of amulets was supposed to reside in their shape and the material from which they were made (their colour being especially important), but to activate them properly the words of spells had to be spoken over them and they had to be placed in prescribed positions on the body. Many amulets were to be put at the throat, a part of the body considered especially vulnerable. The positioning was often related to their symbolic role. The *djed* pillar stood for stability and endurance. It perhaps originally represented a tree or bundle of reeds and was associated with the god Sokar, but it later came to be linked with Osiris, and especially with his backbone. Osiris was often depicted as a composite of human figure and *djed*, with the god's crowned head and arms emerging from the pillar. In spell 155 of the Book of the Dead the connection with Osiris is explicit: 'Raise yourself, O Osiris, you have your backbone ...'. The rubric prescribes that the amulet should be of gold and be placed at the throat. In practice most *djed* pillars were made of other materials; some are found at the throat of the mummy but in the Late Period, when many *djed* pillars were included within the wrappings, they were usually laid in rows on the torso.

The practice of placing amulets on the body became more widespread over time, and there was a connection with the status of the deceased. On the mummy of Tutankhamun there were 150 objects, although only about 25 of these were amulets in the strict sense, but for other people in the New Kingdom the range was limited, often to the heart scarab (see pp. 44–5, 226–7) and a few of the commonest types of amulet mentioned above. Between the Third Intermediate Period and the Ptolemaic era the range of funerary amulets widened enormously and many new types were introduced. From these later centuries come many scarabs, *wedjat* eyes, two fingers, deity figures, miniature crowns and sceptres, and other divine emblems. These might be positioned in groups or distributed over the body in elaborate arrangements, mostly on the front from the neck to the abdomen and sometimes in more than one layer. Most of the 'newer' amulets did not have associated spells in the Book of the Dead, though on some papyri there is a diagram showing the 'recommended' positioning of amulets on a mummy.[9]

In spite of the care and protection which had been lavished on the mummy, it was not expected to be the final form which the dead would assume. Its wrappings served as a cocoon, inside which regeneration took place; the person would emerge from this transition ready to make full use of his limbs. The bandages, in fact, had ambivalent meaning; while they ensured the physical integrity of the body and protected it, they also confined it in a state of rigid immobility. As early as the Old Kingdom, passages in the Pyramid Texts assure the dead king that he will loosen his bandages and throw them off.[10] They did not of course envisage a literal resurrection of the corpse, but a figurative release from the bonds of death. In keeping with this concept, the dead enjoying the afterlife are depicted not as mummies but as people in daily dress and having full command of their faculties.

43 Spell 151 from the Book of the Dead of Nakht

Painted papyrus
H 36.0 cm
Late 18th or early 19th Dynasty, c. 1350–1290 BC
Provenance not recorded (probably Thebes)
London, British Museum, EA 10471/20

Nakht was a king's scribe and general (see also cat. nos 70, 104, 127–8). His papyrus contains a simple version of the vignette of spell 151 (see pp. 106–7). All of the figures and texts are located within a shrine-like canopy, although the artist has included only a selection from the full range of protective forces which the spell enumerates. In the centre Nakht's mummy lies on a lion-bier, attended by Anubis. Isis and Nephthys kneel at each end, resting their hands on the *shen*-ring, a symbol of eternity. Two of the four emblems of the 'magic bricks' – the *djed* pillar and Anubis jackal – appear flanking the mummy, and the Sons of Horus squat at the four corners of the chamber. The *ba*-birds and shabti figure which are features of the more complete versions of the scene (see cat. no. 44) are omitted, but in their place the ibis-headed Thoth is represented, with a short speech in which he declares that he will protect Nakht and will 'open his face'. At the far right, outside the sacred confines of the burial chamber, Nakht stands with arms raised in jubilation, his name and titles written in front of him.

Glanville 1927; Faulkner 1985, 146–7; Munro 1988, 300, no. b.20; Quirke 1993, 46, no. 119.

44 Spell 151 from the Book of the Dead of Muthetepty

Painted papyrus
H 34.0 cm
21st Dynasty, *c.* 1050 BC
Provenance not recorded (probably Thebes)
London, British Museum, EA 10010/5

The Chantress of Amun Muthetepty possessed a
papyrus (see also cat. no. 94) which contained a finely
detailed example of the spell 151 vignette. The internal
space of the burial chamber is more precisely defined
than that of Nakht (previous page) by means of
rectangular compartments. At the centre the mummy
of the dead woman lies on its bier beneath a shrine-
shaped canopy, while Anubis stands in attendance.
Beside the mummy, but depicted as if below it, is
Muthetepty's *ba*, which will leave and return to the
tomb each day. Isis and Nephthys kneel at the ends of
the bier. On all four sides are the amulets of the 'magic
bricks', together with the words of their recitations.
The Sons of Horus stand at the corners, and a pair of
ba spirits raise their hands in token of adoration of
the sun-god. At the lower left and right of the vignette
the text of the shabti spell appears in two variant
forms. That at the left is accompanied by a mummiform
figure which probably represents a shabti. Unusually,
a jackal-headed figure stands by the other text.

Faulkner 1985, 148; Munro 1988, 299, no. b.15; Niwinski 1989,
328; Quirke 1993, 45, 77, no. 115.

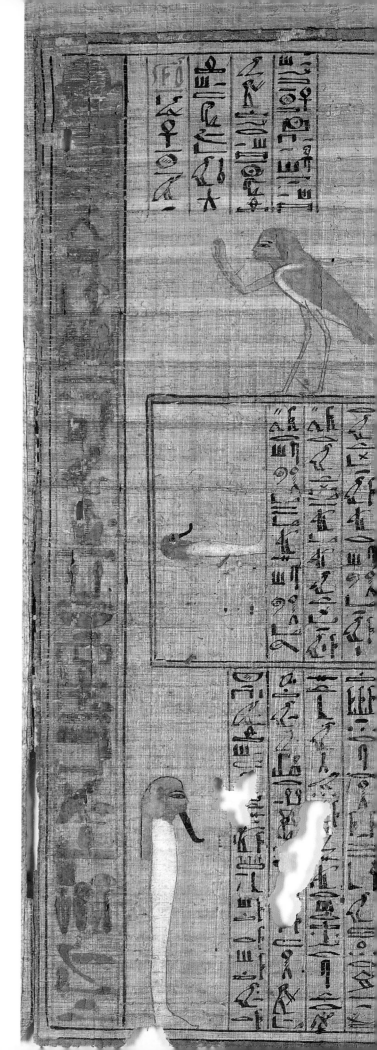

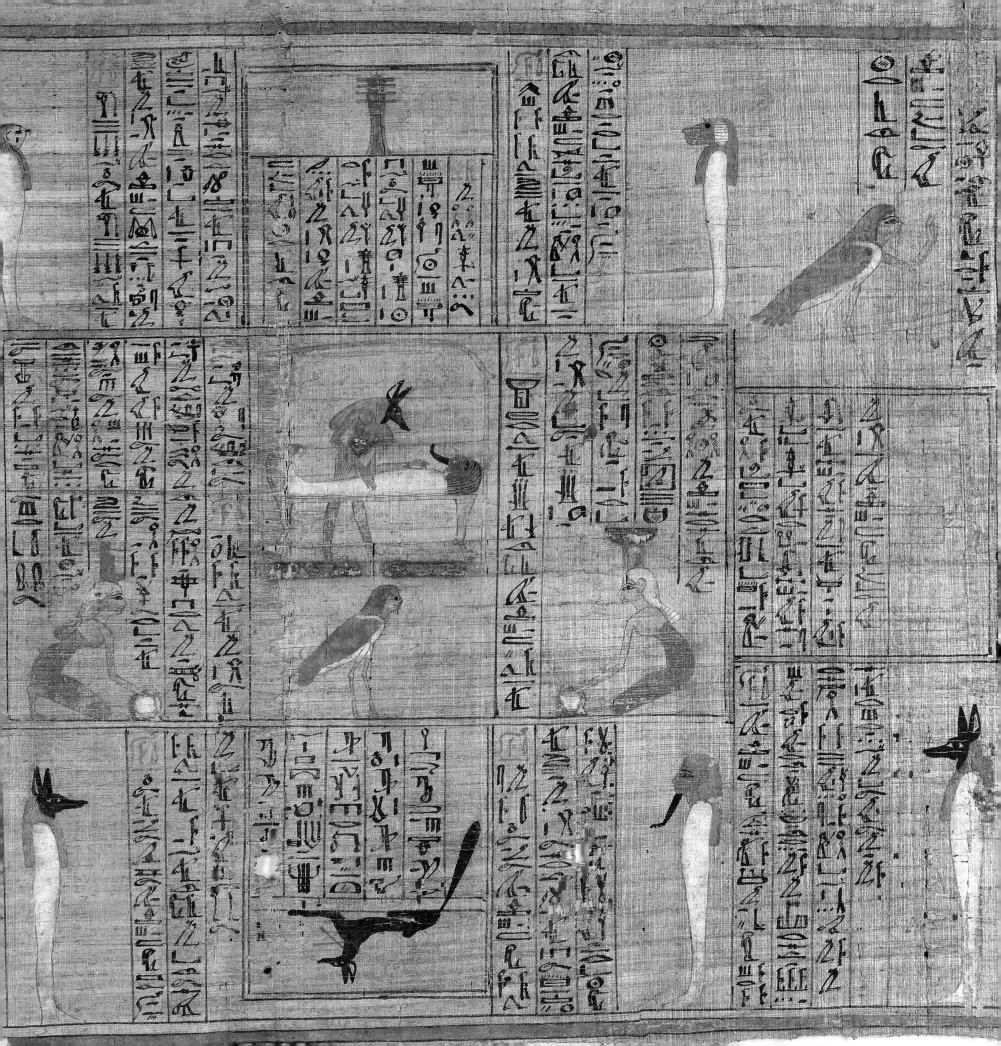

45 Spell 161 from the Book of the Dead of Hor

(Not exhibited)
Painted papyrus
H 36.0 cm
Ptolemaic Period, c. 305–30 BC
Akhmim
London, British Museum, EA 10479/1

Spell 161 of the Book of the Dead describes how the north, south, east and
west winds are released through openings in the sky in order to bring the
breath of life to the deceased (see p. 108). On coffins of the New Kingdom
passages from this spell were often combined with extracts from spell
151, forming a consistent programme of decoration around the mummy.
Usually four figures of the god Thoth appear as well, each one holding
the hieroglyphic sign for 'sky' on a pole (see cat. no. 46). Although these
Thoth figures are clearly related to the text about the four winds, they
do not appear in Book of the Dead papyri until after the New Kingdom.
The papyrus of Hor presents a late interpretation of the motif, in which
the four Thoths are grouped together. The sky signs have disappeared
and their poles have been reinterpreted by the painter so that the god
appears to be grasping the edges of door leaves – presumably to release
the four winds.

Quirke 1993, 39, no. 72; Mosher 2001, 108, pl. 12.

46 Outer coffin of Henutmehyt

Painted and gilded wood; eyes inlaid
H 207.0 cm; W 63.0 cm
19th Dynasty, c. 1250 BC
Thebes
London, British Museum, EA 48001

In terms of its design, Henutmehyt's outer coffin closely resembles her inner case (see cat. no. 38), although instead of tamarisk wood, it is made chiefly from imported cedar. The pictorial and inscriptional decoration on both of these anthropoid coffins consists mainly of elements taken from spells 151 and 161 of the Book of the Dead. The four Sons of Horus are arranged in pairs on the sides, accompanied by the words they were to speak, and Anubis is also depicted in the middle of each side, distinguished by his different epithets, *Imywet* and *Khenty-seh-netjer*, both of which refer to the embalming place over which he presided. Isis appears at the foot; her sister Nephthys is often painted at the head of the coffin, but has been omitted in this case. These figures and texts reproduce the arrangement of the main components of the vignette of spell 151 (see pp. 106–7). The place occupied by the deceased in the vignette is here taken by the mummy itself in the coffin. The coffin is therefore a three-dimensional realization of the diagram, but the spatial arrangement of some of the figures and texts also recalls that on rectangular coffins of the Middle Kingdom, where they are named (and sometimes depicted). At the four 'corners' of the coffin are figures of Thoth holding a pole bearing the sign for the sky. These figures come from spell 161, part of the text of which is included on Henutmehyt's coffin: 'Ra lives, the tortoise is dead, the corpse is interred and the

deceased's bones are reunited ...'. The words magically affirm the ideal situation in which the sun-god is triumphant over his foes (represented by the tortoise), while the deceased, like Osiris, has regained bodily integrity and lies within the protection of the coffin. The full text of spell 161 adds that four openings in the sky would be made, releasing the north, south, east and west winds to bring the breath of life to the deceased (see p. 116).

Taylor 1999, 61, col. pls IX–X; Strudwick 2006, 214–15; Cooney 2007, 398–400, figs 1, 4–9.

47 **Mummy of Katebet**

Human remains, linen, cartonnage
H 165.0 cm
End of 18th or beginning of 19th Dynasty, *c.* 1300–1275 BC
Thebes
London, British Museum, EA 6665

Radiographic investigations of Katebet's mummy have shown that she died at an advanced age. The embalming of her body was evidently carried out in a rudimentary fashion, since traces of desiccated brain are visible in the skull cavity, and the embalmers seem to have applied large quantities of dense mud to the corpse, perhaps to prevent it from falling to pieces. The outer trappings of the mummy are comparatively rich, perhaps indicating that Katebet's relatives chose to devote more resources to the fashioning of her eternal image than to the physical preparation of her remains. The cartonnage mask is gilded and real rings are placed on the fingers of the carved wooden hands. The linen wrappings are retained by transverse bands spaced at intervals; these had been dyed and when first discovered were brightly coloured, but have now faded to a uniform brown. The pectoral ornaments, heart-scarab amulet and shabti figure which lie on the front of the wrappings were not made specifically for Katebet (her coffin was also adapted, having been originally designed for a man). This may indicate either a hasty burial with second-hand goods or that the contents of the tomb were disturbed and later rearranged.

Dawson and Gray 1968, 28–9, pls XIV b, XXXIV a, b (no. 52); Cooney 2007, 406–7, figs 23–4.

A set of magic bricks

19th Dynasty, c. 1250 BC
Thebes
London, British Museum

48 Brick with reed torch (south)
Brick 4.0 x 10.8 cm; H of reed 19.5 cm
EA 41544

49 Brick with wooden mummiform figure (north)
Brick 3.7 x 9.8 cm; H of figure 14.5 cm
EA 41546

50 Brick with faience *djed* pillar (west)
Brick 4.3 x 9.5 cm; H of *djed* pillar 5.8 cm
EA 41547

51 Brick with mud jackal of Anubis (east)
Brick 2.5 x 9.2 cm; H of jackal 7.2 cm
EA 41545

Spell 151 of the Book of the Dead prescribes the use of four magical amulets, each mounted on a brick of unbaked mud, which were to be hidden in niches around the burial chamber to repel evil from the cardinal points (see p. 107). This set was made for the Chantress of Amun Henutmehyt (see cat. nos 15, 38, 46, 54 and 134–5). Each amulet has a speech, in which its function is explained. The figure on the northern brick overthrows the one who would overthrow the deceased. The torch (southern brick) prevents sand from choking the burial chamber. The Anubis jackal (eastern brick) repels the rage of a hostile being, and the *djed* pillar (western brick) 'keeps off the one whose steps are backward and whose face is hidden'. Instructions explain how these amulets should be prepared (see below).

Taylor 1999, 63, col. pl. xv.

This spell is to be spoken over an Anubis of unbaked clay mixed with incense, set firmly on a brick of clay, with this spell incised on it. Make for it a niche in the east wall, its face toward the west and cover its face.

(Spell 151, 'instruction for the brick with the Anubis figure')

Stelae of the general Kasa

19th Dynasty, reign of Sety I, *c.* 1290–1279 BC
Saqqara

The four 'magic bricks' were supposed to be placed in niches in the walls of the burial chamber, oriented north, south, east and west (see p. 107). The King's Scribe and General Kasa was provided with a more elaborate version of this protective device. In his tomb at Saqqara were four painted limestone stelae, inscribed with the spells belonging to the four amulets. On each stela is a hollowed-out depression, into which the appropriate amulet was inlaid. These are now lost, but the shape of their sockets shows clearly that they were the standard amulets known from spell 151 and from other sets of magic bricks. On three of the stelae Kasa is shown adoring the amulet, and to ensure correct placement in the tomb, the hieroglyphic words for north, south, east and west are carved at the upper corners of each stela. The location of Kasa's tomb is now unknown, and it remains uncertain whether the stelae were built into the walls of the burial chamber or were simply erected around the coffin.

PM III, 2, 745; Nelson 1978, 70–72; Meeks and Pierini n.d., 27, 77–9; de Cenival 1992, 98, 99.

52 Stela for the northern wall

H 51.8 cm; W 34.0 cm
Marseilles, Musée d'Archéologie Méditerranéenne, 240

At the top a pair of jackals faces a *shen*-ring (symbolizing eternity), the sign for water and a pot (a group which also appears on the stela for the eastern wall). The text in horizontal lines begins: 'To be placed on the northern wall', and continues with the words of the formula belonging to the amulet of the mummiform figure. Below, Kasa kneels in adoration before a silhouette of the figure on its brick support.

53 **Stela for the western wall**

H 45.7 cm; W 28.8 cm

Marseilles, Musée d'Archéologie Méditerranéenne, 242

At the top the central arrangement of *shen*-ring, water and pot is flanked by a pair of eyes. The main text of the stela is put into the mouth of the owner himself and consists of the words of the spell for the *djed* pillar. Below, Kasa is shown twice adoring the pillar.

54 **Chest and canopic jars of Henutmehyt**

Painted wood
H of chest 46.0 cm; H of jars 37.5–42.0 cm
19th Dynasty, *c.* 1250 BC
Thebes
London, British Museum, EA 51813

Next to the mummy itself, the preserved internal organs of the deceased formed one of the most important parts of the tomb's contents. These organs, stored in four vessels known to Egyptologists as canopic jars, were usually placed in a shrine-shaped chest, which is often depicted being dragged to the tomb in vignettes of spell 1 of the Book of the Dead. The canopic containers were placed close to the foot of the coffin in the burial chamber.

This set of jars, belonging to Henutmehyt (see cat. nos 15, 38, 46, 48–51 and 134–5), is typical of its period. Each jar contained a different organ of the body (usually the liver, lungs, stomach and intestines) and each was magically protected by one of the four Sons of Horus, who are represented in the vignette of spell 151 as guardians of the deceased (see p. 107). The lids of Henutmehyt's jars represent the distinctive heads of these deities: a human head for Imsety, that of a baboon for Hapy, and a jackal and a falcon respectively for Duamutef and Qebehsenuef. The black colouring of the jars and chest symbolically evoke the concept of rejuvenation. These jars were filled to the brim with a mixture of plaster and organic materials after the preserved body parts had been inserted; this substance has been removed from the jackal-headed jar, revealing a miniature anthropoid coffin which enclosed the organ package inside.

Taylor 1999, 63, pls 14–15; Strudwick 2006, 214.

55 Shabti of a Chantress of Amun

Painted limestone
H 25.3 cm; W 7.5 cm
19th Dynasty, *c.* 1295–1186 BC
Probably from Thebes
London, British Museum, EA 24428

The shabti figure had become an important part of the burial outfit during
the Middle Kingdom, and possessed its own distinct magical text, which
was incorporated into the Book of the Dead as spell 6 (see p. 245). The words
explain the function of the figure, which was to act as a substitute for its
owner in case he or she should be summoned to carry out menial labour in
the fields of the Netherworld (see p. 245). The shabti text was also included
in the composite spell 151 and an image of the mummy-shaped figurine is
often found in the associated vignette of the burial chamber.

This shabti is a particularly fine specimen which was inscribed for
a Chantress of Amun. She holds a hoe and mattock in her hands, and
also grasps two small seed baskets. The eight lines of hieroglyphic texts
carved around her body include her name and title, and a version of
the spell. Her headdress is heavy and elaborate, including a small fringe
of curls around the brow, probably representing the natural hair worn
beneath a wig. Despite the fine workmanship of the figure, the lack
of detail in the collar and the absence of paint on the tools may indicate
that it was left unfinished.

Russmann 2001, 211, no. 111.

56 **Miniature stela of Ruiu with spell for a shabti**

Granite
H 8.6 cm; w 6.6 cm
18th or 19th Dynasty, c. 1400–1250 BC
Provenance unrecorded
London, British Museum, EA 66850

This small tablet, shaped like a stela, is inscribed with the shabti spell in four vertical columns, on behalf of the Lady of the House Ruiu, of whom nothing is otherwise known. Next to the text is a depiction of a mummiform figure, probably representing a shabti. The function of this unusual piece is unknown. The disposition of text and image recalls that of the shabti in the vignette of spell 151 of the Book of the Dead (see cat no. 44). Possibly this stela – like those of the general Kasa (see cat. nos 52–3) – was placed within the burial chamber of Ruiu to form part of a rendering of the components of the vignette in stone.

57 Spell for a mummy mask from the papyrus of Nebseny

Ink on papyrus
H 33.0 cm
18th Dynasty, *c.* 1400 BC
Memphite necropolis
London, British Museum, EA 9900/21

The spell for the 'head of mystery' or mummy mask (see p. 109) is given in the Book of the Dead of Nebseny, with a small vignette illustrating the mask, complete with wig, collar and beard.

Lapp 2004, pl. 62.

58 The 'head of mystery': a mummy mask with its spell

Cartonnage, painted and gilded
H 44.0 cm; D 28.0 cm; D 23.0 cm
Ptolemaic/Roman Period, first century BC–first century AD
Provenance unrecorded
EA 29472

This mask presents a bland and idealized eternal image of the deceased owner, with the shining golden skin which denoted his newly acquired divine status. A small *ankh* amulet (signifying life) is depicted at the throat, and a winged scarab beetle propelling the solar disc appears on the crown of the head. The painted rear panel shows a row of unnamed gods (the second being clearly Osiris), a *ba*-bird and a falcon representing the sun-god. The seven columns of text at the bottom include repetitions of the name Osiris and other hieroglyphic signs, randomly arranged and without meaning. The raised-relief inscription around the brow-band, however, is recognizable as an abbreviated version of the 'mask text' from spell 151 of the Book of the Dead (see p. 109). This spell is only rarely found on the masks themselves in the New Kingdom (that of Tutankhamun being a notable exception), but it returned to prominence in the Late Period, and extracts from the text were sometimes inscribed on masks as late as the first century BC, although often in an incomplete or garbled form.

Andrews 1998, 186–9, no. 57; Andrews 2000, 140–1.

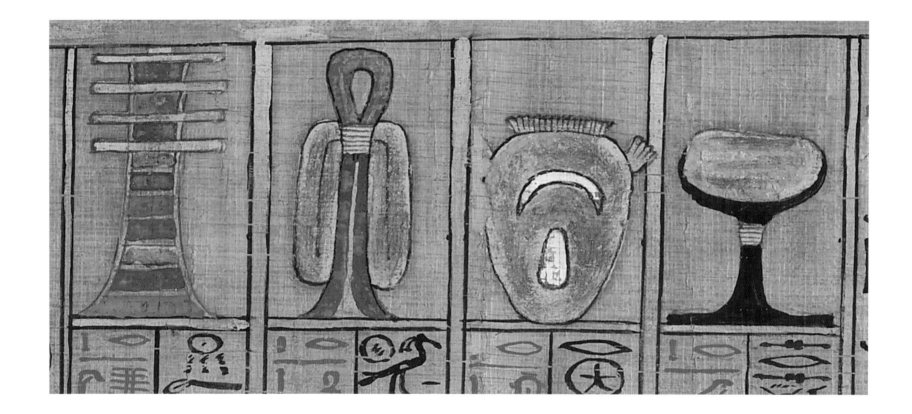

59 Spells for amulets from the papyrus of Ani

Painted papyrus
H 42.0 cm
19th Dynasty, c. 1275 BC
Thebes
London, British Museum, EA 10470/33

Towards the end of the Book of the Dead of Ani come four short spells for the *djed* pillar, Isis knot, heart and headrest amulets (spells 155, 156, 29B and 166). Large examples of the first three amulets were commonly placed on mummies in the New Kingdom. They proliferated in burials of the first millennium BC (see pp. 109–10), when numerous *djed* pillars (now often small in size) were provided for a single mummy. The amulet representing a headrest was less widely used in the New Kingdom but became popular in the Late Period.

British Museum 1890, pl. 33; British Museum 1894, pl. 33; Faulkner 1985, 158; Andrews 1994, fig. 68.

60 *Djed* pillar, Isis knot, heart and headrest amulets

Djed pillar amulet: blue glass; H 5.7 cm; 18th–19th Dynasties, *c.* 1550–1186 BC
Isis knot amulet: red jasper; H 7.0 cm; New Kingdom, *c.* 1550–1069 BC
Heart amulet: feldspar; H 4.6 cm; 19th Dynasty, *c.* 1295–1186 BC
Headrest amulet: haematite; L 3.9 cm; 26th Dynasty, *c.* 664–525 BC
Provenances not recorded
London, British Museum, EA 20623, 20646, 20647, 59589

Djed-pillar amulets were usually positioned at the neck. This example is
inscribed with the name of the embalmer Nebmehyt. Isis-knot (*tit*) amulets
were made from jasper and carnelian and also positioned at the neck. This
one bears the name of the *sem*-priest of Ptah and priest of Thoth, Iryiry.
Heart amulets were made from various stones or glass and usually
positioned on the chest. This one bears the name of Iuty. Headrest amulets
were made from haematite. This one carries the text of spell 166 and bears
the name of the storehouse-keeper Ahmose.

Djed: Cooney 1976, 24, no. 245; Isis knot: Andrews 1994, 45, fig. 49 (e); headrest:
Andrews 1994, 93, fig. 95 (d).

61 **Hypocephalus of Tasheritkhons**

Linen, plaster, ink.
Diameter 18.7 cm
Ptolemaic Period, 305–30 BC
Provenance unrecorded.
London, British Museum, EA 37909

Spell 162 of the Book of the Dead was 'for providing heat under the head of the deceased'. The spell contains the words supposedly spoken by the *ihet*, a divine cow which is described in this text as the mother of Ra. The heat which was to be created beneath the head was intended to bring new life to the dead person. The colophon states that the spell should be spoken over an amulet in the form of a cow, placed on the mummy's throat, or 'put in writing on a new sheet of papyrus placed under his/her head'.

These instructions led to the practice of placing an amulet in the coffin under the mummy's head. These are found mainly in the burials of high-status priestly families in Upper Egypt.

This amulet, the hypocephalus ('under the head'), consisted of a disc, usually made of linen, but occasionally of bronze or papyrus, on which were texts and images relating to the content of spell 162. The images vary and are only partly intelligible; the texts which accompany them do not always explain their full meaning. On this example, the inscribed border names the deceased as Tasheritkhons. At the top is a deity with two heads, holding a staff bearing an image of the jackal-god Wepwawet. At each side are boats containing divine entities, including the sun-god as a scarab beetle on the right. In the central compartment the god Amun-Ra appears with four ram-heads, denoting his multiple divine attributes. Four baboons are stated to be 'adoring the god'. Another scene, orientated at 180 degrees to the rest, shows a cow (perhaps the *ihet* mentioned in the spell) with other deities.

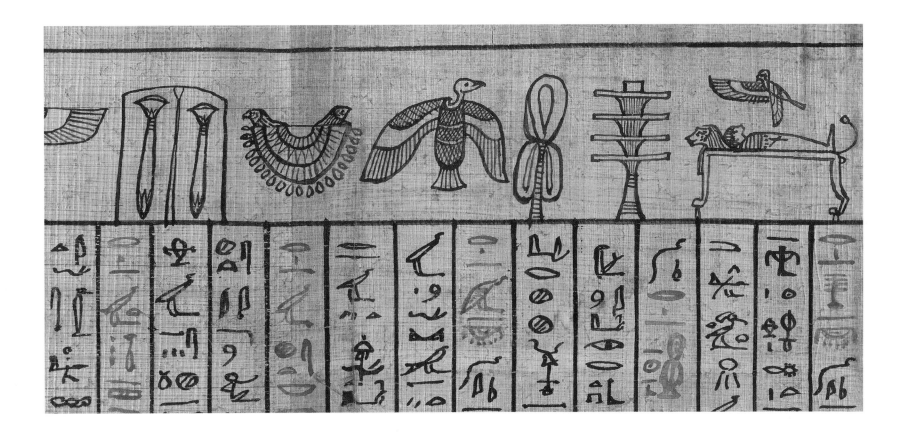

62 Papyrus-column amulet

Faience
H 5.2 cm
Late Period, 664–305 BC
Provenance not recorded
London, British Museum, EA 7445

The papyrus plant had connotations of freshness, and hence by extension the renewal of life. One of the commonest amulets took the form of papyrus stems bound together at the top in the form of a column or sceptre. Two spells in the Book of the Dead relate to amulets of this type. Spell 160 is for 'a papyrus column of green feldspar'; the green colour expressed part of the power of the amulet, and most examples are made of faience with a green or blue-green glaze. Spell 159 directed that the amulet be placed on the throat of the deceased. Such an amulet, of gold inlaid with green feldspar, was found at the neck of Tutankhamun's mummy.

Taylor and Strudwick 2005, 94–5.

63 Spells for amulets and collars from the papyrus of Tentawy

Ink on papyrus
H 37.8 cm
Ptolemaic Period, 305–30 BC
Thebes
London, British Museum, EA 9902/4

This Book of the Dead includes the familiar amulet spells for the *djed* pillar and Isis knot (*tit*) (visible at the right in the vignette), and also spells for amuletic collars: the golden vulture collar (spell 157) and a golden falcon collar (spell 158). Full-size examples of these collars as well as miniature versions have been found on mummies. The falcon collar was also regularly depicted on the breast of the deceased on mummy masks and coffins. They conferred protection on the deceased. To the left of the collars in the vignette are two depictions of papyrus-column amulets, which are described in spells 159 and 160.

Quirke 1993, 66, no. 261.

6 The Landscape of the Hereafter

John H. Taylor

O you door-keepers who guard your portals, who swallow souls and who gulp down the corpses of the dead who pass by you when they are allotted to the House of Destruction ... May you guide [the deceased], may you open the portals for him, may the earth open its caverns to him, may you make him triumphant over his enemies ...

(Spell 127, 'worshipping the gods of the caverns; what a man should say there when he reaches them ...')

Conceptions of the beyond

The tomb was the interface between worlds, a point of access between the realm of the living and that of the dead. This role commenced at the Opening of the Mouth ritual and the placing of the mummy in the burial chamber, events which marked a fundamental change in the dead person's status from inanimate corpse to a functioning complex of physical and spiritual components. On their side, the family of the deceased would help to sustain his *ka* and his *ba* by means of the mortuary cult, regularly presenting offerings at the tomb chapel and reciting prayers in which, by pronouncing his name, they would perpetuate his existence. But the dead person himself was now to enter the hereafter and to make his passage to the other world quite alone. Living relatives could not ensure that he would reach his goal. In this endeavour, the knowledge and magical power which the Book of the Dead gave him were his chief support.

Where did the dead dwell? The Egyptians had different responses to this question. The dwelling place of the dead could be viewed as a part of the real world, with the tomb as the permanent residence of both mummy and spirits, and from it the spirit might now and then come out to commune with the living, or even to bring harm. Alternatively, the realm of the dead was a world of the imagination, to which the tomb was merely the threshold.

This imaginary world is the setting for the experiences described in the Book of the Dead. It was called the Duat (most English translations of the term reflect its separation from the everyday realm: 'Otherworld', 'Netherworld', 'Farworld', 'Underworld'). In the Egyptian view of the universe there were three main regions: the land of the living (with Egypt at its centre); the sky, a watery expanse stretched above the earth and supported like a canopy at four points; and the Duat, which was usually imagined as lying beneath the earth, though it could also be located inside the body of the sky-goddess Nut.[1] Sky, earth and Duat formed a kind of bubble, outside of which were limitless expanses of waters – the original chaos, Nun, from which the universe had been formed by the creator-god. The sun-god travelled across the sky during the day, bathing the earth in his light, and at night he passed into the Duat – which might be envisaged as a journey underground or through the body of the sky-goddess, depending

Fig. 39 A map-like diagram of features in the Netherworld, including paths and watercourses, from the Book of Two Ways. Interior of the inner coffin of Seni from el-Bersha (see cat. no. 20), 12th Dynasty, *c*. 1850 BC. EA 30842.

on which mythology was adopted. He and other gods were present in all three parts of the cosmos.

The Duat was itself a complex region with many different parts. Notions of its character developed through time, with changing emphasis on different aspects. A recurrent theme is that it possessed many of the features of the everyday world. From the very earliest times the Egyptians imagined an afterlife in an environment which resembled the one they knew in life. The gifts for the dead which were placed in the simple graves of the Predynastic period were familiar things – clothes, cosmetic pots and palettes, tools, weapons – all ready for continued use when their owner should awaken to his or her new life. At the most basic level the Duat reflected the natural world the Egyptians knew – chiefly the fertile Nile valley and the Delta rather than the desert. It had earth, watercourses, islands and mounds, fields, lakes, pathways, caverns, air, fire, light, darkness and living creatures (see fig. 39). But it also included fantastic elements – lakes of fire, walls of iron, trees of turquoise – which emphasized its strangeness. The dimensions of some features are quoted in the Book of the Dead; they are larger than their earthly counterparts but not by very much (the barley growing in the Field of Reeds stands 5 cubits, or 2.5 metres, high); instead of intimidating the traveller there is rather a comforting sense of abundance.

The Book of the Dead and other funerary texts refer to many topographical features and inhabitants of the Duat, but it is not easy to visualize that fantastic realm. It has no consistent geography; there is no reliable 'map', on which everything is located. Among the Coffin Texts – the precursor of the Book of the Dead – is a composition called the Book of Two Ways, which describes features of the hereafter and includes a diagram which has been likened to a map. But although it shows paths and waterways it is not a map in the modern sense of an accurate rendering of a three-dimensional landscape at a consistent scale (even if the landscape is imaginary). The 'journey' which the dead take in this region is no more clearly defined in the Book of the Dead. There is no consistent path to be

followed, no fixed sequence of steps or stages which must be passed, and no clear indication of the lapse of time involved. Nor is there a single goal to be reached. Several different outcomes of the journey are mentioned in the spells. One is to dwell in the kingdom of Osiris; this is said to be a place somewhere within the Duat and yet it was also the Duat in its entirety. The dead might also travel through the Duat with the sun-god as he made his nightly passage to the eastern horizon, or they might end their journey in the pastoral paradise called the Field of Reeds (see pp. 241–4).

This lack of consistency can be explained in part by the fact that the rich Egyptian funerary literature encompassed texts of different ages and diverse origins, which were never fully synthesized or rendered uniform. Variants and apparent contradictions were tolerantly accepted. Different interpretations of the texts were equally valid, as the glosses of spell 17 (see pp. 51–3) show. The Book of the Dead was by no means the only text which described the hereafter; there were other compositions, such as the books of Amduat, Gates and Caverns, which illustrated and described the Netherworld in more consistent terms, notably as a sequence of gated chambers or caverns, each with specific topographical features and inhabitants. However, these works arose from different roots, being mainly concerned with charting the nightly journey of the sun-god, and they do not accommodate all the features of the landscape which are mentioned in the Book of the Dead, although there are some 'overlaps'. For the Egyptians the authority which these varied 'books' held, as works of the gods or ancestors, outweighed the inconsistencies which seem so troublesome and frustrating to the modern mind.

Rites of passage: gates, mounds and caverns

The Book of the Dead, then, is not concerned with presenting a complete and 'accurate' picture of the Duat. Those spells which 'describe' its features focus on specific details about which the deceased needs to know in order to make a safe journey. These features – gates, mounds, caverns – are not to be understood too literally. Some of them are equated with sacred places in Egypt but they do not resemble the real localities. To some extent the descriptions are duplicated, probably because the Book of the Dead enshrines several alternative traditions side by side. The factor common to them all is that they are places of supernatural power, points where the deceased must face a challenge. He must demonstrate his worthiness and negotiate his way forward. In every one of these encounters his principal equipment is the special knowledge which the Book of the Dead provides him with, about the appearance of the mounds or other features, and particularly the names of their divine guardians and attendants.

All of these points are well illustrated by the gates (see cat. nos 64–5). For the Egyptians, 'the gate is a most pregnant symbol of transition'.[1] Papyrus Westcar mentions the *ba* knowing the paths of the beyond leading to the gate of 'he who conceals the weary one'.[2] In the Book of the Dead the concept is expressed in several spells (notably 144–7), which describe the multiple gates that are to be passed through in order to reach 'the one whom they conceal' or 'the weary one' (Osiris).[3] The gates are guarded by apotropaic deities of frightening aspect, animal-headed and armed with knives (see fig. 40). The deceased can only pass by speaking their names and the names of the gates. The number of gates varies from spell to spell – twenty-one, fourteen, fifteen, seven. The key idea is that of a concentric ring of protective walls around Osiris at the

Fig. 40 'He who cuts up the foe' and 'He who was joined together', the guardians of the fifth and sixth portals of the 'House of Osiris' (spell 146). Papyrus of Ani, 19th Dynasty, *c.* 1275 BC. EA 10470/11.

Fig. 42 The sixth gate of the Netherworld and its three attendant gods (spell 144). Papyrus of Ani, 19th Dynasty, *c.* 1275 BC. EA 10470/12.

Fig. 41 Gateway of the temple of Horus at Edfu. Ptolemaic Period, 305–30 BC.

centre, and the aim of the deceased is to reach this centre and become identified with Osiris. The idea of a series of gates guarded by animal deities in the Netherworld is found as early as the Middle Kingdom in a unique composition on a fragmentary papyrus which describes and illustrates this,[4] but the full graphic potential of the concept was not explored until the New Kingdom, when the gates and their guardians feature strongly in the Book of the Dead and the Book of Gates.

Spells 144 and 146 of the Book of the Dead provide a clear view of the procedure which the deceased must follow. In spell 144 seven gates are listed, each with the name of its keeper, its guard and its announcer (fig. 42). Thus 'He who lives on snakes' is the name of the keeper of the fifth gate; 'Fiery' is the name of he who guards it; 'Hippopotamus-faced, raging of power' is the name of he who makes report in it. Armed with this information, the deceased begins his speech: 'O you gates, you who keep the gates because of Osiris, O you who guard them and who report the affairs of the Two Lands to Osiris every day: I know you and I know your names.' He declares that he was born in the sacred place Rosetjau (the Netherworld), that he has performed various ritual acts and that he enjoys the protection of powerful deities. By uttering these words he lays claim to the experiences he describes and thereby assures the gate-guardians of his probity. To make doubly sure that the gods will admit him, he even claims superior status: 'Mine is a name greater than yours, mightier than yours upon the road of righteousness.' The colophon informs us that if this spell is recited in accordance with the instructions 'it means that he will not be driven off or turned away at the portals of the Netherworld'.

Spell 146 follows a similar pattern. This is a longer text, describing the twenty-one 'mysterious portals of the House of Osiris in the Field of Reeds'. Again, each portal is guarded by a deity and a door-keeper with bizarre-sounding names, and in this case the names are more elaborate than those in spell 144:

What is to be said by the deceased when arriving at the sixth portal of Osiris: make a way for me, for I know you, I know your name, and I know the name of the god who guards you. 'Mistress of Darkness, loud of shouts; its height cannot be known from its breadth, and its extent in space cannot be discovered. Snakes are on it, of which the number is not known; it was fashioned before the Inert One' is your name. 'He who was joined together' is the name of her door-keeper.

The terrifying character of the gate-keepers is hammered home repeatedly – 'who burns up the rebellious', 'who takes hearts for food', 'sharp of knife against the talker', 'who dances in blood', 'who hacks up human dead' – and this gave the artist scope to create some truly monstrous images in the vignettes which accompany these spells. Some of the gods are semi-human in form, with the heads of lions, cows, rams, snakes, crocodiles and hares. Others are still more nightmarish: a dwarf-like figure with a distended human head, a lion with the head of a hippopotamus. Grasping enormous knives, they squat on their haunches as if eagerly awaiting their chance to spring forward. They belong to a type already familiar from the ivory 'wands' of the Middle Kingdom (see cat. no. 6) which kept children safe in the home: their role is as much to protect as it is to repel, but to pass inside their protective environment one must pacify them with words. Having achieved this goal, the deceased will then be within the protection of the very creatures who had threatened him.[5]

The content of these spells brings to mind the layout of Egyptian temples, the earthly dwellings of the gods (fig. 43). Symbolically, both temple and Duat were worlds in themselves, at the core of which was a god who held the power of creation. The temple sanctuary in which the god dwelt was surrounded by numerous walls pierced with gateways, as may still be seen at Karnak, and each gateway was guarded by an attendant. The priests, in order to enter and perform their duties in the temples, had to pass an initiation involving the demonstration of their purity and special knowledge. The texts for some of these procedures survive and display close affinities with passages from the Book of the Dead, a further indication that some of the texts used by the living and the dead shared a common origin. Just as in the spells for the Netherworld gateways, only those priests who possessed the correct ritual knowledge were able to penetrate successive thresholds into the holy of holies, the spot at which life was eternally renewed.

Another prominent element of the Netherworld topography were features called *iat*, a word which is usually translated 'mound' (see cat. nos 66–7). Natural mounds of sand and gravel rising above the floodplain were a common feature of the Egyptian landscape, especially in the Nile delta, and settlements grew on them. Mounds also had strong religious connotations. In the mythology of the creation of the universe the primeval mound was the first land to emerge from the waters of chaos, bearing upon it the first of the gods (Atum in the oldest

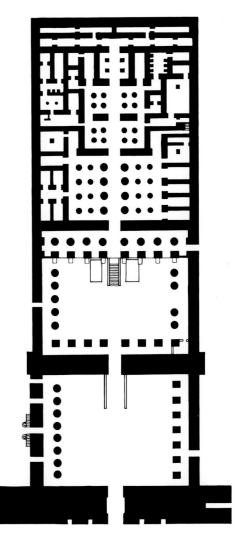

Fig. 43 Plan of the memorial temple of Ramesses III at Medinet Habu. 20th Dynasty, *c.* 1170 BC.

versions), who created the world and all living things. The form and decoration of temples made symbolic reference to this mythology: the sanctuary which housed the cult image of the god symbolized the mound of creation, having a raised floor and being surrounded with architectural features and images drawn from nature (columns and wall-friezes representing papyrus clumps and lotuses). In view of these powerful associations it is hardly surprising to find that mounds featured in the Netherworld. Spell 149 of the Book of the Dead is a list of fourteen mounds, with descriptions and illustrations:

> The fourth mound: green. The very high twin mountains. [The deceased] says: 'As for the Chief of the mysterious mound, as for the very high mountain, which is in the realm of the dead, on which the sky rests, it is 300 rods long by 150 rods wide; a snake is on it called 'Caster of knives', and it is 70 cubits when it glides; it lives by decapitating the spirits of the dead in the realm of the dead. I rise up against you [the snake], so that navigation may be carried out aright; I have seen the way to you and I will gather myself together against you, for I am the male. Cover your head, for I am hale, hale, I am one mighty of magic, and my eyes have caused me to benefit therefrom ...'

In papyri of the New Kingdom spell 149 is often followed directly by spell 150, a second list of mounds, this time numbering fifteen and differing slightly in appearance. As these are sacred places, none of them bears much resemblance to natural features. Most of the illustrations are spatial diagrams, drawn like Egyptian ground-plans of buildings: rectangular, T-shaped, cruciform, S-shaped.[6] Most are inhabited by a god or other supernatural creatures such as a crocodile or snake, all of threatening aspect until pacified (fig. 44).

The deceased could also expect to encounter caverns. The word used means holes or cavities, but as with the mounds their situation and physical appearance are not very clearly defined. Each cavern was occupied by a god or gods – not the well-known deities but rather obscure ones. The deceased's encounters with them were of the same kind as those with the guardians of the gates and mounds, as is clear from the introduction to spell 127, for worshipping the gods of the caverns, which appears at the beginning of this chapter. The rare spell 168 lists and illustrates a different series of caverns (see cat. no. 68), and yet others are described in the Book of Caverns (one of the Netherworld Books inscribed in royal tombs of the New Kingdom).

None of these places is set in a clear spatial context. There is no clue as to whether gates, mounds and caverns are located in distinct regions or are widely dispersed, what the distance between them is, or how the deceased gets from one gate or mound to the next. To attempt a literal reading of these spells would be to miss the point: the Book of the Dead does not attach importance to recording the spatial geography of the Duat. Each gate, mound and cavern is a separate rite of passage, and it is 'the act of passing' which really matters.[7] Perhaps the varied mounds and caverns symbolize the diversity of the hereafter. Experience of the familiar landscape of earth would not be adequate preparation for it, and this might explain the frequent inclusion of the mound spells in the manuscripts of the Book of the Dead.

Fig. 44 The sixth mound, described as 'green' in colour and represented as an enclosure in which lives an eel-like creature. Papyrus of Nu, 18th Dynasty, c. 1400 BC. EA 10477/29.

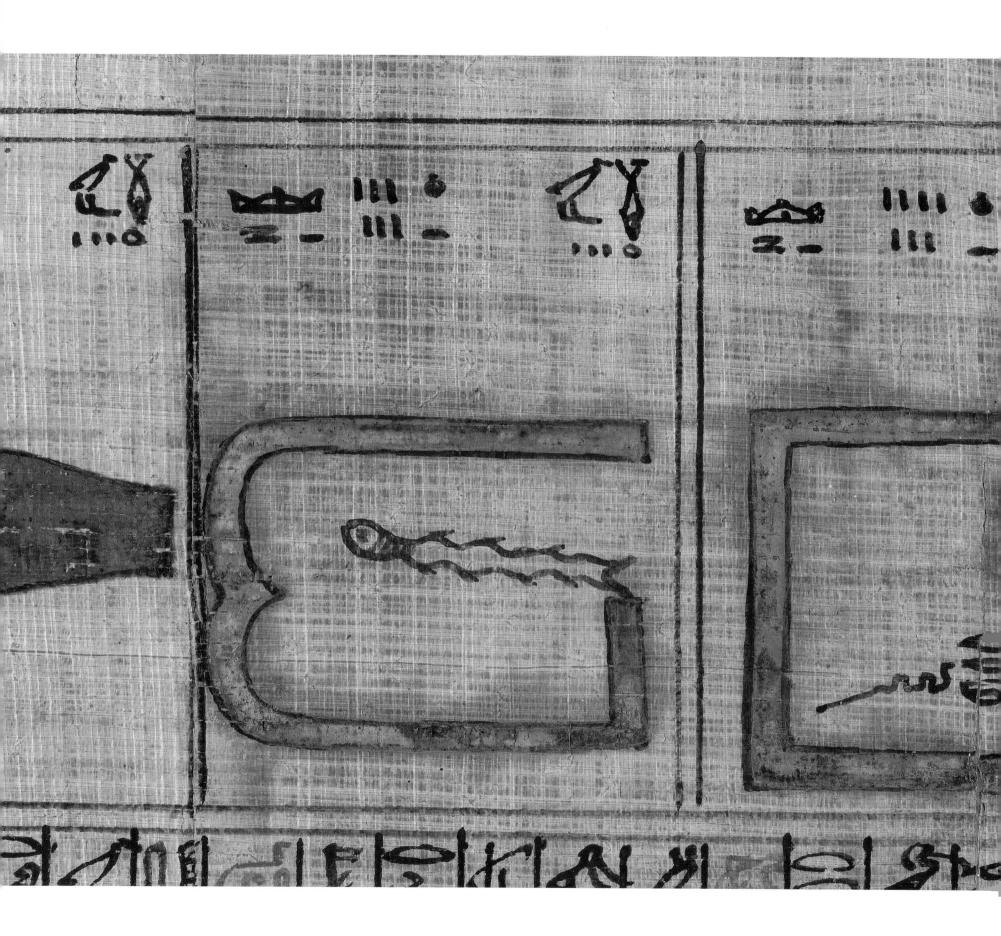

Fig. 46 (opposite) Queen Nefertary, wife of Ramesses II, playing *senet* in the afterlife. Painting from her tomb in the Valley of the Queens, Thebes. 19th Dynasty, *c.* 1250 BC.

Besides possessing a knowledge of exotic places and their guardians, the deceased also had to know about other beings. Spells 108–9 and 112–6 all equipped him for knowing the 'souls' or 'powers' (*ba*s) of various places (see cat. no. 69): the souls of 'the East' and 'the West' (108–9) and those of Pe, Nekhen, Hermopolis and Heliopolis (112–16). The last four were actual sacred localities in Egypt, and the relationship of these places to the landscape of the Duat is not entirely clear. Nor are the texts consistent: the words of spells 108 and 109 duplicate passages describing two of the mounds in spell 149. As with the other spells described earlier, it would be inappropriate to search for a literal interpretation of these texts. What is of paramount importance for the dead person is the knowledge of the names of sacred places and entities – and, in addition, the measurements of various features which are also specified in those spells, knowledge of a thing's dimensions being another means of manifesting one's control of it.[8] The dead person in the Duat then might not really encounter the 'souls/powers of the West', but perhaps there was a greater likelihood of meeting the bull of heaven and his seven cows (spell 148), the reciting of whose names would gain him access to an eternal supply of food (see pp. 152–3).

The game of *senet*

Our picture of the Duat is that of a transitional zone between worlds, the site of a series of supernatural encounters in which one must demonstrate that one is qualified to move forward. The Egyptians found many metaphors for this experience, one of which is regularly depicted in spell 17 of the Book of the Dead (see cat. nos 72–3). Here the deceased is represented playing a board-game called *senet*, a name which means 'passage' or 'passing'. It was popular in Egypt for 3,000 years, and although the exact rules of play are lost it was clearly a race between two players who moved their pieces along a path of thirty squares. From a very early period *senet* acquired religious significance (fig. 46); the playing of it was often depicted in tombs and it was thought of as bridging the worlds of the living and the dead, and as helping to give a person's *ba* the capacity for free movement which would enable it to 'come forth'. Significantly, the scenes of the game in the Book of the Dead are often closely juxtaposed with images of the *ba*-bird. Ultimately the sequence of squares came to be seen as analogous to the sun-god's journey through the night, in which the *ba* also participated, and thus as an allegory of the passage from death to new life. The obstacles and challenges which that journey entailed were seen as being reflected in the game. Many *senet* boards survive (fig. 45; see also cat. no. 74) and on some the individual squares have inscriptions or images which designate them as good or bad, the ultimate object being to reach the god who will provide food and drink, and vindication.[9]

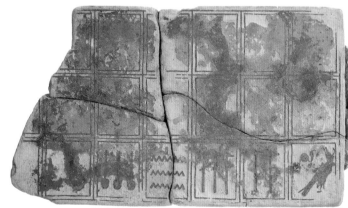

Fig. 45 Fragmentary *senet* boards, with inscriptions in the final squares indicating benefits or hazards. Above: 20th Dynasty (?), *c.* 1186–1069 BC; L 28.5 cm. ME 102396. Right: 20th–21st Dynasty, *c.* 1186–945 BC; L 34.5 cm. EA 38429.

64 Spell 145: the gates of the Netherworld from the Book of the Dead of Nu

Painted papyrus
H 34.5 cm
18th Dynasty, *c.* 1400 BC
Probably from Thebes
London, British Museum, EA 10477/25

Nu was the Steward, or Estate Manager, of an unidentified Treasurer. Recent studies have dated his Book of the Dead to the middle years of the 18th Dynasty, between the joint reign of Hatshepsut/Thutmose III and that of Amenhotep III, on the grounds of the palaeography and other internal details of the spells. An official called Nu is depicted in the tomb of the Treasurer Sebekhotep at Thebes. It is uncertain whether this is the same Nu as the owner of the papyrus, but since Sebekhotep held office in the reign of Thutmose IV, which falls within the date range mentioned above, the possibility is attractive. The papyrus of Nu contains a large number of spells (see also cat. nos 66, 88 and 102). Only a relatively small proportion of these are illustrated, and some of these vignettes are of simple style, as this example shows. The gates of the Netherworld, which are drawn in complex detail in the later papyrus of Ani (see cat. no. 65) are here represented schematically. One side and the top of each gate is shown, with a crenellated *kheker*-frieze along the top. The fearsome guardians described in the text appear here as rather innocuous-looking mummiform figures, without the animal heads and weapons of their later counterparts.

Munro 1988, 280, no. a.25; Quirke 1993, 51, no. 148; Lapp 1997, pls 71–3.

65 Extracts from two spells describing gates from the Book of the Dead of Ani

Painted papyrus
H 42.0 cm
19th Dynasty, c. 1275 BC
Thebes
London, British Museum, EA 10470/11

The papyrus of Ani contains extracts from two of the spells which detail gates of the Netherworld. The artist has arranged these in two parallel rows, one above the other, recognizing the thematic similarity of their content while maintaining the distinction of the individual texts.

The upper row shows Ani and Tutu standing before the 'seven gates of the House of Osiris'. The description of these portals occurs as spell 144 in the New Kingdom, and reappears in later manuscripts in slightly different form as spell 147. Each gate has three attendants – a keeper, a guard and an announcer – all of whom are named in the texts. They are mummiform figures with various heads (hare, snake, crocodile, lion, etc.), and each holds either a knife or an ear of corn. The actual gateways are drawn in simple form, except for the first, which is architecturally more elaborate, adorned with a repeating frieze of *ankh*, *was* and *djed* signs (symbolizing life, dominion and stability).

The lower compartment contains an extract from the spell for the 'mysterious portals of the House of Osiris in the Field of Reeds'. This spell also exists in two versions (145 and 146). Again Ani and his wife stand in adoration before the gates. The full text of this spell lists twenty-one gates, but no New Kingdom papyri include all of them, and only the first ten are given here. In this spell the word used for gate is *sebkhet*, whereas in spells 144 and 147 the term *areret* is used. The precise distinction between them is not clearly understood.

British Museum 1890, pl. 11; British Museum 1894, pl. 11; Budge 1895; Budge 1913; Faulkner 1985, 134–5, 138–9.

66 The mounds of the Netherworld from the Book of the Dead of Nu

Painted papyrus
H 34.5 cm
18th Dynasty, *c.* 1400 BC
Probably from Thebes
London, British Museum, EA 10477/28–30

A number of 18th Dynasty Book of the Dead papyri conclude with the two spells concerning the mounds – mysterious sacred places of the Netherworld that the deceased could pass in safety only by naming the deities and monsters which inhabited them. The full description of these regions is given in the lengthy spell 149, and individual illustrations of the mounds are arranged in a line along the top of the papyrus (here they are preceded by spell 136B, with its vignette of the sun-god's barque). Each pictorial compartment is carefully annotated with the number of

the mound and its colour (eleven are green and three yellow).

The ninth mound (p. 147, top left) is illustrated with a crocodile, above which is written the name 'He who watches what he would seize'. Above the crocodile's snout is an enclosure which represents a 'town', named in the short inscription as Ikesy. The spell relates that Ikesy is a dangerous place, except to the followers of 'that august god who is in his egg' (i.e. the creator god), and the deceased aspires to become one of these privileged followers himself. The eleventh mound (p. 147, top right) is shown as a stepped feature, inside which lurks a jackal-headed god holding knives. The steps may be a depiction of a 'ladder to the sky', which the deceased says he has set up, in the text of the spell.

Spell 149 is followed (at right) by spell 150, which has no text but serves as a pictorial summary of the mounds. It evidently derived from a different tradition to that underlying spell 149, since the mounds differ in detail and number (fifteen instead of fourteen).

Munro 1988, 280, no. a.25; Quirke 1993, 51, no. 148; Lapp 1997, pls 81–7.

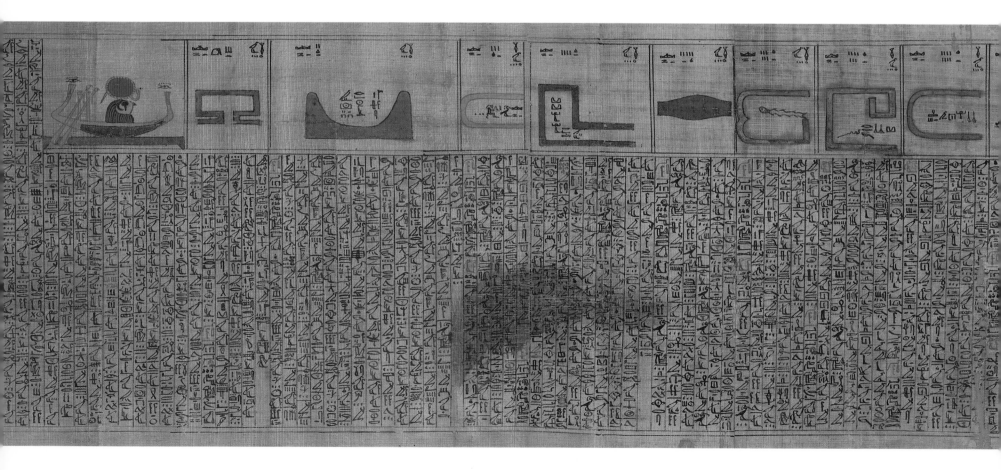

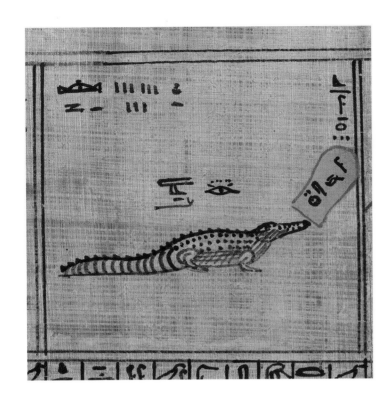

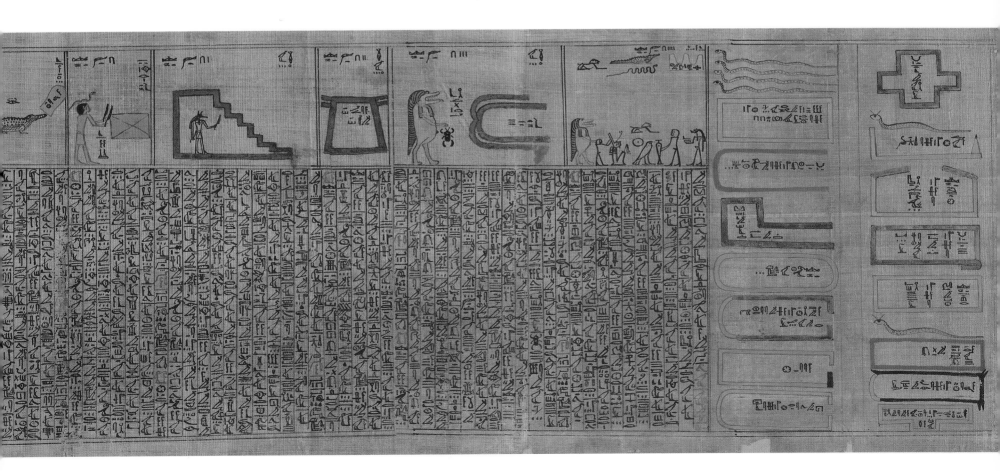

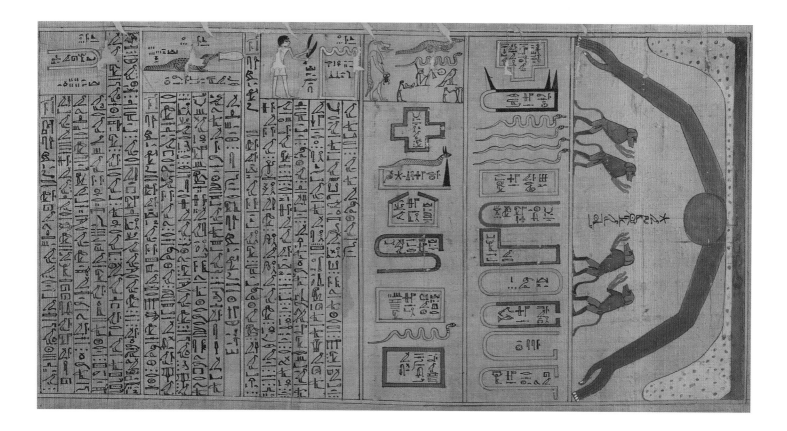

67 The mounds of the Netherworld from the Book of the Dead of Userhat

Painted papyrus
H 41.0 cm
18th Dynasty, c. 1450 BC
Provenance unrecorded
London, British Museum, EA 10009/1

The papyrus of the scribe Userhat ends – as do many 18th Dynasty Books of the Dead – with the description and illustrations of the mounds. In this manuscript there is also a sunrise vignette at the extreme right (p. 239). The papyrus conforms to a standard pattern, in that spell 149 is followed directly by spell 150. This has no texts but consists simply of a set of labelled illustrations of the mounds (here arranged in two columns to the left of the sunrise scene). It is a kind of supplement to spell 149, presenting an alternative set of diagrams, evidently based on a different ancient source. In the 21st Dynasty papyrus of Gatseshen (Cairo J 95838), the spell 149 vignettes are stated to be derived from 'old manuscripts', which suggests that spell 150 represents a later tradition.

There are a number of differences: spell 149 describes fourteen mounds, whereas spell 150 includes fifteen. Some differ in appearance and have different names. Thus, the ninth mound of spell 149 (pp. 146–7) appears here as the second diagram in the right-hand column, an enclosure with three pointed projections and recognizable only by the inscription inside: 'Ikeset [i.e. Ikesy]. The god who is in it is "He who watches what he would seize".' The four snakes beneath this mound, another distinguishing feature of spell 150, may represent the cardinal points.

Munro 1988, 90, no. a.66; Quirke 1993, 67–8, no. 274; Faulkner 1985, 146.

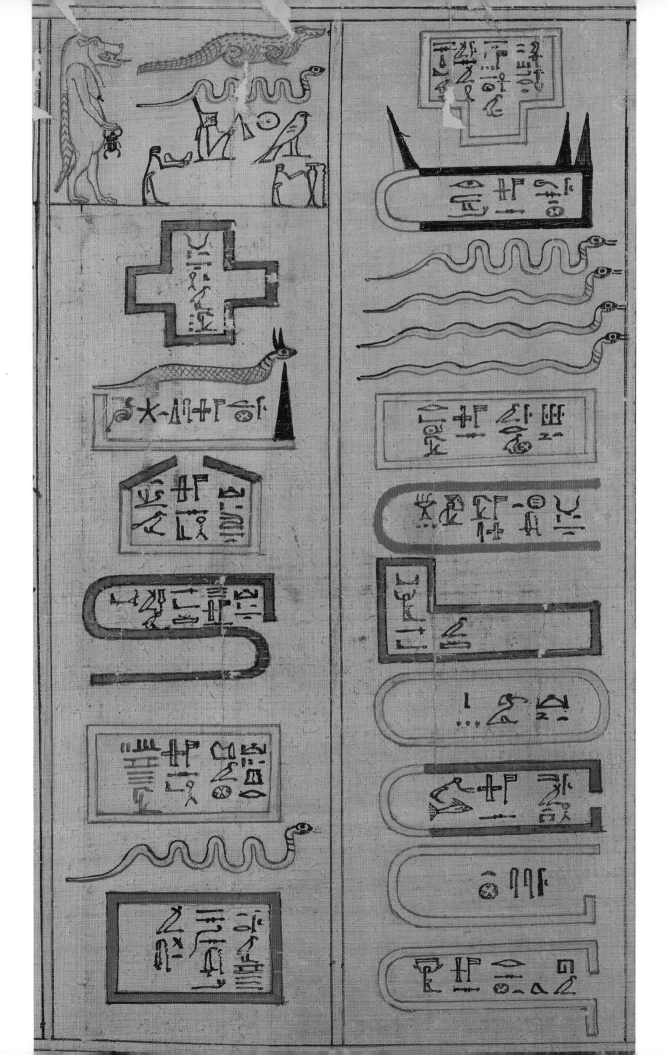

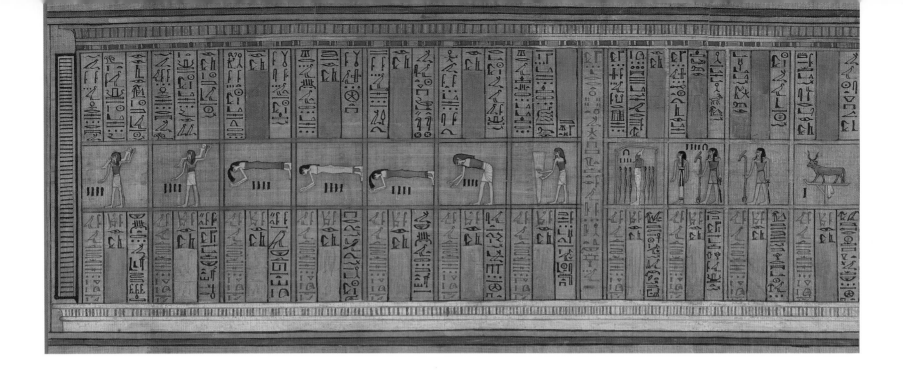

68 Spell 168: the caverns of the Netherworld

Painted papyrus
H 36.3 cm
19th Dynasty, c. 1250 BC
Provenance unrecorded
London, British Museum, EA 10478/6

Spell 168, although included in the corpus of the Book of the Dead, is really a separate composition. This text lists the numerous caverns of the hereafter and the groups of gods who inhabited them. Two versions of the composition are known. This papyrus, which contains version one, describes the eighth to twelfth caverns and their deities. A long shrine with open doors acts as a frame for the text. Within this, the section illustrated shows (from left to right) the names and characteristics of the seven groups of deities who inhabit the eighth cavern, followed by the first four of twenty groups associated with the ninth cavern. Each group is represented by a figure. The first two carry on their shoulders children who are to be taken to heaven; three female figures lie face downwards, mourning the sun-god and assuring the deceased that he will pass safely through the hall of judgement. Further figures depict gods who provide food and other benefits for the deceased, while the bull at the far right ensures that he will be 'powerful in the broad hall of Geb [the earth-god]'. The information given in the spell is complex and would have been challenging to learn by heart. Possession of the text in written form was perhaps thought to be sufficient to have mastery of this special knowledge.

The name of the original owner of this papyrus was in every place so carefully covered with a layer of yellow paint that his identity has long remained a mystery. Infrared imaging technology has now revealed the hidden texts, enabling the owner to be identified as Bakenmut, a scribe of the temple of the goddess Mut (see cat. no. 149). The reason for this alteration is unknown; perhaps the papyrus was never paid for and the crafts-men removed the names so that it could be used for a different person.

Piankoff 1974, 41–114, pls 17–33; Faulkner 1985, 9, 166, 167, 182–3.

69 Knowing the souls of sacred places

Ink on papyrus
H 35.8 cm
18th Dynasty, *c.* 1400 BC
Memphite necropolis
London, British Museum, EA 9900/7

The papyrus of Nebseny contains several spells which gave the deceased knowledge of groups of divine beings, known as the *bau* ('souls' or 'powers') of various sacred localities (see p. 140). Here, from left to right, are the souls of Hermopolis (spell 114), the souls of Pe (spell 112), the souls of Nekhen (spell 113) and the souls of the Westerners (spell 108). The souls of Hermopolis, the cult centre of the god Thoth, are depicted as ibis-headed figures but they are not named individually. However, the souls of Pe are identified as Horus, Imsety and Hapy, and those of Nekhen as Horus, Duamutef and Qebehsenuef. The four sons of Horus are thus divided into complementary pairs, associated with the two religious centres. The souls of the Westerners are named as three major deities, Atum, Sobek and Hathor.

Faulkner 1985, 103, 109; Lapp 2004, pls 19–21.

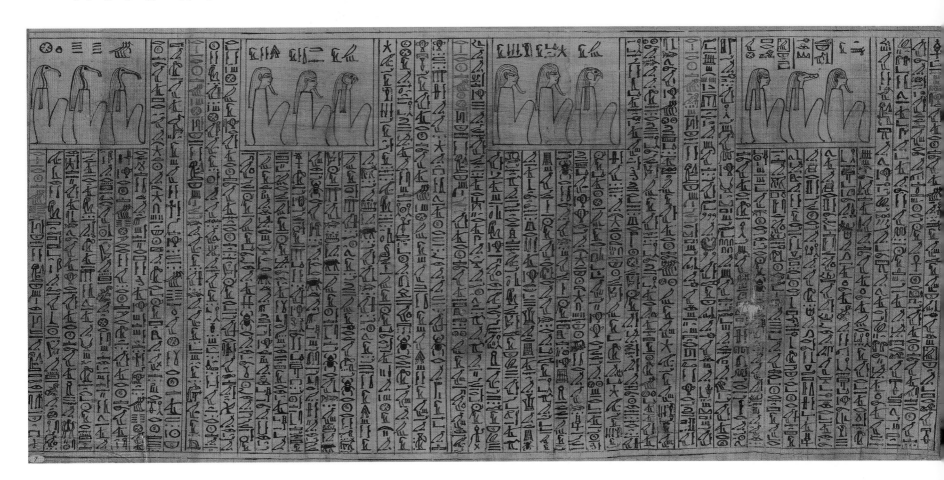

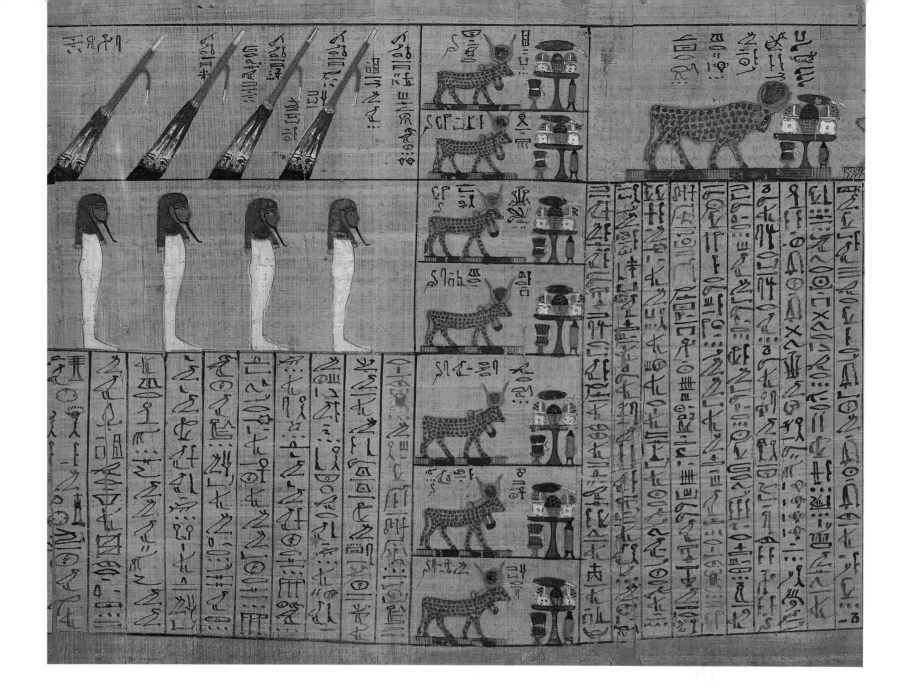

70 The celestial herd and rudders of heaven from the Book of the Dead of Nakht

Painted papyrus
H 36.0 cm
Late 18th or early 19th Dynasty, *c.* 1350–1290 BC
Provenance not recorded (probably Thebes)
London, British Museum, EA 10471/9

Spell 148 was 'for making provision for a spirit in the realm of the dead'. Although in theory the dead would be supplied by means of a cult at the tomb, the Egyptians were unwilling to rely solely on this mechanism for their eternal sustenance. Numerous spells gave the dead the ability to be self-sufficient. This one depended on having detailed knowledge of the bull and his seven cows 'who give bread and beer' and 'who provide daily portions'. As in other encounters with divine beings, the deceased had to know their names, listed in the spell (see cat. 71).

Similarly the dead man had to address by name the four steering oars of the sky, which are also depicted in the vignette, accompanied by mummiform deities.

Glanville 1927; Faulkner 1985, 142; Munro 1988, 300, no. b.20; Quirke 1993, 46, no. 119.

71 The celestial herd and rudders of heaven from the Book of the Dead of Ankhwahibra

Not exhibited
Ink on papyrus
H 27.0 cm
Late 26th Dynasty, c. 550–525 BC
Provenance unrecorded (probably Memphite necropolis)
London, British Museum, EA 10558/24

This late version of spell 148 sets the celestial herd and the rudders within an architectural framework of lotus columns supporting a canopy. Only the bull now stands; his seven cows appear in a more passive pose, reclining on pedestals, and in front of each stands an offering table loaded with food. At right, the deceased stands in adoration before Sokar-Osiris, who is supported by the goddess of the West.

Quirke 1993, 32, no. 23.

The names of the cattle are:
Mansion of Kas, Mistress of All.
Silent One who dwells in her place.
She of Chemmis whom the god ennobled.
The Much Beloved, red of hair.
She who protects in life, the particoloured.
She whose name has power in her craft.
Storm in the sky which wafts the god aloft.
The Bull, husband of the cows.

(Spell 148)

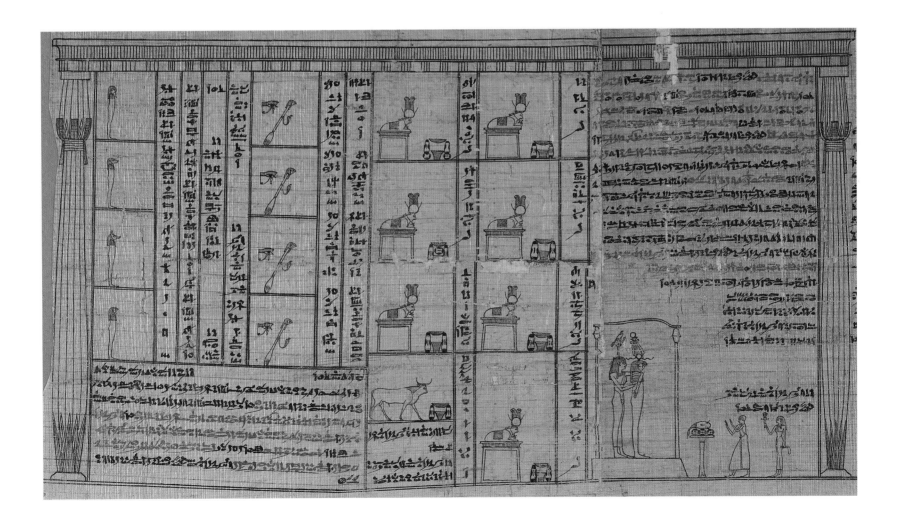

72 **Ani and Tutu playing** *senet*

Painted papyrus
H 42.0 cm
19th Dynasty, *c.* 1275 BC
Thebes
London, British Museum, EA 10470/7

The board-game *senet* was often depicted in tombs, where it conveyed the symbolic notion of continued contact between the living and the dead, and the possibility of crossing the permeable boundary between their worlds. In the New Kingdom the game, with its clearly defined path of thirty squares, acquired a more precise association with the passage of the deceased from this world to the next. Spell 17 of the Book of the Dead, with its long and multi-faceted vignette, usually includes a scene of the dead person playing this game – sometimes with his wife in attendance, as here. Ani's papyrus includes a finely detailed chair and stool for the couple to sit on, while the game itself has been rendered accurately, with the distinctive gaming pieces of the two opposing players carefully delineated.

British Museum 1890, pl. 7; British Museum 1894, pl. 7; Budge 1895; Budge 1913; Pusch 1979, 126–7, Taf. 35a; Quirke 1993, 32, no. 24.

73 **Animals playing *senet*: satirical papyrus**

Painted papyrus
H 8.3 cm
19th–20th Dynasties, *c*. 1295–1069 BC
Deir el-Medina
London, British Museum, EA 10016/1

Scenes of animals engaged in human activities are typical of ancient
Egyptian satire, as is the reversal of roles. On this papyrus, among a cat
and a hyena herding ducks and goats, is a depiction of a lion and a gazelle
playing *senet*. The lion holds an animal knucklebone, which serves as a
dice, to determine his move. The concept and the face-to-face depiction is
perhaps based on the image of the king playing the game with the queen
or a minor wife.

Pusch 1979, 132–4, Taf. 36a; Russmann 2001, 167–9, no. 78.

74 *Senet* board of Amenmes

Wood
H 7.0 cm; W 12.0 cm; L 36.0 cm
19th Dynasty, *c.* 1295–1186 BC
Saqqara?
Paris, Musée du Louvre, E 2710 (N 1605)

Senet boards were frequently placed among the burial equipment of elite individuals in the New Kingdom – both for continued use in the afterlife and on account of their role symbolizing the deceased's successful progress from this world to the next. This finely carved specimen was made for Amenmes, a Deputy of the Harem and 'Child of the *kap*' – the latter title indicating that Amenmes had enjoyed a privileged upbringing among the children of the king. At one end of the board is a depiction of Amenmes

seated and playing the game, while an attendant offers him a cup. Beneath the table are two *astragali* (animal knucklebones) which were used as dice to determine the number of a player's moves (see cat. no. 73). The sides of the box are covered with hieroglyphic texts requesting offerings from various gods, including Amun-Ra, Ptah and Ra-Horakhty.

The upper surface of the board is divided into twenty squares. The name and epithets of Amenmes are inscribed in every fourth square and two longer inscriptions contain further assurances that the owner will receive offerings..

On the bottom is a thirty-square board for playing *senet*. Squares 26–29 have inscriptions denoting 'goodness', water, *ba*-spirits and two men. These relate to the religious significance of the game (see p. 140).

Pusch 1979, 64–6, 208–13, Taf. 18, 49–51; Piccione 2007, 56; Ziegler 2008, 295, no. 112.

7 Empowering the Dead

John H. Taylor

Obey me, my heart, I am your lord, you are in my body, you do not oppose me, I command you to obey me in the god's domain.

(Spell 27, 'for not permitting a man's heart to be taken from him in the realm of the dead')[1]

As for him who knows this pure spell, it means going out into the day after death and being transformed at will, being in the suite of Wennefer, being content with the food of Osiris, having invocation offerings, seeing the sun; it means being hale on earth with Ra and being vindicated with Osiris, and nothing evil shall have power over him.

(Spell 83, 'for being transformed into a *benu*-bird')

MAGIC was a means of harnessing power. The spells in the Book of the Dead gave the Egyptians a wide range of powers to make a person self-sufficient and to avert the many dangers that threatened them in the unfamiliar world of the beyond. Many of these concerns are encapsulated in spell 68. Although it is blandly entitled 'for going out into the day' it is designed to combat a host of fears:

May I have power in my heart, may I have power in my arms, may I have power in my legs, may I have power in my mouth, may I have power in all my members, may I have power over invocation-offerings, may I have power over water ... air ... the waters ... streams ... riparian lands ... men who would harm me ... women who would harm me in the realm of the dead ... those who would give orders to harm me upon earth.

Control of the person

Individual spells which would resolve most of these issues were contained within the Book of the Dead. Having full control over the body was considered to be of prime importance. The rituals and processes of mummification were meant to transform the corpse into a *sah*, a perfect eternal image (see p. 20), but the Egyptians were still haunted by the fear that their bodies would rot away (fig. 47). Spell 154, entitled 'for not letting the corpse perish', gives a gruesome description of physical decay:

Such is he who is decayed; all his bones are corrupt, his flesh is slain, his bones are softened, his flesh is made into foul water, his corruption stinks and he turns into many worms.

The text goes on to assure that the deceased, like Osiris, will be triumphant over the process of decomposition:

> I will possess my body for ever, for I will not become corrupt, I will not decay,
> I will not be putrid, I will not become worms ... there is no destruction in my
> viscera, I have not been injured, my eye has not rotted, my skull has not been
> crushed ... My corpse is permanent, it will not perish nor be destroyed in this
> land for ever.

It is the kind of incantation which we can imagine being recited during mummification, but there is no evidence that this actually happened. Perhaps the spell was meant to perpetuate the preservation of the body throughout eternity.

Among the body parts which required special protection were the head and the heart. The head, as the focal point for most of the senses, was always accorded careful treatment during mummification. As early as the Pyramid Texts, there are repeated assurances that the dead king's head will be joined to his body. Decapitation was more than a misfortune; it was a punishment, a fate reserved for the enemies of the gods, as described in the Books of the Netherworld. Spell 43 in the Book of the Dead prevented decapitation after death. Once again, it identifies the deceased with Osiris, whose body was dismembered by Seth but was afterwards reconstituted:

> I am a flame, the son of a flame, to whom was given his head after it had been cut
> off. The head of Osiris shall not be taken from him, and my head shall not be taken
> from me.

Scarcely less important than the head was the heart, which the Egyptians recognized as the most important organ of the human body, not on account of its true function – the notion of the circulation of the blood was unknown to them – but because it was considered to be the location of the intelligence and memory. It was one of the *kheperu*, manifestations of human existence (see p. 17), and together with the head, the heart was the body part whose preservation after death was held to be most necessary. In an abstract sense it was the centre of the person's being. Of all the internal organs the heart alone remained in its place during mummification. Not only was it essential to a person's existence, his safe passage through the judgement would depend on it (see pp. 209–12).

Because of its importance to the destiny of the individual there was a fear that the deceased might be deprived of his heart. Several spells in the Book of the Dead are aimed at dealing with this threat (see cat. nos 75 and 77). In the manuscripts of the New Kingdom they already occur as a closely related group, spells 26–30, and they remained prominent in the papyri of the Late Period. Spell 26, 'for giving [the deceased's] heart to him in the realm of the dead', was perhaps designed to reinforce the preservation of the heart during mummification; its vignette sometimes shows the embalmer-god Anubis handing the heart to the deceased. Spells 27, 28, 29 and 29A guarded against the loss of the heart (their titles are all variants on a 'spell for not permitting a man's heart to be taken from him in the realm of the dead'). The

Fig. 47 The mummy of Ani, preserved and wrapped in *sah*-form by Anubis. Vignette of spell 45 (for 'not putrefying'). Papyrus of Ani, 19th Dynasty, *c.* 1275 BC. EA 10470/16.

Fig. 48 Ani's heart rests on a support while he adores a group of deities, probably those 'who seize hearts' (spell 27). Papyrus of Ani, 19th Dynasty, *c.* 1275 BC. EA 10470/16.

context in which these spells were supposed to work seems to be the deceased's existence in the Netherworld where potentially hostile forces might oppose him. The vignettes of spells 27 and 28 show the deceased and his heart confronting various deities, and the nature of the threat is most explicit in spell 27, a text against those 'who seize hearts' (fig. 48). The danger here is not simply that the person might lose an essential organ. It emerges that the deities 'who seize hearts' have the power to 'fashion one's heart out of what he has done, so that he would not know him[self] because of you'; as a result the heart might 'fashion evil' against its owner.[2] The implication is that the heart could be made to act against its owner at the judgement (see p. 209), condemning him to destruction.

The ritual aim of mummification was to transform the earthly body into a divine form which would endure for ever. In the process the products of corruption were to be removed and replaced with oils, resins, natron and incense – all substances which had connotations of purity and divinity, making the body wholly divine. The intellectual counterpart to this procedure was the identification of all parts of the body with those of gods and goddesses. A number of texts dwell on this theme of the divinization of the body, including Book of the Dead spell 151 (see p. 109). Spell 42 deals with the same subject (see cat. no. 86). Although it is entitled 'to escape slaughter' and is grouped with other spells which save the deceased from violence, a large part of the text is an enumeration of all the essential parts of the body, each one being associated with the corresponding member of a deity:

My hair is Nun; my face is Ra; my eyes are Hathor; my ears are Wepwawet; my
nose is She who presides over her lotus leaf; my lips are Anubis; my molars are
Selkis; my incisors are Isis the goddess; my arms are the Ram, the Lord of Mendes;
my breast is Neith, Lady of Sais; my back is Seth; my phallus is Osiris; my muscles
are the Lords of Kheraha; my chest is he who is greatly majestic; my belly and my
spine are Sekhmet; my buttocks are the Eye of Horus; my thighs and my calves
are Nut; my feet are Ptah; my toes are living falcons; there is no member of mine
devoid of a god, and Thoth is the protection of all my flesh.

Not only the physical form but also the other 'modes of existence' had to be secured in order for
the person to survive. Several spells are concerned with the maintenance of the non-physical
constituents of the personality. One of the most important was the name, the embodiment of
individuality (see also p. 30). As long as the name was pronounced the person survived, even
after death, so remembrance of the name was crucial to existence in the afterlife. It was to be
spoken aloud during the rituals at the tomb, and by writing or carving the name on the tomb
or coffin its owner's posthumous existence was perpetuated. Conversely, to erase or deface the
written name harmed the individual's chances of survival; this act was sometimes performed
as a formal means of punishing enemies or those who had incurred the displeasure of the king;
it could also be done out of malevolence. Book of the Dead spell 25 is 'for causing [the deceased]
to remember his name in the necropolis' and begins:

I have put my name in the Upper Egyptian shrine, I [have] made my name to be
remembered in the Lower Egyptian shrine, on this night of counting the years and
of numbering the months ...[3]

The spirit components also had to be controlled. The *ka*, which dwelt in the tomb, required
constant nourishment with offerings (see p. 17). To free the deceased from dependence on relatives or priests for this duty, the Book of the Dead contained a 'spell for satisfying the *ka*' (105).

Fig. 49 Nesitanebisheru seated before offering tables
which take the form of the hieroglyph for *ka* (a pair of
upraised human arms). Papyrus of Nesitanebisheru, late
21st or early 22nd Dynasty, *c.* 950–930 BC. EA 10554/17.

Vignettes of this spell show the *ka*-hieroglyph as the recipient of food offerings or being purified with water and incense (fig. 49). The text goes further, by assuring the *ka* that it will be cleansed of any impurity which might have resulted from its owner's improper actions: 'I have brought to you natron and incense that I may cleanse you with them … even this evil phrase which I have spoken, this evil impurity which I have done.' This hints at the judgement to come, where the deceased expects to escape punishment 'because to me belongs that papyrus amulet which is on the neck of Ra'. The allusion is to the practice of wearing around the neck a small rolled papyrus inscribed with a protective text (see cat. no. 9). No less important was the preservation of the *ba*-spirit. Spell 61 was 'for preventing a man's *ba* from being taken from him in the necropolis', while spell 89 ensured the crucial union of the *ba* with the corpse. The *shut*, or shadow, another mode of human existence, was often closely associated with the *ba*, and their survival together is mentioned in spells 91, 92 and 188, particularly in connection with freedom of movement and the ability to leave and re-enter the tomb.

If all of these constituents of the self were successfully reunited, the deceased became an 'effective spirit', or *akh*. This is clearly stated in a text which was a late addition to the Book of the Dead, spell 191:

Fig. 50 Ani and his wife Tutu stand in a pool shaded by palm trees, drinking the water and holding sails, which symbolize air for them to breathe. Vignette of spell 58. Papyrus of Ani, 19th Dynasty, *c.* 1275 BC. EA 10470/16.

Bring Osiris [deceased's] soul [to him], that it may unite with his body, that his heart may be glad, that his soul may come to his body [and] to his heart. Bring his soul into his body [and] into his heart; provide his soul with his body [and] with [his] heart.[4]

Spell 130 made the *akh* efficacious and made a *ba* live forever.

Control of the elements and free movement

The deceased also needed to exercise control over the elements. Several spells (54–9) gave him the power to breathe the air and to have power over water (figs 50–51). Water could be beneficial or dangerous: spell 62 allowed the deceased to drink water, while spell 63B saved him from being scalded. Spell 63A prevented him from being burnt by fire (see cat. nos 76 and 83–4).

Armed with these spells the deceased was assured that all the aspects of his personality would be maintained, the mummy being the central focus from which the *ba* would rise at will. Within its burial chamber, however, the mummy was immobile, the limbs cocooned in the wrappings. The deceased did not want to be confined like this for ever: his aim was to gain freedom of movement. In the New Kingdom the ability to 'come forth by day' – i.e. to move

Fig. 51 Ani kneels by a pool and receives food and water from a goddess who emerges from the branches of a sycomore fig. Vignette of spell 59. Papyrus of Ani, 19th Dynasty, *c.* 1275 BC. EA 10470/16.

Fig. 52 A swallow perching on a support. Spell 86 enabled the deceased to transform himself into this bird. Papyrus of Ani, 19th Dynasty, *c.* 1275 BC. EA 10470/25.

in spirit form out of the tomb – became enormously important. It is no coincidence that this expression occurs in the titles of many of the spells of the Book of the Dead, and that it was even used as the collective title for the whole composition.

In the New Kingdom the notion of going forth is closely connected with the power of transformation into different forms. Transformation gave freedom to move anywhere in the cosmos, including the world of the living. The deceased could assume the form of the *ba* to do this – it was itself capable of free movement – but more than this, the *ba* concept concerns power, 'the capacity to assume or breathe life into various forms'.[5]

In the Book of the Dead there are a number of spells for transformation (76–88) which usually occur grouped together, as if they formed 'a book in its own right'. Earlier versions of these spells were included in the Coffin Texts, where they were already regarded as especially important, and this importance continued in the Book of the Dead. These spells are included in almost every known manuscript of the New Kingdom and they are usually provided with vignettes, even in sparsely illustrated rolls such as that of Nu (see cat. no. 88).

The spells allowed the deceased to assume many different forms. Some are those of wild creatures: a golden falcon, a divine falcon, a heron, a swallow, a snake, a crocodile; one is a lotus flower, and others are divine beings – the god Ptah, the Greatest of the Divine Tribunal, an unspecified 'god', a living *ba*, a *benu*-bird. Spell 76, which serves as a kind of introduction to this group, covers all eventualities by enabling transformation into 'any form one wishes'. These spells are particularly concerned with the notion that the spirit should be able to travel back and forth repeatedly between the realm of the living and that of the dead, departing from the Netherworld every morning and returning in the evening. So by turning into a swallow, the deceased is enabled to 'enter [again] after going forth by day, in any form in which he wishes to emerge from the Field of Reeds'. It is not surprising that many of the creatures involved are distinguished by their capacity for free movement. In the Pyramid Texts the king transforms himself into birds to fly to heaven. There were more such spells in the Coffin Texts, but those in the Book of the Dead received special prominence, and new ones were added. Among the additions to this group is the spell for transforming into a lotus (81A). The flower symbolized regeneration as it opens each day when the sun shines on it.

Travelling the paths to the hereafter

Although the deceased was provided with the power to assume different forms, many of the spells in the Book of the Dead envisage his journey as taking place in human shape, often on foot. Pathways had to be opened for him, as mentioned in spell 9 (see p. 31). This spell also enabled him to drive away darkness. Pathlessness and darkness were two of the constituent features of primordial chaos, and in overcoming these the deceased not only eased his passage to the beyond, he also participated in the creation of the cosmos, in which Maat (Order) triumphs over Isfet (Disorder).

Several spells envisage travel by boat. Navigation was the main means of transport in ancient Egypt, with the Nile the chief thoroughfare, and not surprisingly the gods were thought to travel by boat – above all, the sun-god, who sailed across the sky and through the Netherworld. One of the ultimate aims of the deceased was to enter the barque of the sun-god and to travel with him as a member of his company. Numerous spells in the Book of the Dead make reference to this, and once again empowerment plays a key role in the deceased's success. The long spell 99 explains how the deceased gains control of a boat in the hereafter. It is termed a ferryboat, but any hint that it is the precursor of the ferryboat across the River Styx of Greek tradition is dispelled, as the aim of the journey is to cross to the eastern side of the sky. The spell includes a long dialogue in which the deceased must demonstrate his knowledge of the parts of a boat and their symbolic associations. The boat is in the charge of Aqen and his assistant Mahaf ('He who looks behind him'):

'O Mahaf, as you are provided with life, awaken Aqen for me, for see, I have come.'
'Who are you that comes?'
'I am the beloved of my father …'
'Do you say that you would cross to the eastern side of the sky? If you cross, what will you do?'
'I will raise up his head …'
'O Mahaf, as you are endowed with life, awaken Aqen for me, for see, I have come.'
'Why should I awaken Aqen for you?'
'That he may bring me the built-up boat of Khnum from the Lake of Feet.'
'But she is in pieces and stored in the dockyard.'
'Take her larboard side and fix it to the stern; take her starboard side and fix it to the bow.'
'But she has no planks, she has no end-pieces, she has no rubbing-pieces, she has no oar-loops.'
'Her planks are the drops of moisture which are on the lips of Babai …'

Here all kinds of obstacles are placed in the deceased's way, but by knowing the answers in the correct form of words, the speaker is able to circumvent the difficulties and to have the boat constructed and launched. Finally, in a passage which echoes the challenges of the gate-keepers (see pp. 136–7), he must pronounce the symbolic names not only of every part of the boat but even of the wind, the river and the bank:

'Tell me my name,' say the oars.
'"The fingers of Horus the Elder" are your names.'
'Tell me my name,' says the hogging-beam.
'"She who presides over gardens" is your name.'
'Tell me my name,' says the wind, 'since you are carried thereby.'
'"North wind which went forth from Atum to the nose of the Foremost of the Westerners" is your name.'

During these exchanges the deceased asserts that he is 'a magician'. Through wielding magic power and sacred knowledge he is able to command and control as he needs to take him on his way. But much power will also be required to ward off danger and attack.

Fig. 53 (overleaf) The vignettes of spells 136A and B. At the left, Thoth steers the boat of the sun-god, who appears in two forms – as falcon-headed Ra-Horakhty and as scarab-headed Khepri. A goddess, perhaps Isis, stands at the prow. To the right, Nakht pilots the solar boat, in which the sun-god is represented in the form of a large falcon head. Papyrus of Nakht, late 18th or early 19th Dynasty, c. 1350–1290 BC. EA 10471/9.

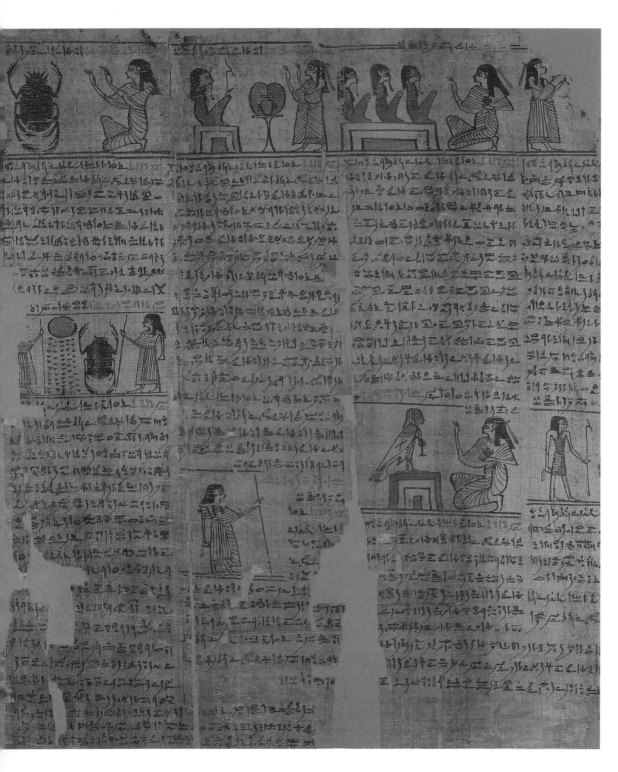

75 Spells for the protection of the heart from the Book of the Dead of Tentameniy

Ink and paint on papyrus
H 47.0 cm
Ptolemaic Period, 305–30 BC
Provenance unrecorded
London, British Museum, EA 10086/5

The spells which gave protection to the heart were often grouped together, even in the early papyri of the New Kingdom, and they continued to form a consecutive sequence in the Saite recension of the Book of the Dead (see p. 58), as in this papyrus of Tentameniy, daughter of Neshorpakhered (see also cat. nos 31 and 76). The spells run in columns from right to left. Spell 26 (lower right) is illustrated with an image of Tentameniy kneeling and cupping her heart in her left hand, while she faces her own *ba*, perching on a plinth. Above this is spell 27, which shows the deceased again holding her heart and adoring three deities (probably those 'who seize hearts'; see p. 162). Directly left of this is the vignette of spell 28, where Tentameniy stands before her own heart, which is depicted both in its conventional 'hieroglyphic' form, as a miniature vessel, and in a more naturalistic manner. In the next vignette to the left (that of spell 30), she adores the scarab beetle. The text ensures that the heart will not betray its owner at the judgement.

Faulkner 1985, 52–3; Quirke 1993, 65–6, no. 258.

76 Spells to control natural forces from the Book of the Dead of Tentameniy

Ink and paint on papyrus
H 47.0 cm
Ptolemaic Period, 305–30 BC
Provenance unrecorded
London, British Museum, EA 10086/7

This section of Tentameniy's papyrus includes, at the right, spells 57 and 59, both of which enable her to 'breathe air and have power over water'. Spells 60–62 in the next column continue the same theme; then, at the top of the next column, is spell 63A, 'for drinking water and not being burnt by fire'. Beneath this comes spell 65, 'for coming forth by day' and having power over one's enemy. The left-hand column has spells 68 and 71, both entitled 'for coming forth by day'.

Quirke 1993, 65–6, no. 258.

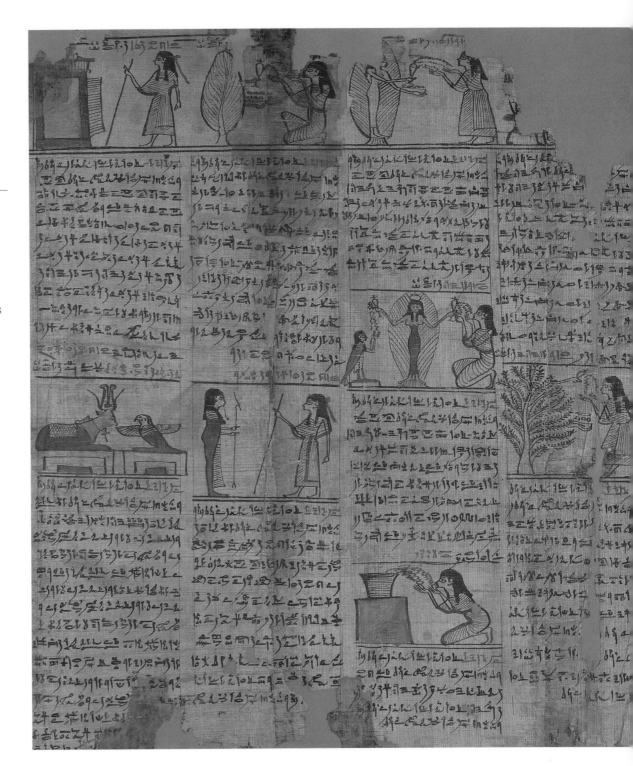

77 Controlling the heart: spell 26 on the coffin of Nesbanebdjed

Cedarwood, acacia and Christ's thorn and bronze
L 212.0 cm; W 57.0 cm
Late 22nd Dynasty, c. 750 BC
Thebes
London, British Museum, EA 6657 (lid) and EA 6886 (face)

This coffin was probably part of a set which belonged to Nesbanebdjed, one of the highest-ranking dignitaries at Thebes. The inscriptions, carved into the surface and originally filled with blue pigment, record his main titles, which include those of Priest of Montu and 'Great Controller who keeps the city in check'. This latter title was usually borne by the governor of Thebes, and Nesbanebdjed's high status is reflected in the use of costly imported cedarwood for his coffin, and in the excellent quality of the carving of the inscriptions.

In Nesbanebdjed's time the Book of the Dead was in decline. No papyri were placed in tombs and only a few selected spells appeared on coffins. The inscriptions on this coffin, however, are drawn mainly from the Book of the Dead. Since Nesbanebdjed was also chief temple scribe of the domain of Amun he may have had privileged access to these religious texts. On the lid is a long inscription in three columns. The first records the owner's titles and the name of his father Ankhpakhered, and the remaining columns contain the first part of the text of spell 26, for 'giving the deceased's heart to him in the realm of the dead'.

The spell is chiefly concerned with ensuring that the deceased possesses his heart, but also emphasizes that by means of his heart his members are unified and he has the use of his bodily faculties. Through these and with the help of various gods he enjoys free movement and power over his enemies in the hereafter.

Whereas the words of the spell are usually put into the mouth of the deceased, on this coffin he is referred to in the second person, and the text breaks off in the middle, illustrating the *pars pro toto* principle whereby a part of a text could magically function as effectively as the complete version.

PM I, ii, 828; Payraudeau 2003, 140–41.

Amulets for the protection of the heart

78 Heart amulet with spell 29B

Jasper?
L 3.3 cm
New Kingdom, *c.* 1550–1069 BC
London, British Museum, EA 15601

79 Heart amulet with crescent and egg-shaped markings and spell 30B

Basalt
L 5.6 cm
New Kingdom, *c.* 1550–1069 BC
London, British Museum, EA 24740

80 Heart amulet

Breccia
L 4.8 cm
Late Period, *c.* 664–305 BC
London, British Museum, EA 24393

81 Heart-shaped amulet

Red glass
L 5.3 cm
Late Period, *c.* 664–305 BC
London, British Museum, EA 8088
Andrews 1994, fig. 61b.

82 Heart amulet of the royal scribe Nakhtamun with the text of spell 30B

Jasper
L 5.2 cm
Late 18th or early 19th Dynasty, *c.* 1350–1250 BC
London, British Museum, EA 15619
Andrews 1994, fig. 61a.

Spell 29B of the Book of the Dead was called the 'spell for a heart amulet of *seheret*-stone', the role of which was apparently to protect the heart. The amulets themselves are often in the shape of a heart, and are made from a variety of stones and other materials, including glass. Some are inscribed with spell 29B: 'I am the *benu* [a mythical bird], the soul of Ra, who guides gods to the Netherworld when they go forth. The souls on earth will do what they desire, and the soul of [the deceased] will go forth at his desire.' Some have an image of the *benu* (see also p. 229); others are inscribed with spell 30B.

83 **Book of the Dead spells on a headrest**

Wood, painted and inscribed in ink
H 15.5 cm; W 25.7 cm; D 8.8 cm
26th Dynasty, c. 625 BC
Provenance unrecorded, but probably from Thebes
London, British Museum, EA 35804

Headrest amulets were associated with spell 166 of the Book of the Dead and were commonly used in the Late Period (see pp. 109–10). A full-sized wooden headrest, however, was a rarity in burials at this period. This example bears the name of Ta-aa, daughter of Hor and Nesmut, a collateral relative of the Theban priests Besenmut and Nespasefy (see cat. nos 29 and 151). The upper surfaces of the headrest are decorated with lotus and papyrus plants, and a *wedjat* eye. An inscription on the under-surface and edges of the base includes three extracts from the Book of the Dead: spell 55 'for giving breath', spell 61 'for not letting a man's soul be taken away' and spell 62 'for drinking water in the realm of the dead'. These spells helped the deceased to control her environment and sustain herself in the Netherworld, but it remains unclear why they should have been inscribed on a headrest.

PM I, ii, 842.

84 Spell 59: for breathing air and having power over water from the coffin of Nesbanebdjed

Cedarwood
L of sides 180.0 and 182.0 cm
Late 22nd Dynasty, c. 750 BC
Thebes
London, British Museum, EA 6657

On the sides of the coffin of Nesbanebdjed (for lid, see cat. no. 77) a text was carved into the wood, beginning with his name and titles and continuing with a passage from spell 59 of the Book of the Dead, for 'breathing air and having power over water'. The full text runs:

'O you sycomore of the sky, may there be given to me the air which is in it, for I am he who sought out that throne in the midst of Wenu [Hermopolis]. I have guarded this egg of the Great Cackler. If it grows, I grow; if it lives, I live; if it breathes air, I breathe air.'

The tree referred to is the sycomore fig in which the goddess Nut is often depicted, providing the dead person with food and drink (see cat. nos 85 and 140). It was a popular image in tombs and on coffins, papyri and offering tables. On this coffin the first part of the spell is missing. Some words were probably inscribed on the head end, which has not survived, but since this would hardly have allowed sufficient space for all the missing text it may be that the spell was abbreviated. Although the signs have been carved with skill, the craftsman accidentally omitted part of the name of Osiris at the beginning, and attempted to correct the error by recarving this part of the text.

PM I, ii, 828; Payraudeau 2003, 140–41.

85 Air and water: spell 59 of the Book of the Dead on an offering table

Limestone
H 48.5 cm; W 51.0 cm
Ptolemaic Period, c. 305–30 BC
Akhmim
London, British Museum, EA 1215

An offering table was one of the most important features of a well-appointed tomb, since on these slabs (usually of stone) food and drink would be placed to sustain the *ka*-spirit of the deceased. In the Ptolemaic Period a series of funerary offering tables from Akhmim were inscribed with passages from the Book of the Dead. These texts are usually spell 59 'for breathing air and having power over water' and spell 62 'for drinking water in the realm of the dead'. On this example, belonging to the Stolist Dudu, son of Padikhonsiat(?) and Asetweret, the text of spell 59 is inscribed in vertical columns in the upper half of the decorated area. The spell addresses the sycomore fig tree of the sky-goddess Nut, and appropriately the vignette shows the goddess standing within the foliage of a tree. Some versions of this scene show only the goddess's arms, reaching out from the branches, but on Dudu's offering table the complete figure of Nut is represented. She pours life-giving water into the hands of the deceased, whose *ba* perches on his head. The deceased's parentage is repeated in the texts of the lower compartment, followed by passages from spell 62.

Budge 1909, 278, no. 1036; Buhl 1947, 93–4.

Fig. 54 Detail from the papyrus of Ankhwahibra, 26th Dynasty (see cat. no. 30), c. 550–525 BC. EA 10558/10.

86 The divine body: spell 42 on the coffin of Itineb

Painted wood
H 183.0 cm
Late Period, *c.* 600–300 BC
Saqqara
London, British Museum, EA 6693

The deceased became divine through the process of mummification and the rites of burial, but the Egyptians sought further reassurance that the mummy would survive as a perfect and indestructible form. One method of achieving this was to equate the individual body-parts with those of deities.

An important passage in spell 42 of the Book of the Dead enumerates the parts of the deceased person's body, identifying each one with a deity and emphasizing that there was no part of the individual which had not become divine (see pp. 162–3). On this coffin of Itineb the space below the scene of judgement is divided into twenty compartments, in each of which the deceased appears adoring a different deity. The accompanying texts, from spell 42, refer to the divinization of the body. One reads 'The eyes of the Osiris Itineb are [those of] Hathor', and the others continue from head to foot, itemizing hair, ears, lips, teeth, breast, belly, phallus, arms, toes. Among the associated deities are Anubis, Neith, Selkis, Sekhmet, Wepwawet and Osiris.

The remainder of the coffin's decoration provides the occupant with other types of power and protection. The green colouring of the face identifies Itineb with Osiris. An amuletic collar with falcon-clasps covers the breast. The sky-goddess Nut spreads her wings over the body, and below is a scene of the judgement from spell 125 of the Book of the Dead. Two figures of Anubis on the feet are painted 'upside down' so as to be clearly visible to the dead man, looking out through the eyes of his coffin mask.

Taylor 2001, 240, fig. 177.

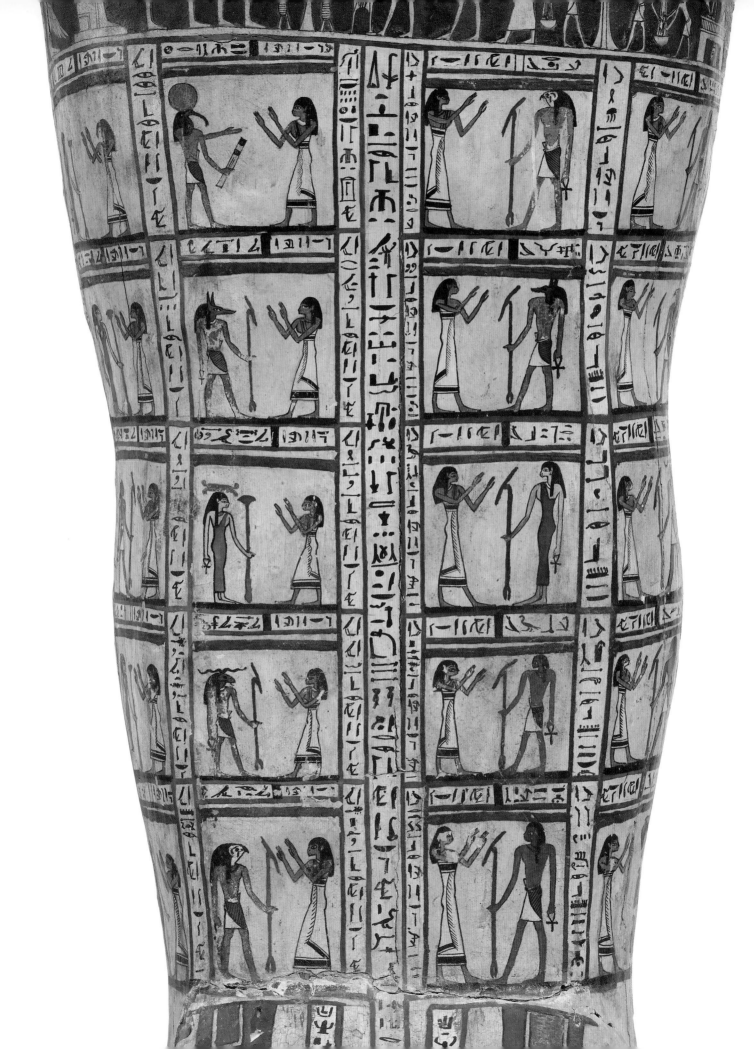

87 Transformation spells from the papyrus of Ani

Painted papyrus
H 42.0 cm
19th Dynasty, c. 1275 BC
Thebes
London, British Museum, EA 10470/27

The transformation spells are illustrated in Ani's papyrus with unusually fine coloured vignettes. At left is spell 87 'for transforming into a snake' (see p. 182) which reads: 'I am the *Sata*-snake, long of years, who sleeps and is reborn each day. I am the *Sata*-snake, dwelling in the limits of the earth. I sleep and I am reborn, renewed and rejuvenated each day.' This is followed by spells 88, 82, 85 and 83, which allow transformation into a crocodile (see p. 183, left), the god Ptah, a 'living soul' and the *benu*-bird – the soul of the god Ra (left).

British Museum 1890, pl. 27; British Museum 1894, pl. 27; Budge 1895; Budge 1913; Faulkner 1985, 82, 84, 86.

88 Transformation spells from the papyrus of Nu

Painted papyrus
H 33.5 cm
18th Dynasty, c. 1400 BC
Provenance unrecorded
London, British Museum, EA 10477/10–11

The papyrus of Nu contains the largest number of spells of any 18th Dynasty Book of the Dead manuscript. All the texts were copied with exceptional accuracy. Günther Lapp has recognized eight thematic sequences of spells in this papyrus, the third of which comprises the transformation spells. The order of the individual spells is unusual: 76, 85, 82, 77, 86, 124, 83, 84, 81, 87 and 88. Their importance, however, is emphasized by the fact that they are provided with vignettes in full colour, an exceptional feature in this otherwise formal and austere manuscript.

Munro 1988, 280, no. a.25; Quirke 1993, 51, no. 148; Lapp 1997, pls 25–31.

Overleaf: p. 182, vignette of spell 87, papyrus of Ani; p. 183, vignettes of spell 88, papyrus of Ani, and spells 81A and 87, papyrus of Nu. See cat. nos 87 and 88.

8 Avoiding Disaster

John H. Taylor

THE Egyptians envisaged the Netherworld as a place of many dangers. Besides the challenges which the deceased faced at gates and caverns (see pp. 134–40), he was vulnerable to threats of different kinds. He might be attacked by dangerous creatures, or fall victim to the terrifying punishments which were reserved for the unrighteous. Many tortures and painful deaths were imagined to be inflicted by frightening entities. These were not all emissaries of evil; many were the agents of gods such as Osiris or Ra whose task was to punish their enemies. The Netherworld was the place where these scenes of hellish violence took place, and the deceased would have to pass by regions such as the 'slaughter place' of the god (spell 50). He was therefore anxious to distance himself from the gods' foes, to make sure that he was not numbered with them and condemned to torment.

Spells in the older funerary literature, the Coffin Texts, helped the deceased to avoid falling into the clutches of these frightening punishers, and many of these texts were absorbed into the Book of the Dead. Some protect against specific fears, such as attacks by snakes and crocodiles. These were dangers which the living might face, and many of the spells to repel them are of types which were used in life, simply transferred into the context of the realm of the dead. Other dangers are more varied in nature – dying again, decapitation, the decay of the body. As if in recognition that these spells shared a common aim, many of them (spells 31–53) were grouped closely together in the Late Period 'recension' of the Book of the Dead. In most of these the deceased takes an active role in keeping himself free from harm.

Controlling and neutralizing hostile forces

Dangerous animals were a constant threat to life in Egypt, so it is not surprising that they were expected to exist also in the Duat. Book of the Dead spells 7, 31–7, 39 and 40 all deal with dangers of this kind (see cat. nos 89–91). Spells 31 and 32 enabled the deceased to drive away crocodiles (fig. 55). Apart from their predatory nature, the dead person feared that these creatures might take away his 'magic':

> Get back! Retreat! Get back, you dangerous one! Do not come against me, do not
> live by my magic; may I not have to tell this name of yours to the Great God
> who sent you; 'Messenger' is the name of one, and Bedty is the name of the other.
> The crocodile speaks: 'Your face belongs to righteousness. The sky encloses the
> stars, magic encloses its settlements, and my mouth encloses the magic which
> is in it. My teeth are a knife, my tusks are the Viper Mountain.'
> The deceased replies: 'O you with a spine who would work your mouth against
> this magic of mine, no crocodile which lives by magic shall take it away.'
>
> (Spell 31)

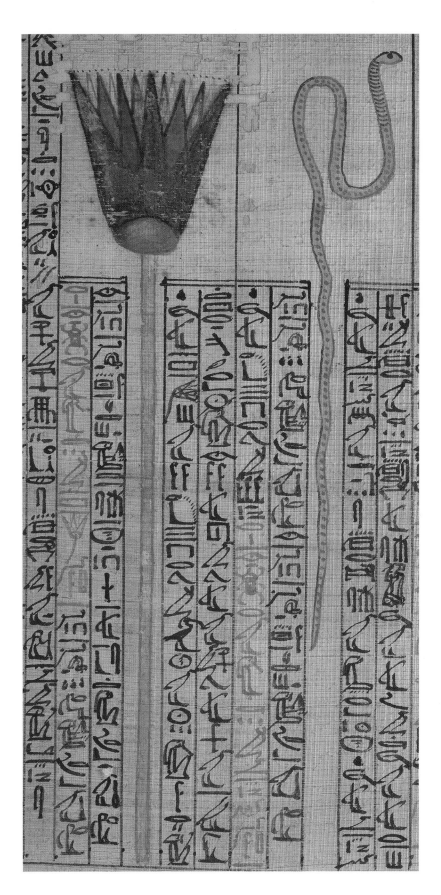

8 Avoiding Disaster

John H. Taylor

THE Egyptians envisaged the Netherworld as a place of many dangers. Besides the challenges which the deceased faced at gates and caverns (see pp. 134–40), he was vulnerable to threats of different kinds. He might be attacked by dangerous creatures, or fall victim to the terrifying punishments which were reserved for the unrighteous. Many tortures and painful deaths were imagined to be inflicted by frightening entities. These were not all emissaries of evil; many were the agents of gods such as Osiris or Ra whose task was to punish their enemies. The Netherworld was the place where these scenes of hellish violence took place, and the deceased would have to pass by regions such as the 'slaughter place' of the god (spell 50). He was therefore anxious to distance himself from the gods' foes, to make sure that he was not numbered with them and condemned to torment.

Spells in the older funerary literature, the Coffin Texts, helped the deceased to avoid falling into the clutches of these frightening punishers, and many of these texts were absorbed into the Book of the Dead. Some protect against specific fears, such as attacks by snakes and crocodiles. These were dangers which the living might face, and many of the spells to repel them are of types which were used in life, simply transferred into the context of the realm of the dead. Other dangers are more varied in nature – dying again, decapitation, the decay of the body. As if in recognition that these spells shared a common aim, many of them (spells 31–53) were grouped closely together in the Late Period 'recension' of the Book of the Dead. In most of these the deceased takes an active role in keeping himself free from harm.

Controlling and neutralizing hostile forces

Dangerous animals were a constant threat to life in Egypt, so it is not surprising that they were expected to exist also in the Duat. Book of the Dead spells 7, 31–7, 39 and 40 all deal with dangers of this kind (see cat. nos 89–91). Spells 31 and 32 enabled the deceased to drive away crocodiles (fig. 55). Apart from their predatory nature, the dead person feared that these creatures might take away his 'magic':

> Get back! Retreat! Get back, you dangerous one! Do not come against me, do not
> live by my magic; may I not have to tell this name of yours to the Great God
> who sent you; 'Messenger' is the name of one, and Bedty is the name of the other.
> The crocodile speaks: 'Your face belongs to righteousness. The sky encloses the
> stars, magic encloses its settlements, and my mouth encloses the magic which
> is in it. My teeth are a knife, my tusks are the Viper Mountain.'
> The deceased replies: 'O you with a spine who would work your mouth against
> this magic of mine, no crocodile which lives by magic shall take it away.'
>
> (Spell 31)

In spell 32 the deceased, speaking as Ra, declares that he will save his father from 'those eight crocodiles'. This is a threat which encompasses the deceased on all sides, two crocodiles being associated with each of the four cardinal points. The vignette of the spell shows the deceased armed with a spear, driving back the creatures (see cat. no. 90), and in the text his words against them are quoted:

Fig. 55 Nakht, armed with a knife, drives away three crocodiles who come to steal his magical powers (spell 31). Papyrus of Nakht, late 18th or early 19th Dynasty, c. 1350–1290 BC. EA 10471/16.

> Get back, you crocodile of the West, who lives on the Unwearying Stars!
> Detestation of you is in my belly, for I have absorbed the power of Osiris, and I am Seth.
> Get back, you crocodile of the West! The *nau*-snake is in my belly, and I have not
> given myself to you; your flame will not be on me.

Fig. 56 Nakht spears a snake, known as 'him who swallowed an ass' (spell 40). Papyrus of Nakht, late 18th or early 19th Dynasty, c. 1350–1290 BC. EA 10471/16.

No fewer than five spells are directed against snakes (33–5, 37, 39, 40) which have different identities and pose different threats (see cat. no. 91). The *rerek*-snake, a demonic snake of the Netherworld, who – like the Apep-serpent (see below) – is an enemy of Ra, is repelled with these words:

> O *rerek*-snake, take yourself off, for Geb protects me; get up, for you have eaten a mouse, which Ra detests, and you have chewed the bones of a putrid cat.

Rerek is mentioned again as the poisonous occupant of the seventh mound in spell 149 (see p. 138). In spells 34 and 35 the danger is that of being bitten and eaten, respectively. Spell 37 wards off a pair of 'songstress snakes', while spell 40 is directed against 'him who swallowed an ass', a snake which is depicted in the vignette biting into an ass's back (fig. 56). The most serious threat is that posed by the Apep-serpent, the great enemy of the sun-god. This gigantic snake features prominently in the Books of the Netherworld, which describe Ra's nightly battles against Apep, who tries to prevent the sun's progress to the eastern horizon. Thanks to the supreme power of Ra, and the assistance of some of his attendant gods, such

Fig. 57 Nakht brandishes a knife to repel the *apshai*-insect (spell 36). Papyrus of Nakht, late 18th or early 19th Dynasty, *c.* 1350–1290 BC. EA 10471/16.

as Seth, Apep is always overcome. In the Books of the Netherworld the dead king journeys with the sun-god and takes part in the destruction of Apep; this conflict is also the basis of spell 39 in the Book of the Dead. In part of the spell the deceased assumes the identity of Ra, and various gods and goddesses are called on to destroy the serpent: 'Your face is turned back by the gods, your heart is cut out by Mafdet, you are put into bonds by the scorpion-goddess, your sentence is carried out by Maat.' Later in the spell the deceased declares that he is Seth, the storm-god who in other texts spears Apep. Through the words of the spell, the deceased participates personally in Ra's nightly progress, ensuring that he will be present at the life-renewing sunrise.

Another creature of the earth which is repelled is the *apshai*-insect or beetle, dealt with in spell 36: 'Begone from me, O Crooked lips! I am Khnum, Lord of Peshnu, who despatches the words of the gods to Ra, and I report affairs to their master.'

The vignettes of these spells show the deceased armed with a spear or knife, actively vanquishing the creatures – in contrast with the purely verbal procedures he uses to pass by obstacles of other kinds (fig. 57). The words stress that he is equipped with magic power, protected by a god such as Geb, or identified with a god such as Ra or Horus.

Slaughter, torture and the world turned upside down

The Duat was the place where the unrighteous were punished at the command of Osiris. Although Osiris is generally presented as benevolent, he could also appear as a threatening figure, particularly in some of the older texts. Punishment involved torture and violent death, carried out by demonic slaughterers, 'slayers of Osiris ... sharp of fingers', who do his bidding.[1] The deceased is understandably anxious not to be numbered with these enemies of the gods, and a group of spells is concerned with saving him from this fate. Spells 41 and 42 are to 'prevent slaughter' (for spell 42, see also pp. 162–3), while spell 50 allows the deceased to escape from the 'slaughter place' of the god (fig. 58). The body is protected from decapitation in spell 43 and from putrefaction in spell 45. The threat of 'perishing' and of having one's rightful place taken are countered by spells 46 and 47 respectively, while spell 44 addresses a danger whose seriousness is hardly reflected by the brevity of the text – 'not dying a second time in the realm

Fig. 58 Ani walks safely past the slaughter-block, represented as a knife dripping with blood, resting on a stand (spell 50). Papyrus of Ani, 19th Dynasty, *c.* 1275 BC. EA 10470/16.

Fig. 59 Nakht escapes from the clap-net in which the divine 'fishermen' seek to trap him (spell 153A). Papyrus of Nakht, late 18th or early 19th Dynasty, c. 1350–1290 BC. EA 10471/15.

of the dead'. This 'second death' was the total extinction of the person which awaited those who did not pass the judgement.

Avoiding danger also meant escaping from traps. The variant spells 153A and B present a situation in which a gigantic net is stretched between heaven and earth to snare the unwary like a catch of fish or birds (fig. 59; see also cat. no. 93). The deceased boldly defies the gods who would entrap him:

> You shall not catch me in this net of yours, in which you catch the inert ones, you shall not trap me in this trap in which you trap the wanderers, the floats of which are in the sky and its weights on earth. I have escaped from its snare, and I have rejoiced as Henu; I have escaped from its clutch, and I have appeared as Sobek, I have used my arms for flying from you, even you who fish and net with hidden fingers.

The passage which follows shows that the deceased's authority over the net comes from his detailed knowledge of all its parts and their symbolic meaning:

> I know the reel in it; it is the middle finger of Sokar. I know the guard-beam in it; it is the shank of Shesmu. I know the name of its cords with which it catches fish; they are sinews of Atum.

Fig. 60 Enemies of the sun-god, decapitated and turned upside down by deities. The text explains: 'They [guard] the bodies of those whom they have decapitated, whose members they have overturned. This god makes them suffer.' A scene in the tomb of Ramesses VI, Valley of the Kings. 20th Dynasty, c. 1140 BC.

A particular fear was that in the hereafter the deceased would encounter a 'world turned upside down'. The graphic images of the Books of the Netherworld from the New Kingdom show that the enemies of the sun-god were turned head down, a very ancient visual metaphor for defeat (fig. 60). A deeply unpleasant consequence of this fate was that the human digestive process was reversed and one would be forced to consume the body's waste products instead of food. This primal fear led to the creation of many spells 'not to eat faeces', which were included in the Coffin Texts. In the Book of the Dead less space is devoted to this, but spells 53 and 189 allude to it, being for not walking upside down and not eating faeces or drinking urine.

A protective armoury: spell 182

Another means of averting attack is given in the rare spell 182. This belongs to the same genre as spell 151 (see pp. 106–8), with a vignette of the burial chamber, showing the mummy on a bier at the centre surrounded by the goddesses Isis and Nephthys, and the Sons of Horus. This vignette differs from the other in that instead of magic bricks, further protection is provided by a series of deities in semi-animal form, armed with knives, snakes and lizards, whose task is to drive away hostile forces (see cat. no. 94). These are members of an extensive category of protectors who appear at several periods of Egyptian history and who are first found safeguarding the living in domestic contexts. Some of them are depicted on the ivory 'wands' of the Middle Kingdom to bring healing and protection in childbirth (see cat. no. 6). Others appear on headrests in the New Kingdom (see cat. no. 7), and in this period also a repertoire of entities of related type is depicted in some royal tombs (either as figures carved on the walls or in the form of carved wooden statues (see cat. nos 95–100). It is these deities who now appear in spell 182 of the Book of the Dead, and in the Third Intermediate and Late Periods their figures are also encountered on royal and non-royal coffins (see cat. no. 101), sarcophagi and papyri, and occasionally as stone statues.

The title of spell 182 is 'Book for the permanence of Osiris, giving breath to the Inert One in the presence of Thoth, and repelling the enemy of Osiris who comes yonder in his various shapes...'. In the text the deceased speaks in the persona of Thoth:

> I cause Ra to enter Osiris, I cause Osiris to enter Ra. I cause him to enter the
> mysterious vault, so as to breathe life into the heart of the Weary of Heart,
> the sheltered *ba* who is in the West.[2]

These words identify the burial chamber ('mysterious vault') as the place where the merging of Ra and Osiris (see p. 20) takes place – the crucial event which brings new life to the dead (the 'Weary of Heart'). Since the deceased takes the place of Osiris, it is to him that the spell will bring renewed life, and him who will be defended from 'the enemy of Osiris who comes ... in his various shapes'. The circle of gods wielding snakes and knives are the agents of this defensive action, who will prevent any attack on the mummy which might frustrate the eternal union of body and *ba*.

89 Repelling hostile creatures from the Book of the Dead of Ankhwahibra

Ink on papyrus
H 27.0 cm
Late 26th Dynasty, c. 550–525 BC
Provenance unrecorded (probably Memphite necropolis)
London, British Museum, EA 10558/7

The spells which enabled the deceased to drive away harmful creatures form a coherent group, numbers 31–40. Several of them are included on this section of the long papyrus of Ankhwahibra, each with its title inscribed in red above compartments containing the text of the spell and the appropriate vignette. Here the dead man, armed with a spear, dispatches crocodiles, snakes and an insect. At the far left of this section is spell 41, 'for preventing slaughter', illustrated by a symbolic motif for 'slaughter' (a snake on top of stylized vertebrae). To the right of this the deceased spears an ass, a variant on earlier versions of this spell (40), in which the ass is bitten by a snake (see p. 186).

Faulkner 1985, 61; Quirke 1993, 32, no. 23.

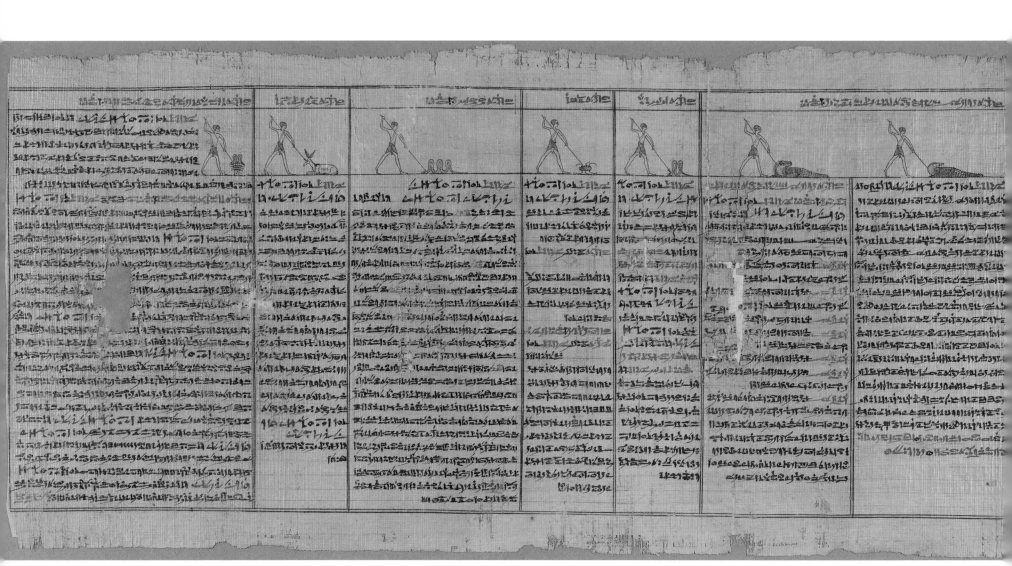

90 Spells for repelling crocodiles from the papyrus of Mutirdis

Painted papyrus
H 18.1 cm
Ptolemaic Period, 305–30 BC
Provenance unrecorded
London, British Museum, EA 9951/4

This illustration combines the vignettes of spells 31 and 32, both of which concern the repulsion of crocodiles who threaten to steal the deceased's magical powers. This Book of the Dead belonged to a woman named Mutirdis, who herself appears in some of the vignettes. In these particular spells, however, it is her husband who wields the spear to drive away the dangerous animals – perhaps an example of decorum, according to which edged or sharpened weapons should only be handled by men in specially sacred contexts (see cat. no. 132).

Faulkner 1985, 56–7; Quirke 1993, 45 (no. 117).

91 Repelling a snake and repelling an insect: spells 33 and 36

Limestone
H 28.2–43.9 cm
Early 26th Dynasty, probably reign of Psamtek I (664–610 BC)
Probably Memphite necropolis
London, British Museum, EA 541–545 and EA 537–540, 546

Two of the spells for repelling hostile creatures were carved on these stone blocks, which also bear the name of a man called Wahibre-em-akhet. The texts are spells 33 and 36 (see pp. 186–7). They read in different directions and were probably positioned on two facing walls of a chamber in their owner's tomb. The end of each text was positioned on a short adjacent wall, perhaps on either side of a doorway. Such spells to ward off dangerous creatures would be especially appropriate at an entrance.

The provenance of the blocks is uncertain. On stylistic grounds a location somewhere in the Memphite necropolis is likely, and both Giza and Saqqara

have been suggested, although neither can be proved. Underground walls in 'Campbell's Tomb' at Giza were inscribed in a similar manner, but it is equally possible that these blocks could have formed part of a structure above ground level. The stylistic features of the figures and texts together with the owner's name (which commemorates a king Wahibre) suggest that the inscriptions date to the reign of Psamtek I.

> O *rerek*-snake, take yourself off, for Geb protects me; get up, for you have eaten a mouse, which Ra detests, and you have chewed the bones of a putrid cat.
>
> (Spell 33, 'for driving off a snake')

> Begone from me, O Crooked-lips! I am Khnum, Lord of Shen, who despatches the words of the gods to Ra, and I report affairs to their master.
>
> (Spell 36, 'for repelling the *apshai*-insect'

Budge 1909, 237; Leahy 1989.

 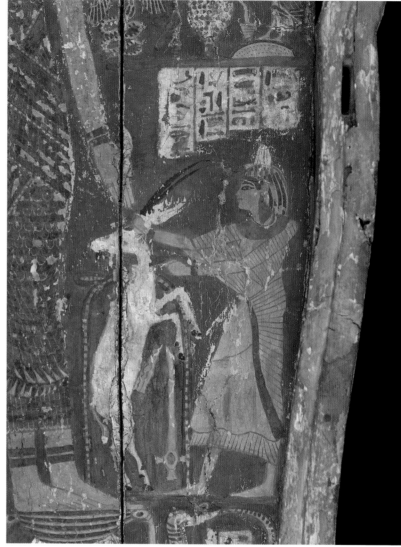

92 The destruction of hostile forces from the coffin of Inpehefnakht

Painted wood
L 187.0 cm; w 54.0 cm
21st Dynasty, c. 1000 BC
Thebes
London, British Museum, EA 29591

During the 21st Dynasty the painted wooden coffins which were made for the priests of Amun at Thebes were decorated with extracts from a rich iconographic repertoire, drawn from various funerary compositions including the Book of the Dead. These scenes were painted both on the outer and inner surfaces of the case, as on this inner coffin made for the chief sailor of the barque of the domain of Amun Inpehefnakht.

Typically scenes from different sources could be combined and adapted to convey symbolic meaning on many levels of interpretation. Hence it is sometimes difficult to be specific as to the origin of a particular image. Among the scenes on the exterior of this coffin are the weighing of the heart, the separation of heaven and earth (see pp. 18–19) and the Lake of Fire (see p. 217). The interior is dominated by the figure of the Goddess of the West, a common feature in the 21st Dynasty. In front of her are scenes which seem to be drawn at least in part from vignettes of the Book of the Dead: the deceased spearing the chaos-snake Apep and cutting the throat of a bound antelope. The latter creature was often associated with the god Seth, and hence this image may symbolize the dead man's successful vanquishing of the powers of evil. In a general sense he is depicted as the defender of order over chaos.

Niwinski 1988, 153, no. 270; Pinch 2006, 158–9, fig. 86.

93 Spells for escaping the net from the Book of the Dead of Nesitanebisheru

Ink on papyrus
H 47.0 cm
Late 21st or early 22nd Dynasty, *c.* 950–930 BC
Royal Cache, Deir el-Bahri
London, British Museum, EA 10554/57–8

On this papyrus the illustrations to two spells, 153A and 153B, appear side-by-side (see p. 189). Both concern the deceased escaping from a net stretched by the gods to entrap her. The vignette of spell 153A, at the right,

shows an open clap-net stretched between two pegs, one of which bears a human head. The text relating to this spell contains the deceased's declaration of knowledge of the components of the net, by means of which she avoids being caught in it. However, the text inscribed below this image is actually that of the unrelated spell 182.

To the left is the vignette of spell 153B, 'for escaping from the catcher of fish'. Three gods are shown hauling on a large net which they are dragging through the water to catch those who are unworthy of entering the next world. The words inscribed below are an address to Osiris, again unconnected to the image at the top.

Budge 1912, 44–6, pl. LXVII–LXVIII; Faulkner 1985, 149.

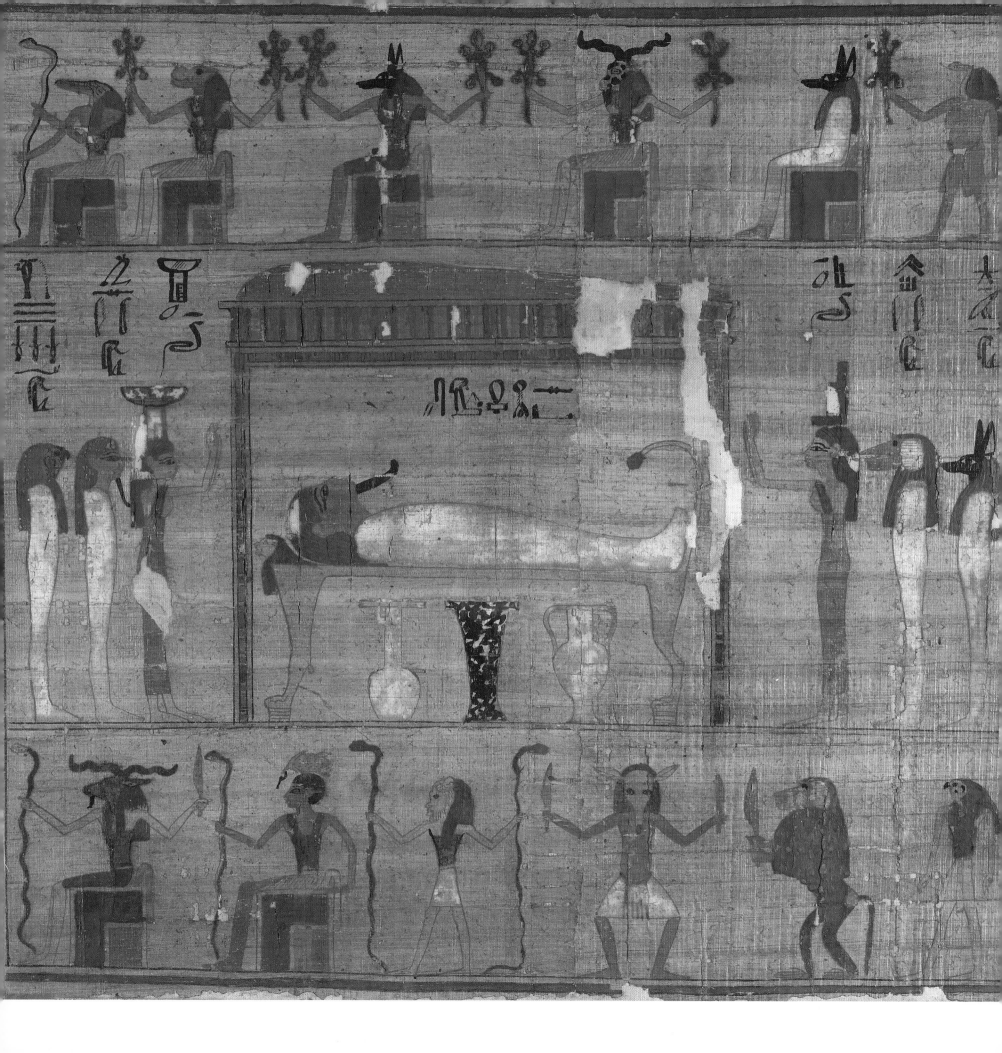

94 Spell 182 from the Book of the Dead of Muthetepty

Painted papyrus
H 34.0 cm
21st Dynasty, *c.* 1050 BC
Provenance unrecorded
London, British Museum, EA 10010/3

Spell 182 is entitled 'Book for the permanence of Osiris, giving breath to the Inert One in the presence of Thoth, and repelling the enemy of Osiris'. The text of the spell focuses on the powers of Thoth, but the vignette is more directly concerned with the creation of a protective environment around the mummy, as alluded to in the title (see p. 190). The papyrus of Muthetepty shows the body, here called 'the noble mummy', on a lion-bier and surrounded by protectors. It is analogous to the vignette of spell 151 and, like that image, it includes the most familiar protectors – Isis and Nephthys and the four Sons of Horus. However, instead of the amulets of the 'magic bricks', the burial chamber is here defended from evil by a large group of deities in human and animal form, grasping snakes, lizards and knives. They belong to the same broad category of 'protectors' who are represented on the ivory wands of the Middle Kingdom (see cat. no. 6). In the New Kingdom they are depicted in some royal tombs, both on the walls and in the form of three-dimensional wooden figures (see cat. nos 95–100), and they reappear in ever-varying shapes and numbers on coffins and sarcophagi in the Third Intermediate and Late periods (see cat. no. 101).

Faulkner 1985, 178–9; Munro 1988, 299, no. b.15; Niwinski 1989, 328; Quirke 1993, 45, no. 115.

Figures of protective entities

Wood, black varnish
Late 18th Dynasty, reign of Horemheb (*c.* 1323–1295 BC)
95–8, 100: Valley of the Kings, tomb of Horemheb (KV 57)

95 Hippopotamus deity

H 32.5 cm
London, British Museum, EA 50699
Waitkus 1987, 81.

96 Turtle-headed deity

H 37.2 cm
London, British Museum, EA 50704
Waitkus 1987, 81; Russmann 2001, 160–61, no. 72.

97 Baboon

H 36.0 cm
London, British Museum, EA 50698
Waitkus 1987, 81.

98 Gazelle(?)-headed deity

H 40.5 cm
London, British Museum, EA 50703
Waitkus 1987, 81; Russmann 2001, 159, no. 71.

99 Lizard from a wooden deity figure

L 13.4 cm
London, British Museum, EA 2018

100 Ram-headed deity

H 57.0 cm
London, British Museum, EA 50702
Waitkus 1987, 82.

The guardian deities of spell 182 were represented
in the form of wooden statues in the tombs of
several kings of the New Kingdom. Examples have
been found in the tombs of Horemheb, Ramesses I,
Sety I and Ramesses IX. The figures were coated
with a shiny black varnish or sometimes just
painted black – the colour symbolizing death and
resurrection. Their poses vary: some stand, some
are seated and others squat on the ground. A few
are depicted in a half-turning posture very rare in
Egyptian sculpture, which was perhaps meant
to suggest that they were moving to confront an
enemy. They may be fully human or fully animal
in form, or a mixture of both. Some of them clearly
resemble figures depicted in spell 182 and on later
coffins (see cat. no. 101). Among the most distinctive
is the deity with the head of a turtle attached to a
human body. He is named on the sarcophagus of
Psusennes I as 'the one who eats putrefaction'. Holes
cut into the hands of some figures show that they
held attributes: these certainly included lizards, and
probably snakes and knives.

101 Protective entities on the coffin of Horaawesheb

Painted wood
L 195.0 cm; W 64.0 cm
22nd Dynasty, *c.* 900 BC
Thebes
London, British Museum, EA 6666

This coffin of the incense-bearer of Khons, Horaawesheb, is covered with images of deities and divine emblems. Those depicted on the lid (not illustrated) include Osiris, the *djed* pillar, Isis and Nephthys. Around the sides is a long series of apotropaic figures, members of the same group who appear in the vignette of spell 182 and as wooden statues in royal tombs (see cat. nos 95–100). They are ranged along both sides of the mummy to provide an impenetrable wall of defence. Protectors are

usually shown moving to indicate their eagerness in going to aid the deceased. Movement in Egyptian art was usually represented by showing one leg advanced, but these figures are more unusual: several of the deities are depicted in a semi-sitting posture with legs bent at the knee, but without seats. This perhaps imitates the pose of some of the New Kingdom royal wooden figures which seem to show the gods rising from the ground and in the act of turning to confront

an enemy who might approach – a more emphatic way of showing the life-force and readiness to act which these deities were believed to possess.

Radiography of the mummy inside the coffin has revealed that it is that of a young woman. It was perhaps placed into Horaawesheb's coffin by antiquities dealers of the early nineteenth century.

Andrews 1998, 182–5; Taylor 2003, pl. 55.

9 Judgement

John H. Taylor

Here I am in your presence, O Lord of the West. There is no wrongdoing in my body, I have not wittingly told lies, there has been no second fault. Grant that I may be like the favoured ones who are in your suite, O Osiris, one greatly favoured by the good god, one loved of the Lord of the Two Lands, [the deceased], vindicated before Osiris. **(Spell 30B)**

THE dead person's experience of the Netherworld, or Duat, involved many encounters with unearthly beings and forces, posing challenges or threats which had to be negotiated. The greatest challenge of all was the judgement, a review of a person's whole life in the presence of Osiris, the key episode being the weighing of the heart. It was this test which determined whether or not one was worthy to be immortal. The good were rewarded with paradise, the evil punished. How a man should behave at this critical moment was the subject of one of the most important parts of the Book of the Dead – spell 125.

By making his way through gates and by repelling dangerous creatures the deceased had demonstrated his command of special knowledge, a strong indication of his worthiness to enter the afterlife. Much of this knowledge, of course, had been imparted to him by the Book of the Dead, and did not necessarily reflect the person's own moral status as indicated by his behaviour on earth. In the hall of judgement the gods considered a man's past conduct as well as his present state of readiness. Here for the first time in Egyptian records the idea is clearly developed that obtaining the benefits of eternal life depended on correct behaviour on earth.

The Egyptians' ideas of good and bad behaviour are known from many texts. They were written down in books of instruction by respected men such as the sage Ptahhotep, or occasionally by kings such as Amenemhat I. Correct behaviour meant maintaining the balance of society and showing reverence to the gods; it was expressed mainly through paying respect to senior figures, supporting the less fortunate (for example, by clothing the naked or feeding the hungry), and observing ritual practices in temples. These precepts were simply based on human experience. There is no Egyptian equivalent of the Bible's Ten Commandments, in which proper conduct is laid down by divine word. Nor was the Egyptian conscious of a need to prove his faith or belief in the gods. Nonetheless, correct behaviour was equated with Maat, the divine principle of right and order, and in spell 125 the deceased asserts that he has conducted himself in a way which conforms with conventional precepts. It was on this basis that the gods would judge him. It has been described as a 'classic situation so often observed by students of religion, i.e. the moral system prevalent in a given society is transposed into the realm of the gods and related beings so that they too become its practitioners and, ipso facto, its guarantors and validation'.[1]

In life, offences usually led to trial before a court. Litigation was a common feature of daily life in ancient Egypt, and every town and village had its tribunal. Since the afterlife was an extension of the earthly existence, the idea of a court and judgement taking place in the hereafter was not strange, and had in fact a long history in Egypt. Texts of the earlier periods of the Old and Middle Kingdoms show that it was believed that this kind of tribunal could be transplanted from the living world to the world of the dead. Thus inscriptions in the tombs of some Old Kingdom officials threaten those who might vandalize their sepulchres with prosecution in the beyond. The idea is that the earthly processes of justice would continue to be available for the deceased to secure his rights even after death. Indeed, the deceased might himself be prosecuted in the afterlife court and might need to be defended. This idea is prominent in the Coffin Texts.[2] There was in theory no limit to the number of such tribunals which could take place after death.

Gradually the possibility of multiple trials for specific offences gave place to the idea of a single moment of posthumous judgement on everyone for their conduct throughout life. There are hints of this in the Pyramid Texts at the end of the Old Kingdom and on the stela of Merer dating from the First Intermediate Period. The first explicit references to the weighing of the heart on scales and the separation of the good from the evil occur in the Coffin Texts in the 12th Dynasty (nineteenth century BC).[3] By the seventeenth century BC the concept was well developed, as the balance is referred to in Book of the Dead spell 30B, first attested on the heart scarab of Nebankh, who lived during the reign of Sebekhotep IV (c. 1720 BC). But only in the 18th Dynasty, with the full emergence of the illustrated Book of the Dead, does the judgement of the dead become fully articulated. Spells 30B and 125 represent the establishment of a new stage in attitudes to immortality. These texts do not present a collective 'day of judgement' for all humanity, as in Christian doctrine, but a single episode undergone by each individual during the passage from life to the afterlife.

In the Hall of the Two Maats

In the Book of the Dead the judgement takes place in the 'Hall of the Two Maats' (see fig. 61). This name probably refers to the twin figures of Maat as goddesses who are sometimes depicted guiding the deceased or seated near the balance.[4] The location of the hall is not clearly stated; nor are we told how or when the deceased reaches it, but specific instructions are given in spell 125 about dress and manner when entering: 'This is the way to act toward the Hall of the Two Maats. A man says this speech when he is pure, clean, dressed in fresh clothes, shod in white sandals, painted with eye paint, anointed with the finest oil of myrrh ...'.

To gain admission he must answer the last of the many probing questions which have been put to him by guardian gods during his journey. At the entrance to the hall the gods ask him to identify himself and pose questions which will reveal his knowledge of mystical matters, in particular with reference to the mysteries of Osiris:

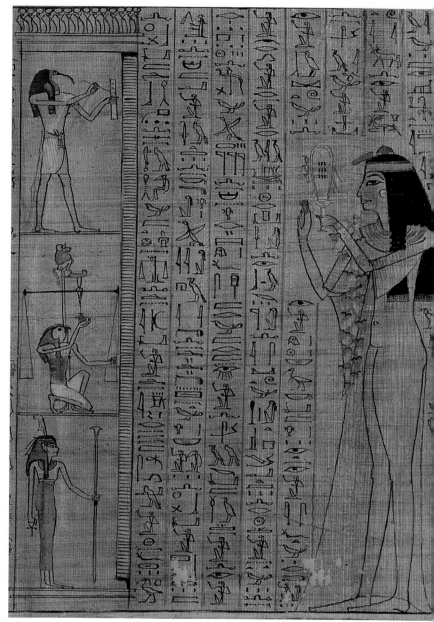

Fig. 61 Anhai shakes her sistrum at the door to the hall of judgement. Within are Thoth, Horus weighing the heart and Maat. Papyrus of Anhai, 20th Dynasty, c. 1100 BC. EA 10472/6.

'Who are you?' they say to me.
'What is your name?' they say to me.
'I am the lower root of the papyrus plant, "He in the olive tree" is my name.'
'Where have you gone past?' they say to me.
'I have gone past the place to the north of the thicket.'
'What have you seen there?'
'It was a leg and a thigh.'
'What have you said to them?'
'I have seen the jubilation in yon lands of the Phoenicians.'
'What have they given you?'
'It was a flaming fire and a faience amulet.'
'What have you done with them?'
'I buried them on the shores of the Maati waters during evening sacrifice.'

(Spell 125)[5]

After further exchanges of the same kind, he is invited to enter: 'Come, then, and step through this gate of the Two Maats, for you know us.' But before he can do this, there is further knowledge to be demonstrated: he must give the names of the individual components of the doorway, names which contain allusions to the events which will take place within.

'We will not let you enter by us,' say the door-posts of this door, 'unless you tell our name.'
'"Plummet of Truth" is your name.'
'I will not let you enter by me,' says the right-hand leaf of this door, 'unless you tell my name.'
'"Scale-pan which weighs Truth" is your name.'

(Spell 125)

And so on for the left-hand door leaf, the floor, the door-bolt, the hasp, the door, the cross-timbers, and then the door-keeper. At last the deceased is announced to the god Thoth, one of the deities most closely associated with the judgement. Besides being the god of writing and knowledge, and the patron of scribes (see cat. no. 138), he played an important part in the protection of the dead and their transition to the afterlife. He acted as a kind of guide and messenger, conducting them on their way, and for this reason he was equated with Hermes by the Greeks. In the Book of the Dead Thoth occurs not only in spell 125, but also in spells 18 and 20 where the deceased appeals to him to vindicate him in the tribunals of the gods.

At the threshold of the hall, Thoth asks four simple questions:

'Why have you come?'
'To be announced.'
'What is your condition?'
'I am free of every sin.'

Fig. 62 Osiris standing within a shrine accompanied by Isis. The four Sons of Horus stand facing him on top of a large lotus flower. Papyrus of Ani, 19th Dynasty, c. 1275 BC. EA 10470/30.

'To whom shall I announce you?'
'To him whose ceiling is fire, whose walls are living *uraeii*, whose house-floor is the flood.'
'Who is that?'
'Osiris.'

(Spell 125)

Now the deceased's name is announced and the judgement proper begins.

The earlier depictions of the judgement do not give much idea of the surroundings, but from the 19th Dynasty onwards the hall is shown with varying details. It is essentially a long room, the roof supported on columns, with doors at each end. It often takes the form of a shrine or chapel; along the top may be an ornamental frieze or a series of Maat feathers alternating with *uraeus* serpents, and sometimes with hieroglyphic signs for 'fire'. These motifs were all ways of repelling the unrighteous, and their depiction may be a graphic rendering of the description just quoted – walls of living *uraeii* and a ceiling of fire. Sometimes these friezes include small images of Thoth as a baboon and a god figure with hands outstretched over a falcon eye or eyes, and a lake; this motif also appears in spell 17 in connection with the purification and rebirth of the deceased (see cat. no. 19) and it is perhaps used here to illustrate what will happen in the judgement hall.[6]

At one end of the hall, often under a canopy approached by steps, is Osiris, enthroned or standing. He presides over the tribunal, often attended by Isis and Nephthys and the four Sons of Horus (see fig. 62). Most depictions of the judgement in the New Kingdom show Osiris in this position, but in the first millennium BC his place is often taken by Ra. Under the watchful eyes of the god, two events unfold – an elaborate denial of wrongdoing, and the weighing of the heart.

The protestation of innocence

In the main part of the text of spell 125, the deceased asserts his good character by declaring himself innocent of a series of offences (see cat. no. 102). This denial

is first made to Osiris, and then before forty-two assessors. They are regularly depicted as mum-miform figures, sometimes standing in a long row within their own shrine or seated in two groups above the weighing scene (fig. 63); the latter depiction probably means that they were imagined as being ranged along two facing walls. These intimidating gods must be addressed each in turn by name. Their names, like those of the guardians of gates and caverns (see pp. 134–7), betoken mystical knowledge, and so to recite them accurately is itself a sign of the deceased's worth. Each deity is concerned with a specific offence which must be denied:

O Far-strider who came forth from Heliopolis, I have done no falsehood.
O Fire-embracer who came forth from Kheraha, I have not robbed.
O Swallower of shades who came forth from the cavern, I have not stolen.
O Dangerous One who came forth from Rosetjau, I have not killed men.
O Flame which came forth backwards, I have not stolen the god's offerings.
O Bone-breaker who came forth from Heracleopolis, I have not told lies.
O Eater of entrails who came forth from the House of Thirty, I have not committed perjury.
O Disturber who came forth from Weryt, I have not been hot-tempered.
O Serpent who brings and gives, who came forth from the Silent Land,
I have not blasphemed god in my city.

(Spell 125)

Fig. 63 The forty-two assessors of the Hall of the Two Maats. All hold knives and wear the Maat feather on their heads, except for the thirteenth figure in the upper row, whose headdress is the lotus flower and plumes of the god Nefertum. Papyrus of Ankhwahibra, late 26th Dynasty, c. 550–525 BC. EA 10558/18.

Several of these acts reflect situations in everyday life, and their categorization as sins would be endorsed by most societies, ancient and modern. Among the total of forty-two, however, there are also numerous offences which relate strongly to religious observance: infringements of correct conduct in cult practices and improper behaviour with regard to the administration of temples.[7] The prominence of these statements in the lists provides a clear hint that this

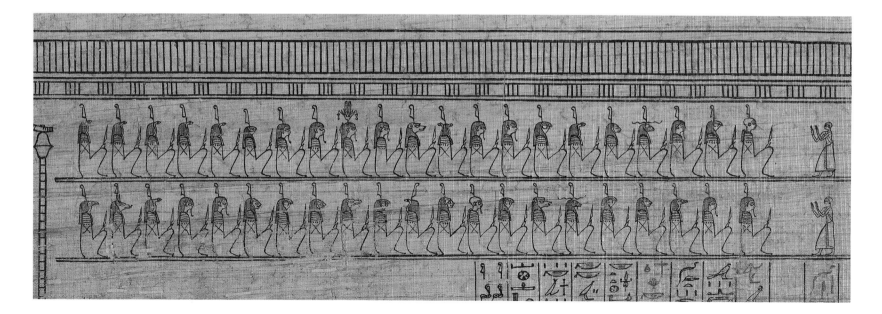

part of the Book of the Dead had its origin in priestly initiation rites where religious personnel had to declare themselves innocent of misdemeanours before entering the sacred precinct of the temple. Statements comparable with those in spell 125 have been found inscribed on some temple doorways, making the connection clear.[8]

The weighing of the heart

The key episode in the judgement is represented by the vignette of spell 125. This image conveys all of the significant details of the weighing of the heart, which is not described in the text of the spell (fig. 64; see also cat. no. 105). A balance stands on the floor of the hall, and from its arms two scale pans are suspended (see cat. no. 108). In one is placed the heart of the deceased; in the other an image of Maat, which may take the form of an ostrich feather (the hieroglyphic sign for the word) or may be personified as a squatting goddess wearing the feather on her head (see cat. nos 109–10). The weighing is conducted under the watchful eye of Thoth. In baboon form, he often squats beside the balance or even on top of the pole. The scale pans and the plummet are carefully manipulated; in early depictions Horus usually performs this task, but in the classic images of the later New Kingdom the role is allotted to the jackal-headed Anubis.

The heart, rather than the brain, was supposed to be the site of the intellect or mind. Here also was the memory, a record of the person's deeds in life (see pp. 161–2). Ideally the heart should balance exactly against Maat. This is not specifically stated, but is implied by the equilibrium shown in the vignettes, which always depict the ideal outcome of the weighing. The demotic story of Setne (see p. 215) gives a slightly different picture, in which the weight of one's good and bad deeds is compared, the result determining one's future state, but this is a very late source and may reflect influence from the Graeco-Roman world.

The heart might not remain entirely passive during the judgement. As an aspect of the person it was considered to have human attributes, notably the ability to speak. This clearly posed a threat to the deceased for the heart might reveal to the gods of the judgement hall some facts about its owner's conduct which would harm his chance of passing the test. Spell 30B of the Book of the Dead was intended to counter this possibility. This crucial text was inscribed on a scarab amulet which would be placed on the mummy (see cat. nos 13, 112–15). It is one of the easiest Book of the Dead texts to understand. Dispensing with mythological allusions, the deceased speaks to his heart in plain language:

> O my heart of my mother! O my heart of my mother! O my heart of my different forms! Do not stand up as a witness against me, do not be opposed to me in the tribunal, do not be hostile to me in the presence of the Keeper of the Balance, for you are my *ka* which was in my body, the protector who made my members hale. Go forth to the happy place whereto we speed; do not make my name stink to the Entourage who make men. Do not tell lies about me in the presence of the god; it is indeed well that you should hear!
>
> (Spell 30B)

Fig. 64 Anubis weighs the heart of Ani, watched by his *ba*, in the presence of Shai ('Fate'), Meskhenet and Renenet. Papyrus of Ani, 19th Dynasty, *c.* 1275 BC. EA 10470/3.

Fig. 65 (opposite) Thoth records the outcome of Ani's judgement. His words are recorded in front of him: 'His *ba* stands as a witness for him. His deeds are true upon the great balance. No sin has been found in him.' Behind Thoth the Devourer waits to swallow the heart if Ani is judged to be sinful. Papyrus of Ani, 19th Dynasty, *c.* 1275 BC. EA 10470/3.

Both spells 30B and 125 offer a revealing insight into the Egyptians' attitude to the judgement. Although moral integrity was regarded as important (as the instructional literature reveals) and although certain deities might turn the heart against its owner and make it 'fashion evil' against him (see pp. 161–2), it was acknowledged that everyone would have done something bad during their lifetime. But to prevent this from condemning the person at the judgement, the evil could be set aside. By denying his guilt of the forty-two sins, the deceased absolved himself from the penalty which they incur. By commanding his heart to be silent he concealed his misdeeds from the gods. In either case, possession of the appropriate knowledge enabled him to escape punishment. The introduction to spell 125 provides a slightly different perspective on the process: 'What should be said when arriving at this Hall of Justice, purging the reader of all the evil which he has done ...'. The judgement hall was a place of purification, but there was no lengthy 'purgatory', no redemption from sin to be gained; ritual knowledge would suffice.

Spell 30B includes the words of Thoth to the Great Ennead (the company of nine primeval gods), announcing the verdict on the dead man (fig. 65):

I have judged the heart of the deceased, and his soul stands as a witness for him. His deeds are righteous in the great balance, and no sin has been found in him. He did not diminish the offerings in the temples, he did not destroy what had been made, he did not go about with deceitful speech while he was on earth.

Fig. 66 A late depiction of the Devourer. It is represented as distinctly female, and the head (usually that of a crocodile in the New Kingdom) now resembles that of a hippopotamus. Papyrus of Ankhwahibra, late 26th Dynasty, *c.* 550–525 BC. EA 10558/18.

The Great Ennead recognize the deceased's good character and declare:

Ammit shall not be permitted to have power over him. Let there be given to him the offerings which are issued in the presence of Osiris, and may a grant of land be established in the Field of Offerings as for the Followers of Horus.

(Spell 30B)

Horus then presents the deceased to Osiris: 'His heart is true, having gone forth from the balance, and he has not sinned against any god or any goddess.' Finally the deceased himself speaks to the god, in the words quoted at the beginning of this chapter (see p. 204).

The Devourer and the punishment of the damned

If all did not go well, the unhappy deceased was handed over to a punisher called 'the Devourer'. This monster was a hybrid beast, with a crocodile's head, the forelegs

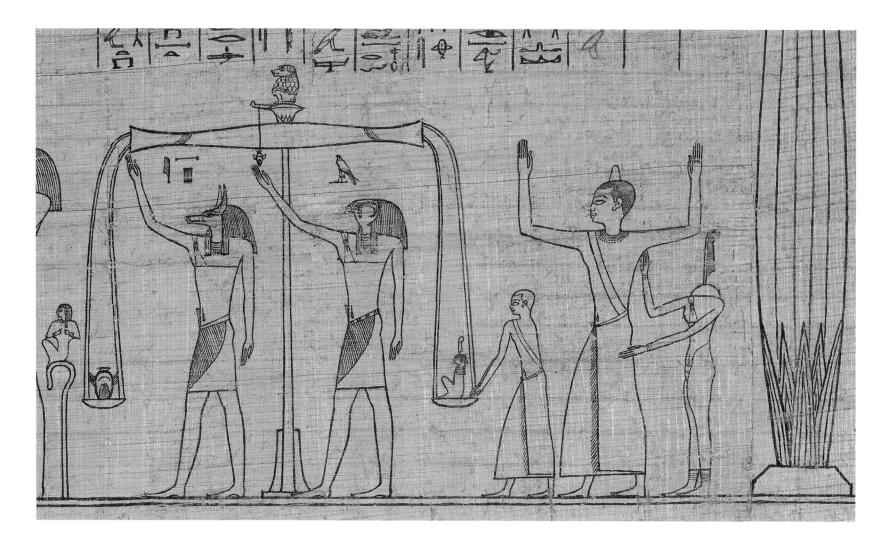

Fig. 67 The deceased Ankhwahibra appears twice: first as a small figure assisting Anubis and Horus in the weighing of the heart, and again at right, raising his arms in the gesture of vindication. He is embraced by Maat, depicted as a goddess with a feather in place of her head. Papyrus of Ankhwahibra, late 26th Dynasty, *c.* 550–525 BC. EA 10558/18.

of a lion and the rear of a hippopotamus (fig. 66; see also cat. no. 104). This fits with the description in the papyrus of Hunefer and in Theban tomb 341: 'Her forepart is that of a crocodile, her rear part of a hippopotamus, her middle a lion.' All three components were creatures who appeared on the ivory 'wands' of the Middle Kingdom (see cat. no. 6), and later in the Books of the Netherworld, as the punishers of wrongdoers and the opponents of hostile powers. Among them the goddess Thoueris – part-hippopotamus, part-human and part-crocodile – may be recognized as a precursor of the Devourer, at least in her physical form.[9] The Devourer first appears in the Book of the Dead in the late fourteenth century BC, after the Amarna period. Early depictions show it lying or squatting under the balance; later it stands before the throne of Osiris, often on a shrine or plinth. After the New Kingdom its tripartite character becomes less obvious and it increasingly resembles a large dog.

In early examples (such as the papyrus of Hunefer) the creature is called *am[et] mutu*, 'the one who devours the dead'. Later the name is generally simplified to Ammit, 'the Devourer', sometimes 'Devourer of the West' or 'Lady of the Duat'.[10] The *mutu* mentioned in the full name are not the dead in general but specifically those who were not vindicated at the judgement; the word could be translated 'the damned' (see p. 23). Elsewhere the Devourer is said to destroy *kheftiu*, 'enemies'. As her name implies, the Devourer's role was to eat the damned, and one very late depiction actually shows her with a human body in her mouth. In the Late Period she is often shown grasping knives, and some late texts also describe her 'slaughtering' and cutting out hearts.[11] These are just a selection of the full range of torments which the gods reserved for the unrighteous; the Books of the Netherworld also detail decapitation, dismemberment and burning in fiery furnaces which seem to prefigure early Christian notions of hell.

Predestination

There are some indications that a person's destiny was established at birth and that the judgement was the fulfilment of this. In a late story written on a demotic papyrus, Setne and his son Si-Osiris travel to the Netherworld and witness the judgement of the dead before Osiris. They find that a man's good deeds are judged 'according to the measure [?] of his term of life that Thoth wrote for him'.[12] Two other texts also mention the notion that a person's fate was decreed for him at birth and was inscribed on a birth brick (*meskhenet*) (see also p. 108). This helps to explain the appearance of birth bricks in the weighing scene on Book of the Dead papyri from the New Kingdom, such as that of Anhai (cat. no. 121), where the human-headed bricks are named as Renenet (a birth-goddess) and Shai ('Destiny'). On Ani's papyrus (cat. no. 105), Meskhenet and Renenet appear by the balance as twin goddesses while Shai is a male figure who stands nearby. The Setne story shows how a poor man and a rich man receive reward and punishment in the hereafter. The poor man is raised to high status, while the rich man suffers a horrific torment – the pivot of the door to the judgement hall is implanted in his eye socket as he lies screaming on the floor. This reversal of their fortunes reflects their deeds on earth. It would seem to emphasize the importance of good behaviour in life, were it not for the context of the tale, which states that their acts had been predetermined. Such an idea is not found specifically in earlier Egyptian sources and may show the influence of Hellenistic culture.

Vindication

Having passed safely through judgement, the deceased is declared *maa-kheru*, 'true of voice', a term for a dead person which can be traced back to the beginning of the second millennium BC. In the Book of the Dead only a successful outcome for the deceased is described or recorded: by having this written and depicted, it would come about through the creative power of word and image. The deceased receives back his heart, which is sometimes shown worn around the neck on a chain. In the vignettes of the Third Intermediate Period and Late Period the actual moment of vindication is sometimes depicted. The dead people stand with arms upraised in jubilation, sometimes supported by Maat (fig. 67; see also cat. no. 111). They are adorned with feathers, stuck in a headband and held in the hands. On Anhai's papyrus (cat. no. 121), she also wears a Maat amulet on a necklace. A small Maat figure was often painted at the throat of anthropoid mummy-cases in the 22nd Dynasty, probably as a 'wish' that the deceased should be vindicated. A further visible sign that one had passed the test was a floral garland called the 'wreath of vindication', which was to be placed on the head, as alluded to in spell 19 of the Book of the Dead.

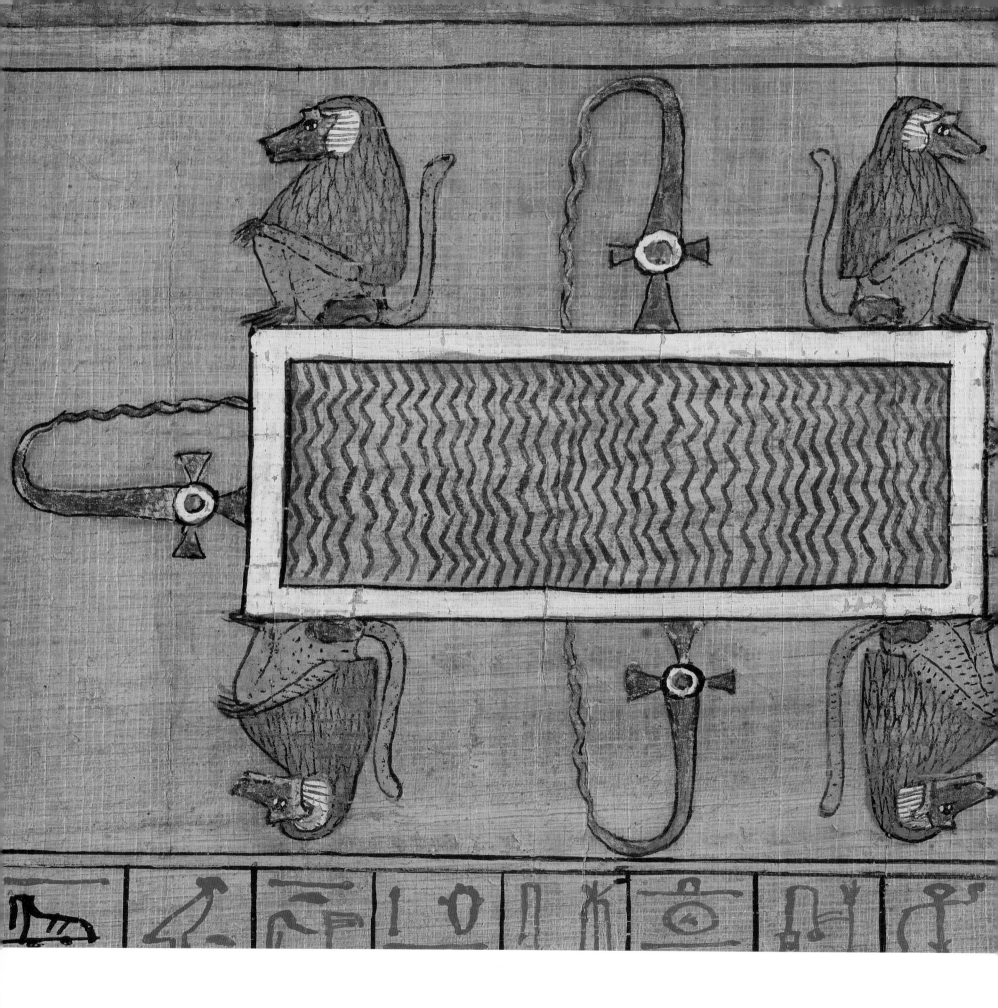

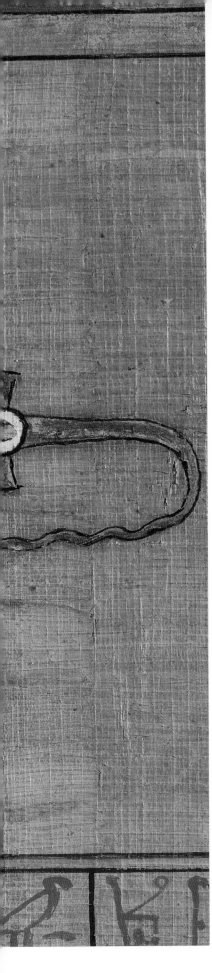

Judgement in the Lake of Fire

Some versions of the vignette of spell 125 include a feature called the Lake of Fire, a rectangular pit with torches on all four sides, baboons at the corners, and sometimes also eight *uraeus* serpents (fig. 68). This lake, located in the Duat, executed a kind of judgement on those who approached it: the evil were burned in its flames, but the blessed dead received nourishment from it. Spell 126 expands on this idea; it, too, has the lake as a vignette and the text is an address to the four baboons, who, we learn, travel in Ra's barque. In their response to the deceased they say:

> Come, so that we may expel your evil and grip hold of your falsehood, so that the dread of you may be on earth, and dispel the evil which was on you on earth. Enter into Rosetjau [the realm of Osiris in the Netherworld], pass by the secret portals of the West, and there shall be given to you a *shens*-cake, a jug of beer and a *persen*-loaf, and you shall go in and out at your desire, just like those favoured spirits who are summoned daily into the horizon.
>
> (Spell 126)

It is not made clear whether the Lake of Fire was an alternative to the weighing of the heart, but both reflect the notion that salvation could be gained by being purged of one's evil deeds.

Fig. 68 The Lake of Fire, surrounded by the four baboons of the sun-god's barque and by flaming torches. Papyrus of Ani, 19th Dynasty, *c.* 1275 BC. EA 10470/33.

102 The protestation of innocence from the Book of the Dead of Nu

Painted papyrus
H 33.8 cm
18th Dynasty, c. 1400 BC
Provenance unrecorded
London, British Museum, EA 10477/23

In one of the earliest depictions of the forty-two judges of the Hall of the Two Maats, the deities appear in a long line, standing within a shrine-like enclosure. The open door leaves of this shrine are depicted at each end. Each god is located in the middle of a narrow column of inscription; the upper part contains the address of the deceased, with the name of the deity concerned; below the figure is the denial of a specific sin, beginning with the words: 'I have not ...'.

Lapp 1997, pls 66–7.

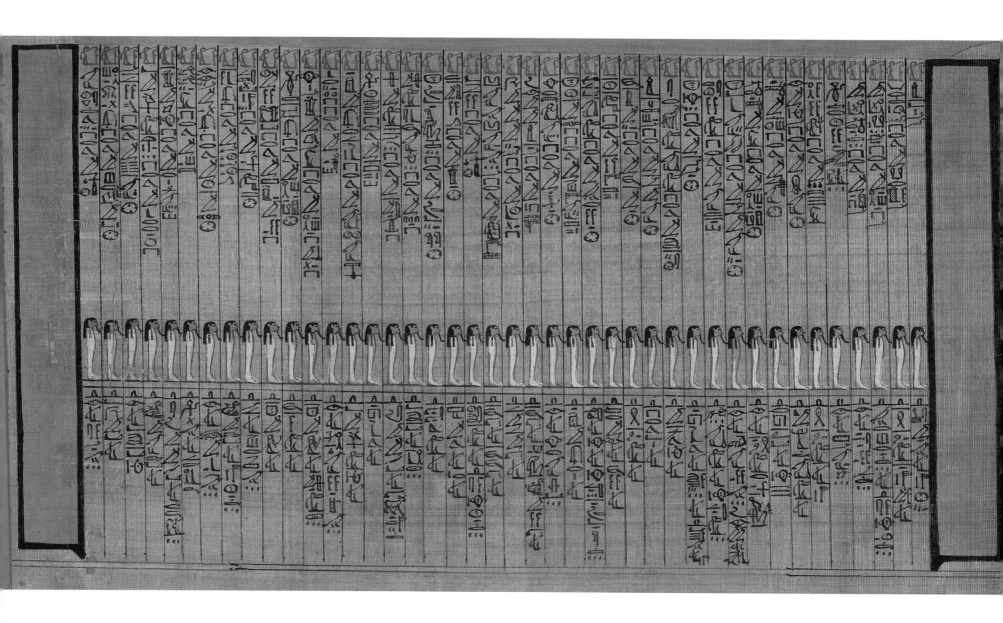

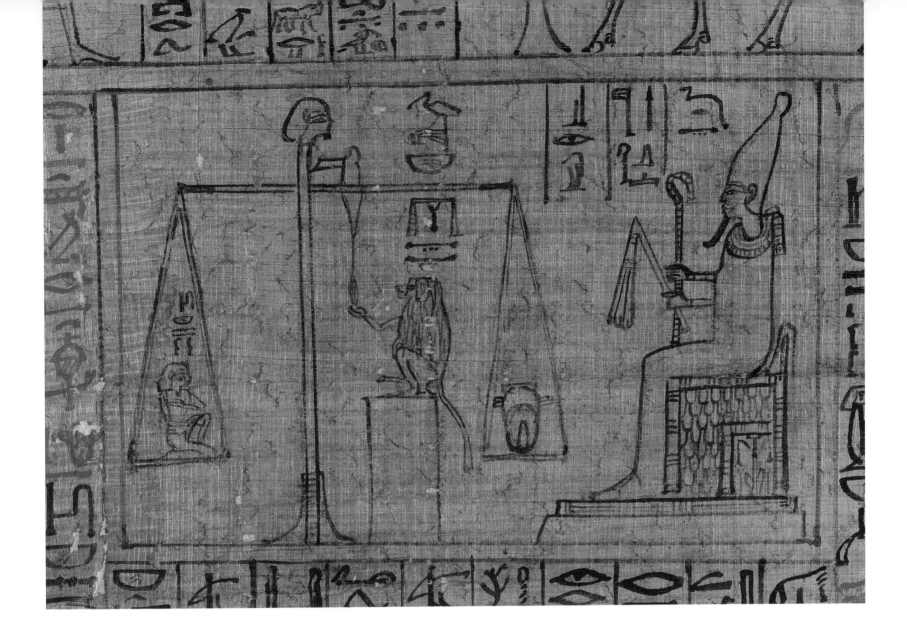

103 The papyrus of Nebseny: an early scene of the weighing of the heart

Ink on papyrus
H 35.8 cm
18th Dynasty, c. 1400 BC
Memphite necropolis
London, British Museum, EA 9900/4

In this papyrus the weighing vignette accompanies spell 30B. It is a small and very simple version of the scene. At the right, Osiris sits enthroned and before him stands the balance. The pole has a human head, but unlike some later depictions, where it is that of Maat (see cat. no. 34), this head is male and has a short beard. The plumb-weight is adjusted by Thoth in baboon form, who squats on a plinth. The right scale-pan holds the heart of Nebseny and in the other is a small human figure – not, as might be expected, Maat, but Nebseny himself, with his name and the title 'scribe' written above him. This depiction of the deceased being weighed against his own heart occurs in several New Kingdom versions of the scene.

Seeber 1976, 201; Lapp 2004, pl. 12.

104 One of the earliest depictions of the Devourer from the Book of the Dead of Nakht

Paint on leather
H 34.5 cm
Late 18th or early 19th Dynasty, c. 1350–1290 BC
Provenance unrecorded (probably Thebes)
London, British Museum, EA 10473/2

The Book of the Dead of the general Nakht (see cat. nos 43, 70, 127–8) was made up of a long roll of papyrus, to which a shorter section of leather was apparently attached – a highly unusual arrangement. On the leather portion of the book is the scene of the weighing of the heart, which is notable for containing an early depiction of the Devourer. Indeed, depending on the dating of Nakht's life, this may be the oldest illustration of the monster so far known. It is made up of the 'standard' components (crocodile, lion and hippopotamus) but is represented as much larger in size than most later examples. Its ruffled mane and wide-open jaws present a more terrifying aspect than the dog-like Devourers of Late Period manuscripts and coffin paintings (see cat. no. 122).

Glanville 1927, pl. xxi b; Quirke 1993, 46, 77, no. 119.

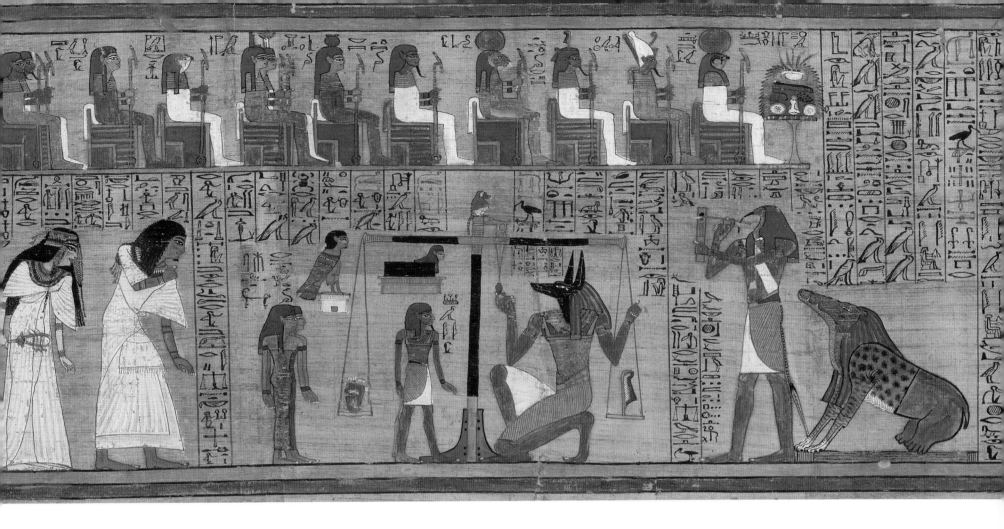

105 The weighing of the heart from the papyrus of Ani

Painted papyrus
H 42.0 cm
19th Dynasty, c. 1275 BC
Thebes
London, British Museum, EA 10470/3

The papyrus of Ani offers the full development of the scene of the weighing of the heart, and includes details which were often omitted from other examples. Ani and his wife Tutu approach at left, bowing, Ani placing his right fist against his left shoulder in a gesture of respect towards the gods. The baboon of Thoth sits on the top of the balance pole, while Anubis kneels adjusting the plummet. On the left scale-pan is the heart of Ani, and on the right the feather of Maat. Ani's *ba* is also present to witness the proceedings. To the left of the balance stands a male figure, Shai ('Fate'), and two female figures, Meskhenet and Renenet, the goddesses who played a part in the birth and nursing of children. They could even be regarded as personal components of the individual, like the other *kheperu* (see p. 17),

and their reappearance here at the judgement marks the end of one cycle of Ani's existence and the beginning of another.

The short columns of text above the scene contain words from spell 30B. In front of Ani is his speech to his heart, telling it not to testify against him (see p. 209). To the right stands Thoth in human form with ibis head, using his scribal palette to record the outcome of the weighing. The words written in front of him record his speech: 'I have judged the heart of the Osiris, and his *ba* stands as a witness for him. His deeds are true upon the great balance, and no sin has been found in him.' At the extreme right is the speech of the Great Ennead (see p. 212), acknowledging Ani's vindication and assuring him that he shall not fall into the power of Ammit. The Devourer herself is represented below, in one of the most graphically vivid images of the creature to have survived. The scene is framed along the top by a row of twelve enthroned deities: Ra-Horakhty, Atum, Shu, Tefnut, Geb, Nut, Isis, Nephthys, Horus, Hathor, Hu and Sia. This group, the occupants of the sun-god's barque, here act as witnesses to Ani's judgement.

British Museum 1890, pl. 3; British Museum 1894, pl. 3; Budge 1895; Budge 1913; Faulkner 1985, 14.

106 **An abbreviated weighing scene**

Ink and paint on papyrus
H 9.5 cm
21st Dynasty, *c.* 1069–945 BC
Thebes
London, British Museum, EA 10008/3

This small papyrus is one of a pair made for the burial of a woman named Tameni (for the other see cat. no. 28). It is a typical 21st-Dynasty example of the abbreviation of passages from the Book of the Dead. Here the weighing of the heart is conducted by Anubis. Others sections of the papyrus (not illustrated) show the Devourer, the dead woman vindicated and adorned with feathers, and an extract from the texts of the protestation of innocence. These elements are intermingled with scenes drawn from other sources – notably the image of the creation of the world, shown here, in which the sky-goddess Nut arches her body above that of the male earth deity Geb. This scene, a powerful evocation of regeneration, appeared prominently on coffins and funerary papyri in the 21st Dynasty.

Seeber 1976, Abb. 16; Niwinski 1989, 328; Quirke 1993, 64, no. 242.

107 A late weighing scene from the Book of the Dead of Ankhwahibra

Ink on papyrus
H 27.0 cm
Late 26th Dynasty, c. 550–525 BC
Provenance unrecorded (probably Memphite necropolis)
London, British Museum, EA 10558/18

In the Late Period the components of the judgement scene and their arrangement in the vignette of spell 125 became relatively standardized. Here the event is located within a columned hall. The forty-two assessors are depicted at a small scale in two rows, each confronted by a figure of the deceased. An enthroned Osiris watches the weighing of the heart. Horus and Anubis tend the balance, and the dead man stretches out a hand to the scale pan containing the image of Maat, as if to ensure a correct outcome. Thoth records the result and the Devourer squats on a pedestal. At the right Ankhwahibra, attended by Maat, raises his arms in the gesture of vindication.

Quirke 1993, 32, no. 23.

108 Silver pans from a set of scales

D 7.6 cm
Ptolemaic or Roman Period, after 305 BC
Probably from the temple of Hathor at Dendera
London, British Museum, EA 57369

The balance which features in the judgement scenes would have been a type of object familiar to most ancient Egyptians. They were commonly used in the marketplace for weighing goods to be bought and sold, while smaller and more accurate sets of scales were to be found in workshops and temples for weighing precious materials. These silver scale pans were probably discovered in the early twentieth century among a hoard of votive objects and other ritual furnishings from the temple of Hathor at Dendera. Each pan bears an incised hieroglyphic inscription, a ritual text naming Hathor, Lady of Iunt. Suspension cords would have been attached by means of small holes at the edges.

Shore 1979, 141, 158.

109 Figurine of Maat

Copper alloy, originally inlaid
H 11.4 cm; W 2.9 cm
Late Period, 664–305 BC
Provenance unrecorded
London, British Museum, EA 60383

Maat was the principle of right by which the cosmos was maintained in order. Everyone was expected to live according to this notion, which encompassed the ideas of truth and justice. In mythological terms Maat was the daughter of the sun-god Ra and could be represented as a female figure wearing the hieroglyphic sign for her name (an ostrich feather) on her head. A squatting mummiform image of Maat is often shown being presented by the king to the gods, and a similar figure may appear in the scale pan of the balance of judgement. This statuette may have formed part of a larger votive group of sculpture.

110 Gold chain with pendant in the form of Maat

L of chain 49.5 cm; H of figure 2.7 cm
26th Dynasty, c. 600 BC
Provenance unrecorded
London, British Museum, EA 48998

This gold-foil figurine of Maat, fashioned over a light core and originally inlaid, is suspended from a chain of small interlocking links of gold wire. A Maat image, worn around the neck like an amulet, is occasionally depicted on statues and also appears at the throat of coffins in the 22nd–25th Dynasties. As the papyrus of Anhai shows (cat. 121), this was a visible indication that one had passed safely through the judgement. Maat amulets were also worn in life by Egyptian judges, according to the Greek historian Diodorus Siculus, and it is possible that this may have been the function of the present example.

Andrews 1998, 120–21, no. 34.

111 The weighing scene from the papyrus of Kerasher

Painted papyrus
H 23.0 cm
Reign of Augustus, late first century BC
Thebes
London, British Museum, EA 9995/4

Kerasher's Book of Breathing contains a very late illustration of the weighing of the heart. In its general outline the scene closely follows the models of earlier periods, although certain details are exceptional. At the top are 'the gods of the hall of the Two Maats', although the artist has erroneously drawn forty-three figures instead of the standard group of forty-two. Under their eyes Kerasher watches as Horus and Anubis perform the weighing. Thoth records the outcome using his scribal palette, and the Devourer, holding two knives, crouches on a plinth; unusually, she is named in the inscription as 'Tem-Isher'. Having successfully passed through the assessment, Kerasher makes an offering to the enthroned Osiris, who is attended by Isis. At the far right, as in the papyrus of Anhai a thousand years earlier (cat. no. 121), the dead man raises his hands in jubilation at his vindication. With him stands a goddess who is named as 'Maat-Hathor who resides in the West', a combination of the personification of Truth and the goddess Hathor, who protected the dead in their tombs. She wears the feather sign in her headband and appears to be represented with her face turned away from the viewer. Although it is tempting to interpret this as an early image of 'blind Justice', the sightless nature of the figure perhaps derives from Maat's role as companion of the sun-god in his journey through the pitch-dark depths of the Netherworld. The vignette is notable for the strong orange-red colouring used by the painter. Analysis has shown that this contained red lead, which is not attested as a pigment in Egypt before the Roman period.

Seeber 1976, 230, no. 3; Quirke 1993, 43, no. 102; Herbin 2008, 40, pl. 24.

112 Heart scarab of King Sebekemsaf

Green jasper and gold
H 3.8 cm W 2.5 cm
17th Dynasty, *c.* 1590 BC
Thebes
EA 7876

The body of the scarab, carved from jasper, has a human face and is set within a gold mount, on to which the insect's legs have been represented in separate strips of gold. Around the sides and on the base of the mount is the text of spell 30B, which, as on the scarab of Nebankh (cat. no. 113), includes 'mutilated' hieroglyphs. The owner of this amulet was one of two kings named Sebekemsaf, and this is the earliest heart scarab made for a royal person that is so far known. Papyrus records of the trials of tomb robbers, about 1110 BC, include the confession of a thief who plundered the tomb of Sebekemsaf II at Thebes; it was perhaps from this tomb that the heart scarab came.

Strudwick 2006, 110–11.

Heart scarabs

Spell 30B, which prevented the heart from testifying against its owner at the judgement (see above, p. 209), was usually inscribed on an amulet in the form of the scarab beetle – hence these objects are known as 'heart scarabs'. They were among the most important and frequently used amulets which were placed on the mummy.

113 Heart scarab of Nebankh

Green jasper
H 3.2 cm
13th Dynasty, *c.* 1720 BC
EA 64378

Nebankh is known to have lived during the reign of King Sebekhotep IV (*c.* 1720 BC), making this the earliest accurately datable heart scarab. The beetle has a human head and the inscription on the base contains the words of spell 30B. As on other funerary objects of this period, hieroglyphic signs representing birds are shown without legs, to prevent them from harming the deceased.

Andrews 1994, fig. 44; Quirke 2002–3, 31.

114 Heart scarab of Ani

Basalt
L 6.1 cm W 4.0 cm
19th Dynasty, *c.* 1295–1186 BC
EA 7878

The text of spell 30B on the base of this scarab includes the name of the owner, Ani (not, apparently, the man of that name who owned the Book of the Dead EA 10470). Carved on the beetle's body is an image of the *benu*-bird, here described as the 'heart of Ra'.

115 Heart scarab

Green basalt
L 6.3 cm W 4.5 cm
18th Dynasty, *c.* 1550–1295 BC
EA 26244

The nine lines of inscription on the base of this scarab contain the text of spell 30B. A space was left for the insertion of the name of the eventual owner, but this was never filled in.

116 Depiction of a heart scarab or amulet from the Book of the Dead of Astemakhbit

Painted papyrus
H 30.0 cm
Mid to late 21st Dynasty, c. 1000–945 BC
Provenance unrecorded
London, British Museum, EA 9904/2

Astemakhbit's short Book of the Dead contains spells 138, 60, 17, 89, 77, 81A, 9, 56 and 1 in hieroglyphic script, and spells 125, 126, 30B, 6 and 61 in hieratic. In keeping with the compression of content into a small space, the vignettes of several spells are grouped together. Among the vignettes for spells 56, 77 and 81A is a detailed drawing of a heart-shaped amulet with the outlines of a scarab beetle's body on the back.

Niwinski 1989, 320, pl. 17b; Quirke 1993, 33, 72, no. 29.

Heart amulets

Amulets shaped like the human heart (see also p. 174) frequently fulfilled a role similar to that of the heart scarab.

Heart amulets became, from the New Kingdom onwards, one of the most important elements of the mummy's trappings. They exhibit varying degrees of realism in their form. Some have a human head, emphasizing the organ's status as the embodiment of the person; some have a *benu*-bird on the front; several actually have the text of spell 30B (as on the heart scarab); and some also have a scarab motif.

117
Schist amulet of Amenhotep

H 6.5 cm W 4.2 cm
New Kingdom, *c.* 1550–1069 BC
EA 27385

The front carries the image of a scarab beetle, and on the back is the text of spell 30B.

Strudwick and Taylor 2005, 98.

118
Faience heart amulet

H 5.8 cm W 3.5 cm
Late 18th or 19th Dynasty, *c.* 1350–1186 BC
EA 29440

This amulet has a human head and a depiction of the *benu*-bird. On the flat back is spell 30B in seven lines. The owner's name is omitted.

Andews 1994, fig. 61f.

119 **Composite heart scarab and heart amulet of a woman named Iuy**

Green feldspar
H 9.5 cm W 4.1 cm
New Kingdom
Thebes
EA 7925

This amulet, owned by a woman named Iuy, combines a scarab with an elongated heart and has spell 30B incised in twelve lines on its flat back. The *ankh*, *djed* and *tit* signs symbolize life, stability and protection. Incised on the scarab's body is a prayer that the deceased shall sail across the sky and have the use of her eyes and ears.

Andrew 1994, fig. 56; Parkinson 1999, 139, no. 52.

120
Obsidian heart amulet of Shedkhons

H 5.2 cm W 3.7 cm
New Kingdom, *c.* 1550–1069 BC
Thebes
EA 8003

A scarab beetle is incised into the front of this amulet, and spell 30B is inscribed in yellow on the back. The owner, Shedkhons, was a priest and scribe of Amun.

Andrews 1994, fig. 61c.

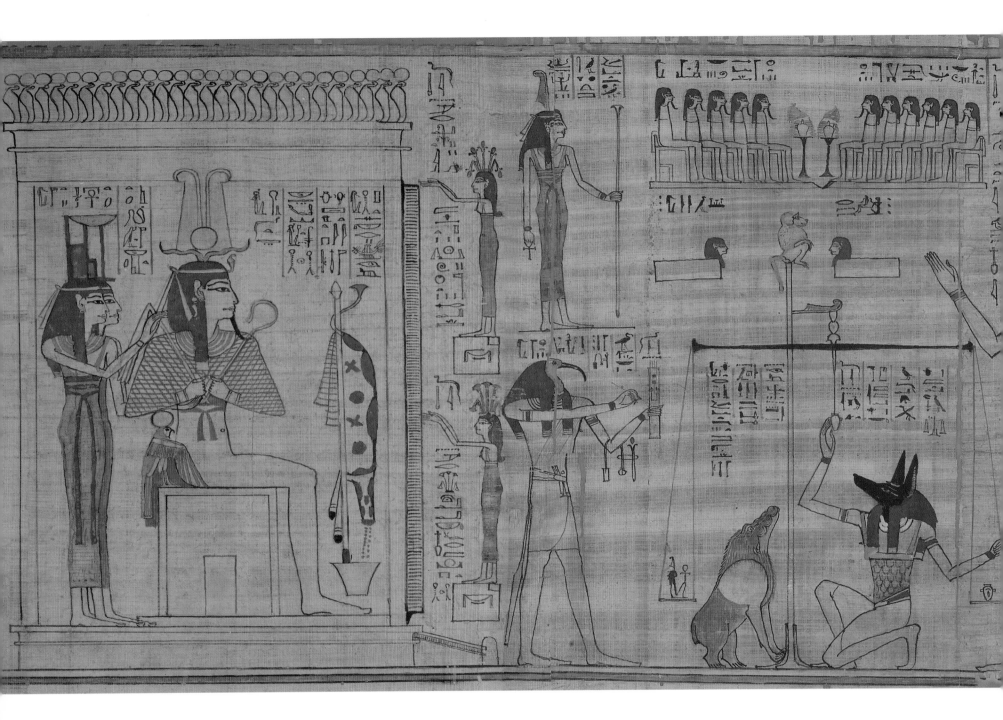

121 The judgement of Anhai

Painted papyrus
H 42.0 cm
20th Dynasty, *c.* 1100 BC
Probably from Thebes
London, British Museum, EA 10472/4–5

The papyrus of Anhai is one of only a small number of Books of the Dead from the New Kingdom that were made specifically for women (see also cat. no. 26). The draughtsmanship of its vignettes is also unusually fine, as this detailed scene of the judgement shows. On the left Anubis crouches beneath the scales to weigh Anhai's heart, watched by the Devourer who will swallow it if she is judged unfit. Above are the deities Shai and Renenet, both of whom were connected with the birth and personal lifespan of the individual, and so are appropriately depicted in the form of birth bricks with human heads (see p. 215). At the top are two groups of deities who preside over the entire process of the judgement. These beings, the Greater and Lesser Enneads, were companies of nine gods, although here the artist has drawn only five on one side and six on the other. Maat stands at the left together with Thoth in his ibis-headed form. Thoth uses a scribal palette to record the result of the weighing, and he carries an additional palette, water pot and pen case (together forming the hieroglyph for 'scribe' or 'to write') hanging in the crook of his arm. Anhai stands watching the weighing, her hand held by the falcon-headed Horus, whose speech, recorded in the text above, announces her to the Lords of Maat.

At the left the composite deity Ptah-Sokar-Osiris sits enthroned in a shrine, attended by Isis and Nephthys. Facing him are the twin Meret goddesses of the north and south. At the far right Anhai appears again, having passed safely through her judgement. In contrast to her appearance by the balance, where she is simply dressed, without collar, bracelets or garlands in her hair, she now appears triumphant, arms raised, embraced by the Goddess of the West and adorned with visible signs of her acceptance by the gods. A narrow band of cloth (perhaps the 'wreath of vindication') has been tied around her head, into which feathers have been tucked, while other feathers are held in each hand and hang suspended from her arms. A figure of Maat around her neck on a chain (see cat. no. 110) emphasizes that she has emerged 'true of voice' from the ordeal of judgement.

Budge 1899, pls 4–5; Seeber 1976, 212.

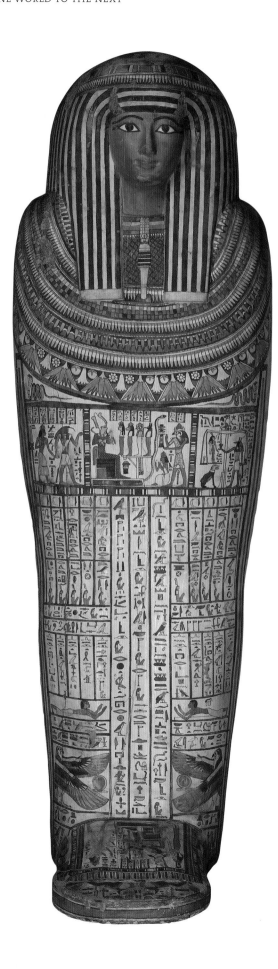

122 The dead man in the hall of judgement: the coffin of Pasenhor

Painted wood
H 203.0 cm; w 67.5 cm
Late 22nd or early 25th Dynasty, *c.* 750–720 BC
Thebes
London, British Museum, EA 24906

Pasenhor, a member of the Libyan Meshwesh tribe, was buried in a coffin which is covered with texts and images relating to the judgement. Across the breast the weighing of the heart is depicted in three scenes. At the right (appropriately located close to the mummy's heart) we see the weighing being performed on the balance by Anubis and Maat, while a small dog-like 'Devourer' crouches below. At the left Pasenhor, having received back his heart, holds it in his right hand and is led by Thoth towards Osiris. In the centre the vindicated Pasenhor appears again, kneeling before Osiris, who is attended by the Sons of Horus and a giant snake. Horus presents a *djed* pillar.

The inscriptions on the lower part of the lid include passages from spell 1 of the Book of the Dead (in the three central columns and the short horizontal bands). At each side of the central text there are extracts from the 'protestation of innocence' from spell 125, as well as images of the deceased, prostrate in adoration, and divine falcons. On the foot Pasenhor appears again in the presence of Osiris. Various deities are painted on the sides of the coffin, beneath an architectural *kheker* frieze. This may be a further allusion to the place of judgement. It is possible that the iconographic 'programme' of this coffin was designed to create the Hall of the Two Maats by magic around the mummy, eternalizing the desired moment of vindication. This might also be reflected in the band of lotus petals which Pasenhor wears around his head, and which may be an early version of the 'wreath of vindication' – a crown of plant material which the dead received as a sign that they had passed the judgement.

Andrews 1998, 58, fig. 56; Taylor 2003, 109, pl. 58.

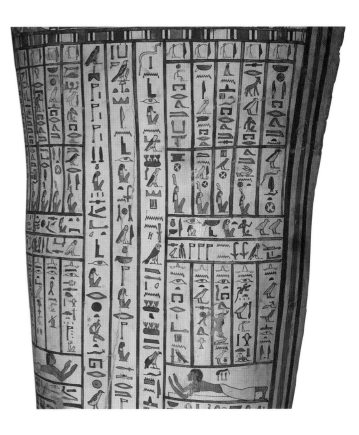

123 **The Book of the Dead of 'Queen' Nodjmet**

Painted papyrus
H 55.0 cm; L 419.0 cm
Early 21st Dynasty, *c.* 1050 BC
Royal Cache, Deir el-Bahri
London, British Museum, EA 10541

Nodjmet was one of the most influential women in Egypt at the end of the New Kingdom. She was married to King Herihor (formerly army commander and high priest), and was also sister of a king and mother of a king, though the identities of these rulers are uncertain. Her original burial place is unknown, but her mummy was found in 1881 in the hidden tomb known as the 'Royal Cache' on the Theban west bank, to which it had been transferred at some time during the 21st or early 22nd Dynasty.

She possessed two funerary papyri (see also, p. 271, fig. 82). The larger roll, of which this is a part, contained spells from the Book of the Dead. The complete papyrus was over 14 metres long; the right-hand end is in the Louvre (E 6258) and the central section was formerly in Munich but is now lost. Although the papyrus belonged to Nodjmet, her husband Herihor is also shown prominently in the vignettes, perhaps reflecting the New Kingdom tradition by which women were usually depicted only alongside their husbands in the Book of the Dead. The British Museum portion includes vignettes and texts of spells 15, 125, 101, 100, 1 and 17, the last of which continued on the Munich section.

Nodjmet is one of very few owners of a Book of the Dead about whose life we know any details. Surviving letters on papyrus (see overleaf), written by the powerful army commander Piankh, show that she was involved in the political murder of two policemen who had made seditious speeches: 'Have these two Medjay [policemen] brought to my house and get to the bottom of their words in short order, and have [them] killed and have them thrown [into] the water by night.' Such an act, if revealed to the gods at the judgement, would in theory have led to her damnation. On her papyrus, she is shown standing by the balance in anticipation of a successful outcome.

Niwinski 1989, 337–8; Quirke 1993, 47, no. 126; Parkinson and Quirke 1995, col. pl. VII; Lenzo 2010.

(left) Nodjmet and Herihor adorning Osiris; (above) part of the funeral procession; (above right) the mummy of Nodjmet, part of the vignette of spell 17; (opposite) Nodjmet stands by the balance of judgement. Fig. 69 (below) Letter from Piankh requesting Nodjmet to arrange a murder. Berlin 10489.

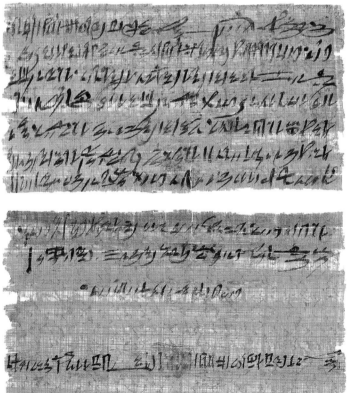

10 The Perfect Afterlife

John H. Taylor

THE Egyptians have left a wealth of texts and objects all testifying to a vivid conception of the afterlife. However, these sources extend over a very long time-span of 3,000 years and come from different localities and different strata of society, so it is not surprising that there is a great deal of variety in the information supplied, as well as much that seems at first sight contradictory. An important reason for this is that the different sources – whether texts, objects or the traces of ritual practices – reflect the status of the person for whom they were originally conceived. The Old Kingdom Pyramid Texts were at first provided only for the dead king (see p. 54); so also (with a few exceptions) were the New Kingdom Books of the Netherworld. Both of these text genres later became accessible to non-royal individuals as well, but the sacred nature of the texts and images was respected and the views of the afterlife which they presented were not significantly changed or adapted to make them consistent with what was contained in other sources such as the Book of the Dead. It was characteristic of the Egyptian attitude to religion that alternative traditions were tolerated simultaneously. All had validity because all possessed independent authority deriving from a particular god or cult centre. Different myths and traditions might be synthesized, yet the older, independent versions, in spite of all their inconsistencies, still remained valid. Among the most obvious expressions of this phenomenon are spells 17 and 18 of the Book of the Dead, in which alternative versions of certain passages are presented within the framework of a single, continuous text.

Because of this approach it is difficult to tell whether there was a single notion of the afterlife which all Egyptians would have recognized, or whether king, courtier and peasant each had different expectations. The afterlife of the king is expounded in detail in different compositions: in the pyramid age of the Old Kingdom he ascends to the sky to become a star or to join his divine father Ra; in the New Kingdom, the Books of the Netherworld elaborate on the dead king's unity with the sun-god and explain that he participates in the god's cyclical journey across the sky by day and through the Netherworld by night. During this passage the king also becomes identified with Osiris, and his existence is perpetuated. But what kind of afterlife did a peasant expect? The contents of the earliest and simplest graves – mainly clothes, food, drink, tools and weapons – suggest that they aspired to enter a world similar to that of the Egypt they had known in life, but we do not know whether they hoped for more than this.

The afterlife that is presented in the Book of the Dead embraces elements of both of these traditions. The spells reveal that the dead person could experience a rarefied existence interacting with the great gods, and also a comforting life in a familiar landscape. Different Book of the Dead spells allude to different aspects of the afterlife, but how these experiences related to each other is not articulated. There is no single goal and no single path to be followed. This does not seem to have troubled the minds of the Egyptians; we must be content to note that a number of different experiences were possible.

Fig. 70 The sunrise scene which concludes the Book of the Dead of Userhat. The inscription between the four baboons reads 'Adoring Ra when he rises'. 18th Dynasty, *c*. 1450 BC. EA 10009/1.

Community with Osiris and the sun-god

A fundamental tenet of the Egyptians' belief, which appears at a very early date, is that the mummy was destined for the earth and the spirit for the sky. In spite of later elaborations this notion was still at the root of the ideas of the afterlife which are reflected in the Book of the Dead. The mummy, surrounded by protective powers, rested in the tomb, which, in symbolic terms, was located in the Duat or Netherworld. The deceased in spirit form – as a *ba* or *akh* – left the mummy to join the gods Osiris and Ra, and to become one with them. A vast amount of Egyptian mortuary literature and practice was devoted to bringing about community between the deceased and these two gods, who were regarded as complementary aspects of a single divine being (see pp. 18–20).

Osiris's realm lay under the ground, and was equated either wholly or partially with the Duat. Osiris lived eternally and one of the goals of the dead person's journey was to penetrate the many gates which led to his domain and to enter into a special relationship with the god (see pp. 134–7 and cat. no. 128). This relationship with Osiris was also brought about by the funeral rituals. By becoming 'an Osiris' he, like the god, triumphed over death. He entered the following of Osiris and worshipped him, as many passages from the Book of the Dead attest, such as this hymn which occurs at the beginning of the papyrus of Ani:

> Hail to you, King of Kings, Lord of Lords, Ruler of Rulers, who took possession of
> the Two Lands even in the womb of Nut ... May you grant power in the sky, might
> on earth and vindication in the realm of the dead, a journeying downstream to

Busiris as a living soul and a journeying upstream to Abydos as a heron; to go
in and out without hindrance at all the gates of the Netherworld. May there be
given to me bread from the House of Cool Water and a table of offerings from
Heliopolis, my toes being firm-planted in the Field of Reeds …

However, to achieve community with Osiris was not the sole aim of the deceased. Osiris never left his subterranean kingdom and existence there was static. Although many hymns and prayers to Osiris emphasize the desirability of dwelling with him, a remarkable text from the Book of the Dead (spell 175) reveals some very human concerns about this type of existence. Part of the spell is a dialogue between the deceased and the creator-god Atum:

Deceased: 'O Atum, how comes it that I travel to a desert which has no water and
no air, and which is deep, dark and unsearchable?'
Atum: 'Live in it in content!'
Deceased: 'But there is no love-making there!'
Atum: 'I have given spirit-being instead of water, air and love-making,
contentment in place of bread and beer – so says Atum. Do not be sorry
for yourself, for I will not suffer you to lack.'

The 'peace of mind and blessedness' which are offered here as compensation for the loss of earthly pleasures were evidently not considered to be enough. It was regarded as important to be able to leave this Netherworld realm periodically, and hence the notion of 'coming forth by day' attained great importance: the idea that the individual could leave the inert body in the darkness of the tomb, travel to the world above and experience the pleasures of life (see pp. 105 and 166). This possibility was closely associated with community with the sun-god. He possessed freedom of movement, passing in his boat through the Netherworld at night, where he was rejuvenated, and then reborn the next morning as he rose on the eastern horizon. Thus many spells in the Book of the Dead are concerned with the deceased gaining admittance to the sun-god's boat and being able to travel in his company (see cat. no. 127). Spells 100 and 102 are to allow the deceased to go aboard the barque of Ra, to navigate it and to drive away the hostile serpent Apep. Spell 101, 'for protecting the barque of Ra' recounts that the god has 'included [the deceased], a worthy spirit, in your crew' and assures the deceased that he will be healthy. Variations on the same theme occur in spells 129–31 and 133–6; some of these spells were also used by the living in rituals in temples, and prescribed the drawing of images of gods on bowls to make the spell effective (see cat. no. 17). In one case the instruction requires that an image of Ra drawn on a bowl be placed before a sacred barque made of pieces of malachite, 4 cubits long, containing an image of the spirit 'which you desire to be made worthy'. If these conditions were fulfilled, 'it means that he will sail in the barque of Ra, and that Ra himself will see him in it … the gods will see him as one of themselves, the dead will see him, and they will fall on their faces when he is seen in the realm of the dead by means of the rays of the sun' (spell 133).

The sun-god's rejuvenation took place each night, deep in the hidden Netherworld, when he met Osiris and the two momentarily merged their beings (see p. 19). This mysterious union does not receive much attention in the Book of the Dead. Much more prominence is given there to the sunrise. This highly visible manifestation of the sun-god's 'rebirth' became a strong feature of the Book of the Dead after the Amarna period, when the sun-disc became for a short time the sole manifestation of divinity throughout Egypt. Most Books of the Dead from the following Ramesside period include a hymn to the sun-god at dawn. Though classified as 'spell 15', there is no standard text for this paean of praise. This passage from the papyrus of Ani is typical:

> O all you gods of the Soul-mansion who judge sky and earth in the balance ...
> give praise to Ra, Lord of the Sky, the Sovereign who made the gods. Worship
> him in his goodly shape when he appears in the Day-barque. May those who are
> above worship you, may those who are below worship you, may Thoth and Maat
> write to you daily; your serpent-foe has been given over to the fire and the rebel-
> serpent is fallen, his arms are bound. Ra has taken away his movements, and the
> Children of Impotence are non-existent ... May he grant that I see the sun-disc
> and behold the moon unceasingly every day; may my soul go forth to travel to
> every place which it desires; may my name be called out, may it be found at
> the board of offerings; may there be given to me loaves in the Presence like the
> Followers of Horus, may a place be made for me in the solar barque on the day
> when the god ferries across, and may I be received into the presence of Osiris in
> the Land of Vindication.
>
> (Spell 15, papyrus of Ani)

These hymns are usually followed by a large vignette of the sunrise (conventionally labelled 'spell 16'; see fig. 70 and cat. nos 124–6). The earlier versions of these images sometimes encapsulate the entire course of the sun's journey in one scene. The sun-god often takes the shape of a falcon with a solar-disc on his head. It may stand upon a *djed* pillar or west sign, denoting the Netherworld realm of Osiris which Ra is leaving, and his emergence into the sky is greeted by the acclamation of gods, *ba*-spirits and jubilant baboons. The later images of spell 16 are divided into registers showing the sun in different guises, including those of a falcon-headed god and shining disc (see cat. no. 126).

Through his presence among the sun-god's entourage the deceased would experience an endless daily cycle of rebirths. The *ba* would leave the tomb for the world of the living by day, and return to the mummy at night. The reuniting of spirit and mummy brought rejuvenation. Although this constant repetition does not seem to allow for much rest, within the course of this journey was a locality which is singled out as a goal: a paradise called the Field of Reeds.

A familiar landscape: the Field of Reeds
The Field of Reeds (or perhaps better, 'Marsh of Reeds')[1] is described in three spells in the Book of the Dead (110, 109 and 149). It is visualized as a landscape of waterways leading past fields

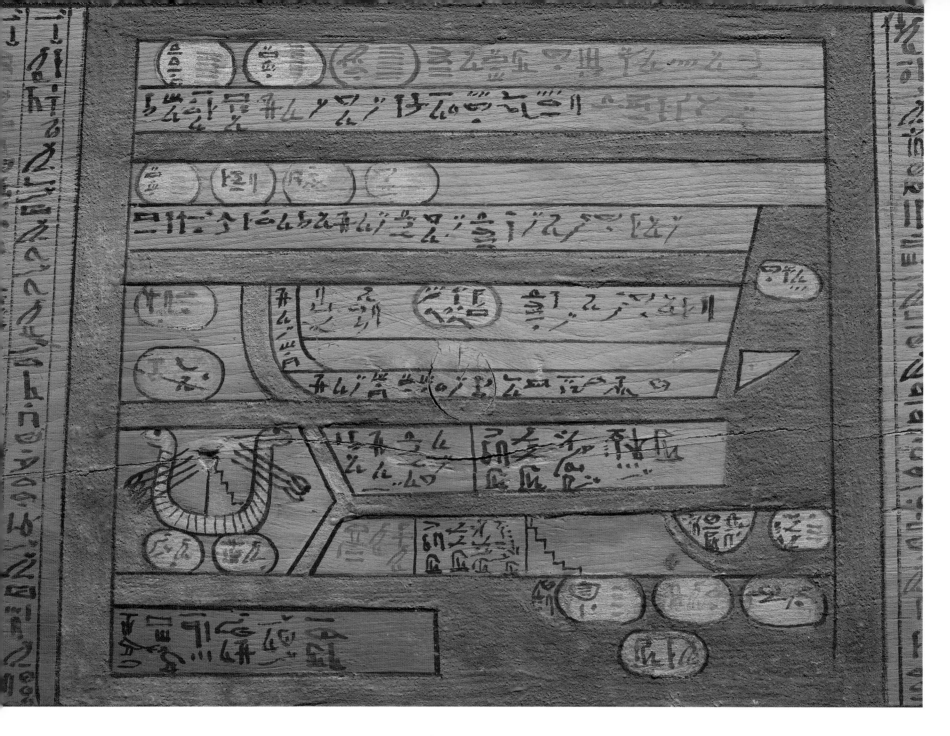

Fig. 71 Spell 466 of the Coffin Texts, a precursor of the vignette showing the Field of Reeds (better known as spell 110 of the Book of the Dead). Interior of the inner coffin of Seni from el-Bersha (see cat. no. 20). 12th Dynasty, *c.* 1850 BC. EA 30842.

where abundant crops grow and where gods and the blessed dead live in peace and contentment (fig. 71).

The idea of an eternal paradise can be traced back long before the Book of the Dead. Its location and role changed over time. Originally, as described in the Pyramid Texts, it was part of the watery expanse of the night sky, on the surface of which the celestial bodies voyaged. The path of the sun, moon and planets, which the Egyptians called the 'Winding Waterway', divided the sky into northern and southern parts. In the northern sky was the Field of Rest (or Offerings), in the southern sky the Field of Reeds.[2] In the Pyramid Texts the Field of Reeds was a place in which the deceased was purified before ascending to the sky, but in the later Coffin Texts it has become a destination for the deceased, a place where crops were grown to provide the dead with food.[3] This was to be its principal role in the Book of the Dead.

In the Book of the Dead tradition it is not entirely clear whether the Field of Reeds is located in the sky or under the earth. It seems, however, to be in the east, at the point where Ra ends his nightly journey. A description of it occurs in the chapter of the mounds, spell 149 (second mound): 'I know the gate in the middle of the Field of Reeds from which Ra goes out into the middle of the sky'. Spells 149 and 109 state that Ra goes forth between 'two trees of turquoise', and they record in similar words the character of the Field: 'Its walls are of iron, its barley stands 5 cubits high, with ears of 2 and stalks of 3 cubits, and its emmer [wheat] stands 7 cubits high, with ears of 3 and stalks of 4 cubits; it is the blessed, each of them 9 cubits tall, who reap them alongside the Eastern Souls.'

The character of the Field of Reeds is a reflection of the Egypt of the living: the green, lush, fertile, well-watered Nile valley and Delta, rather than the burning, lifeless desert. It has been described as 'an exaggerated version of the cultivated fields of the floodplain at harvest time'. When the dead reach this place they have come full-circle from the landscape they loved during life to a similar (but better) environment for eternity. Spell 110 describes what happens in the Field: 'ploughing therein, reaping and eating therein, drinking therein, copulating, and doing everything that was once done on earth by the reader'. It indeed provides those earthly delights which are so conspicuously missing in spell 175. The Field of Reeds was probably the origin of the Elysian Fields of Classical mythology; not only is the concept similar, the name 'Elysian' has been derived from a Greek pronunciation of *iaru* or *ialu*, the Egyptian word for 'reeds'.[4]

The Field of Reeds seems to have a more concrete reality than other regions of the Egyptian afterlife because it is depicted in a large illustration, the vignette to spell 110 of the Book of the Dead – the only true depiction of a landscape in the entire composition (fig. 72). This diagram first appears on some coffins of the Middle Kingdom from el-Bersha, as a rare illustration to Coffin Texts spells 466–7 (the precursors of spell 110 in the Book of the Dead). Here the locality is called the 'Field of (the god) Offering', but the diagram is recognizably the same landscape as the Field of Reeds of the New Kingdom. The arrangement of waterways and islands is basically the same, and although there are no figures of the deceased or the deities he will meet, there are written descriptions of what lies there. The associated Coffin Texts spell 467 explicitly states that the deceased will travel, plough, reap, eat and copulate there.

The vignette of the Field of Reeds in copies of the Book of the Dead varies in detail, but there is a high degree of consistency in the main features (see cat. nos 130–33). It has been pointed out that these can be related closely with the text of spell 110 if the illustration is 'read' from the bottom to the top. Thus the deceased's arrival in the Field with the sun-god is indicated by the boats in the bottom register; one boat is regularly named as the barque of Wennefer (Osiris); the other is the boat of the sun-god. The attribution of the names to the boats fluctuates, but at the temple of Medinet Habu, where this scene is unusually carved on a wall, the double snake-headed boat is explicitly called 'the barque of Ra-Horakhty when he crosses the Field of Reeds'. Also in this register appears the Great Ennead (a company of gods). Here the deceased receives food and drink, and next, moving upwards, we see him engaged in agriculture – ploughing and harvesting and perhaps also seeding the earth (fig. 73). He is supplied with an abundance of

Fig. 72 Nesitanebisheru in the Field of Reeds (spell 110). The usual four divisions of the scene have been reduced to three. The blank spaces in the central and lower registers suggest that the vignette was left unfinished. Papyrus of Nesitanebisheru, late 21st or early 22nd Dynasty, *c.* 950–930 BC. EA 10554/81.

nourishment, symbolized by a fantastical bird, the 'heron of plenty', and we see heaps of grain and oval shapes representing localities where food and offerings are provided. The surplus is given to the *ka*-spirits of the blessed dead. The deceased then arrives at a place called Qenqenet, and here we are told that he is reunited with his deceased parents, a meeting which is depicted in some of the versions of this scene. After this he sails on the waters and finally meets the Great Ennead again. These gods are encountered both at the beginning and end of his passage through the Field of Reeds, which, like other journeys in the hereafter, turns out to be a cyclical one.

Escaping from toil: the shabti spell

So the Egyptians hoped to reach a land that was like the Egypt they knew and loved, with waterways, islands and fields of waving corn; but some aspects of the agricultural life were less pleasant. In the real world the annual inundation of the Nile brought the need for

Fig. 73 Detail of spell 110. The text behind Ani's figure reads 'ploughing' and that above the oxen gives the location of the activity, 'The Field of Reeds'. Papyrus of Ani, 19th Dynasty, *c.* 1275 BC. EA 10470/35.

much hard labour to prepare the land for planting. The flood covered the ground for several months and when the waters receded there was much work to reconstruct banks and field boundaries, to shift sand to unblock canals and irrigation channels, and generally to fine-tune the complex hydraulic network on which the Egyptian economy was based. To do this a corvee system was operated. In every nome (province) men were recruited to take part in this essential work. Yet exemption from this hard labour was possible. Some members of society, such as priests and scribes, could employ a deputy to do the work on their behalf. It was expected that a similar obligation to work would be placed on people in the realm of the dead, and to escape this irksome task a magical figurine called the shabti was devised. These small human images of wax, wood, stone or faience first appeared at the beginning of the Middle Kingdom. A spell in the Coffin Texts explains their basic function, to act as a substitute for the owner if he should be summoned to do work in the hereafter. In the New Kingdom shabtis became a standard part of the well-appointed burial (see cat. nos 2, 12 and 55). The spell was modified and incorporated into the Book of the Dead as spell 6. Its wording varies, but a typical version reads:

> O shabti allotted to me, if I be summoned or if I be detailed to do any work which has to be done in the realm of the dead; if indeed obstacles are implanted for you therewith as a man at his duties, you shall detail yourself for me on every occasion of making arable the fields, of flooding the banks or of conveying sand from east to west; 'Here I am,' you shall say.

Fig. 74 Three of the forty shabti figures of the Chantress of Amun Henutmehyt (see cat. no. 134). 19th Dynasty, *c.* 1250 BC. EA 41548.

The spell was often inscribed on the body of the figure. In the New Kingdom shabtis were usually carved in the form of mummies equipped with agricultural tools – hoes, mattocks, baskets and sometimes water pots (fig. 74; see also cat. no. 134). These items were carved or drawn on the figure, but sometimes the utensils were fully crafted on a miniature scale (see cat. no. 136). The importance attached to shabtis is very clear. The figures remained among the most essential elements of burial equipment; their numbers increased from 1 or 2 per person to 401 (365 'work-ers', plus 36 'overseers', equipped with whips to control every gang of 10); even the king had shabtis, although it would seem unlikely that he would be obliged to labour like his subjects. While shabtis of the New Kingdom are often beautifully sculpted, those of the Late Period are much more stand-ardized in appearance. By the early first millennium BC their meaning had changed. The earlier ones were manifestations of the owner himself, alterna-tive bodies rather like a statue or a mummiform coffin, but the later ones had a more subordinate status; they were 'slaves' to work at the owner's com-mand, and this was reflected in a change in the name, from shabti to ushebti (meaning 'answerer'), a clear indication that their sole duty was to respond to the summons to work.

124 Adoration of the rising sun from the Book of the Dead of Anhai

Painted and gilded papyrus
H 46.0 cm
20th Dynasty, *c.* 1100 BC
Provenance unrecorded (probably Thebes)
London, British Museum, EA 10472/1

Many Book of the Dead papyri include a prominent vignette of the rising sun, usually positioned close to the solar hymn spell 15. This illustration was classified by Richard Lepsius as 'spell 16', though it is not strictly speaking a spell, as it has no text. There are many variants of the scene. In this one the sun-god is depicted as a falcon with a gilded solar disc on his head. It is perched on a large hieroglyphic sign meaning 'West', which in this context represents not the cardinal point but the Netherworld (often described simply as 'the West') from which the sun is emerging at dawn. The scene is framed below by undulating lines and red dots which represent the sandy tracts of the desert at the horizon. The sun is adored by pairs of winged *wedjat* eyes with ostrich-feather fans, and groups of anthropomorphic deities and baboons. Below these are the goddesses Isis and Nephthys, and the lady Anhai in the form of her *ba*, shown twice, standing on a plinth with arms raised in adoration.

Budge 1899, pl. 1; Faulkner 1985, 43.

125 Adoration of the rising sun from the Book of the Dead of Hunefer

Painted papyrus
Height 39.0 cm
19th Dynasty, *c.* 1280 BC
From Thebes
EA 9901/1

In Hunefer's papyrus the 'sunrise' vignette ('spell 16') directly follows the adoration text of spell 15. Here the sun god is again depicted in falcon-shape, with a large solar disc as headdress and a gently curving sky-hieroglyph above. Seven baboons, dancing and waving their paws, are described in the inscription as 'giving praise to Ra when he rises on the horizon.' The Netherworld realm of Osiris, from which the sun is emerging, is represented by the *djed* pillar. Here it is a manifestation of Osiris himself, and is provided with human arms and hands which hold the crook and flail. The sister goddesses Isis and Nephthys flank the pillar.

Budge 1899, pl. 1; Faulkner 1985, 6.

126 Adoration of the rising sun from the Book of the Dead of Hor

Ink and paint on papyrus
H 36.0 cm
Late first century BC
Akhmim
London, British Museum, EA 10479/11

In later papyri the vignette known as 'spell 16' is arranged in a series of horizontal registers (see p. 241), and the contents are more standardized than in the New Kingdom. At the top the deceased kneels adoring the sun-god in a boat. The god appears in three forms – as falcon-headed Ra-Horakhty (the daytime sun), as Atum with a double crown (the evening sun) and as Khepri with a scarab on his head (the morning sun). Horus mans the steering oar and Harpocrates sits at the prow. In the second register the sun is depicted as a disc with shining rays supported by two goddesses, and flanked by the four sons of Horus and the emblems of east and west. In the third register the sun-disc is suggested by a god flanked by pairs of *ba*-birds and baboons; they are surrounded by *ankh* signs with human arms holding feather fans. In the fourth register Hor and his wife are seated; behind them a priest pours a libation and burns incense.

Faulkner 1985, 42; Mosher 2001, 16–17, col. pls 1–2 .

127 Nakht in the celestial barque of Ra

Painted papyrus
H 36.0 cm
Late 18th or early 19th Dynasty, *c.* 1350–1290 BC
Provenance unrecorded (probably Thebes)
London, British Museum, EA 10471/9

The sun-god Ra was the guarantor of eternal life, and to travel in his boat across the sky enabled a dead person to experience endless rejuvenation (see p. 240). The Books of the Netherworld painted on the walls of royal tombs in the Valley of the Kings made it possible for the dead pharaoh to be identified with Ra himself. Lesser mortals sought to go aboard the god's boat and this is the theme of numerous spells in the Book of the Dead. Two images of the boat appear in Nakht's papyrus, where the vignettes of spells 136A and 136B are painted side-by-side. At the right, Nakht uses a long pole to navigate the barque, which is occupied by a large falcon head of the god. A group of enthroned deities pulls a tow-rope at the right. In the second barque the sun-god is seen in two manifestations simultaneously: as the falcon-headed Ra-Horakhty and the scarab-headed Khepri (the daytime and morning sun, respectively). Thoth and an unidentified goddess accompany him.

Faulkner 1985, 126–7.

128 **Nakht and his wife adore Osiris in the hereafter**

Painted papyrus
H 39.7 cm
Late 18th or early 19th Dynasty, c. 1350–1290 BC
Provenance unrecorded (probably Thebes)
London, British Museum, EA 10471/21

This unusually large and detailed vignette comes at the end of the long papyrus of the general Nakht. The text at the top is a hymn to the sun-god (spell 15). At the far left is a mountainous slope which represents the western horizon. The arms of the sky-goddess Nut emerge from the top of this to receive the sun-disc at the close of the day. In front of the slope, enthroned on a stepped dais, sits Osiris, fully accoutred with feathered crown, ram's horns, sun-disc and sceptres. He is attended by Maat, the personification of Order and Truth.

Nakht and his wife Tjuyu stand facing the deities, with their hands raised in adoration. Tjuyu also shakes a sistrum. Both wear on their heads the perfumed ointment cones which are often depicted in the scenes of

banquets and other recreations on the walls of tomb chapels. These details rarely appear in papyri of this date. Also more typical of the genre of 'daily life' scenes are the images of Nakht's house and garden which are included here. The garden is represented by a stylized water pool surrounded by trees; a vine is also growing there, stretching towards the face of Osiris as if to offer its fruit to the god. The house, with its carefully delineated windows and triangular rooftop ventilators, is also shaded by trees. This is one of the most important illustrations of an Egyptian domestic structure to survive from this period.

Glanville 1927; Quirke 1993, 46, 77, no. 119; Russmann 2001, 196–7, no. 100.

129 Conclusion of the Book of the Dead of Ani, showing Sokar-Osiris, Ipet and Hathor

Painted papyrus
H 38.0 cm
19th Dynasty, *c.* 1275 BC
Thebes
London, British Museum, EA 10470/37

The papyrus of Ani ends with two full-height vignettes. At the left stands the composite funerary deity Sokar-Osiris as a falcon-headed mummiform figure. This is the vignette to spell 185, a short hymn to Osiris. To the right of this is the vignette of spell 186, a scene which acts as the conclusion of several Book of the Dead papyri of the 19th Dynasty. First, before an offering table, stands the birth-goddess Ipet in hippopotamus form. In front of her is the hieroglyphic sign *sa* (meaning 'protection') (see cat. no. 6 for a similar figure). She also holds an *ankh* ('life') sign and a flaming torch, with which – as spell 137B states – she drives away Seth. Finally we see the cow of Hathor on the slopes of the western mountains. Her head emerges from a papyrus thicket, behind which is the whitewashed tomb chapel of Ani, topped with a small pyramid.

British Museum 1890, pl. 37; British Museum 1894, pl. 37; Budge 1895; Budge 1913; Faulkner 1985, 186–7; Andrews 1998, 84–7, no. 18.

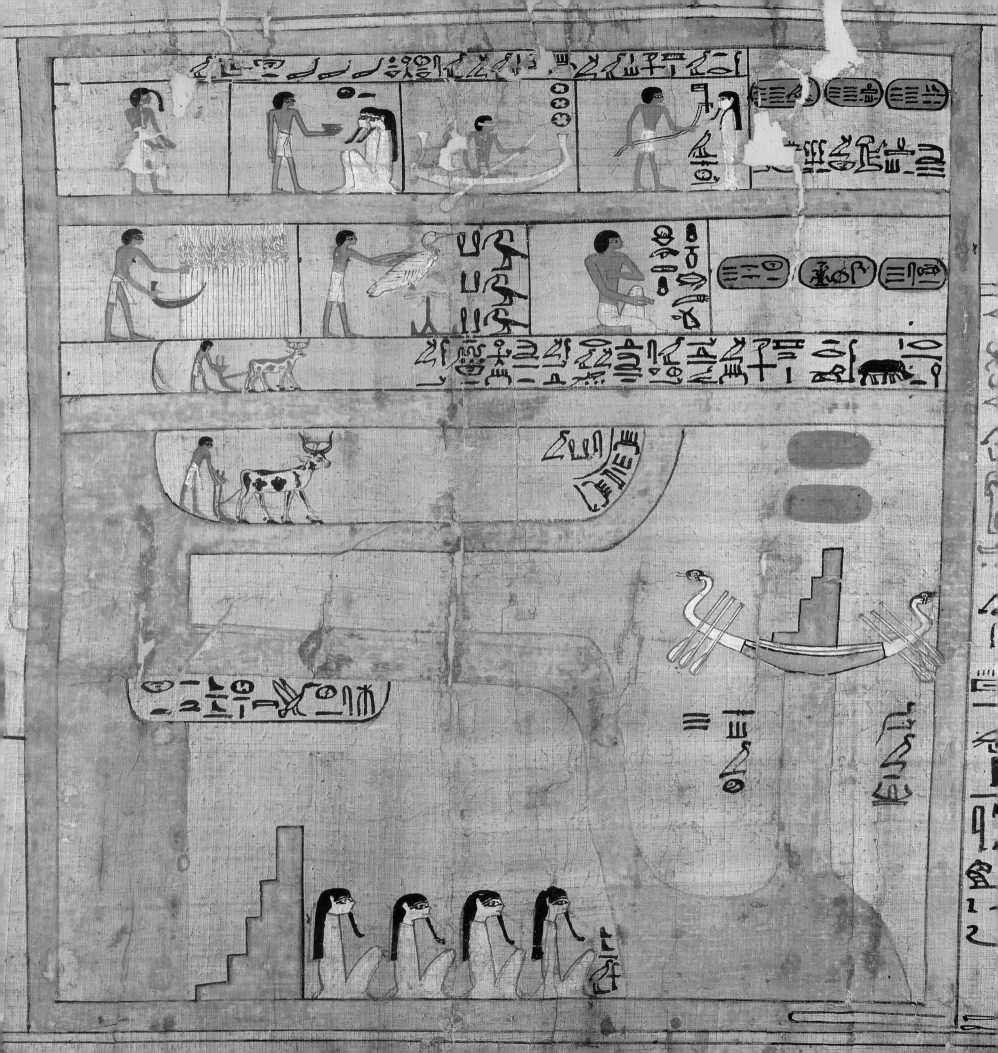

130 The Field of Reeds from the Book of the Dead of Userhat

Painted papyrus
H 35.5 cm
18th Dynasty, c. 1450 BC
Provenance unrecorded
London, British Museum, EA 10009/3

The vignette of the Field of Reeds varies in detail in different papyri. In this early example, the lower portion of the diagram occupies an exceptionally large space. The serpent-headed boat stands at the end of a channel, from which further waters lead past a group of gods to the more rigidly compartmentalized scenes above. Here Userhat is seen ploughing. Two of the watercourses in the upper section have descriptive captions. The lower one is 'the waterway of the white hippopotamus. It is a thousand leagues in length; its breadth has not been told. There are no fish in it; there are not any snakes in it.' The upper one, which is called 'The Horns of the Mistress of Purification', is stated to be a thousand leagues in length and breadth. These 'labels' occur in some of the oldest versions of the diagram, on coffins of the Middle Kingdom, but without the images which are included here. Userhat then harvests his crops, sails in his boat and encounters various deities. The blue ovals represent 'towns', whose names are inscribed within. Next to the Field of Reeds is a large figure of Userhat receiving a purifying libation and an offering of clothing.

Munro 1988, 290, no. a.66; Quirke 1993, 67–8, no. 274.

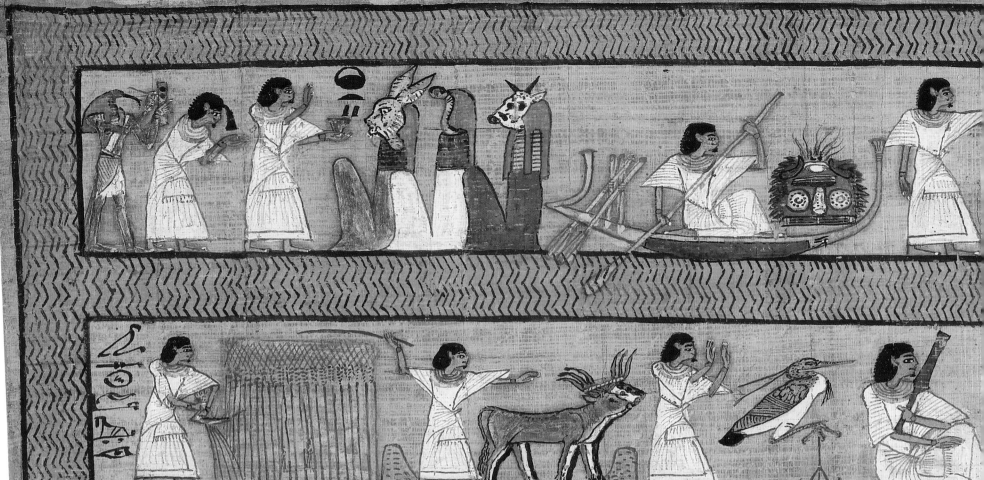

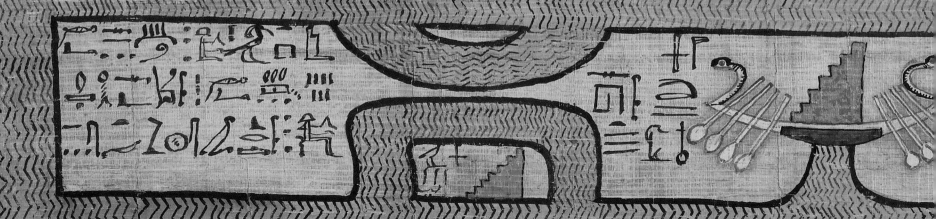

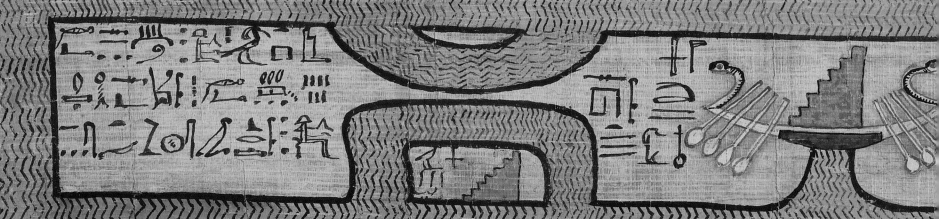

131 The Field of Reeds from the Book of the Dead of Ani

Painted papyrus
H 42.2 cm
19th Dynasty, c. 1275 BC
Thebes
London, British Museum, EA 10470/35

The papyrus of Ani contains an exceptionally clear illustration of the Field of Reeds. Beginning at the bottom, we see the two divine barques and islands. Above, Ani drives oxen who pull a plough. The location is confirmed as 'the Field of Reeds' in the inscription above. The remainder of this space contains a text identifying the water as 'the waterway of the white hippopotamus', the dimensions and description of which are given in almost identical wording to that in the papyrus of Userhat (see cat. no. 130). In the next register Ani harvests flax with a sickle and then drives his cattle over a threshing floor. He adores the 'heron of plenty' and sits by heaps of grain which will provide food for the *akh*-spirits who dwell in the Netherworld. At the top Ani offers to a group of three animal-headed gods, identified as members of the Great Ennead (the company of nine deities). Thoth also appears, holding his scribal palette. Ani then paddles his boat and finally confronts a falcon deity and a mummiform figure which is not specifically identified.

British Museum 1890, pl. 35; British Museum 1894, pl. 35; Budge 1895; Budge 1913; Faulkner 1985, 110–11; Russmann 2001, 199–200, no. 103.

132 Anhai and her husband in the Field of Reeds

Painted papyrus
H 42.0 cm
20th Dynasty, *c.* 1100 BC
Provenance unrecorded (probably Thebes)
London, British Museum, EA 10472/5

In Anhai's version of the Field of Reeds only a single
barque, that of Wennefer, appears at the bottom,
together with stylized town-enclosures and heaps of
grain. Two herons and four gods also appear. Above,
Anhai appears alone in two scenes of ploughing. In the
third register she pulls stalks of flax, while a male
figure, representing her husband, the Stablemaster of
the Residence, Nebsumenu, harvests grain with a
sickle. To the right Anhai worships a god and the heron
of plenty. The topmost register shows Nebsumenu
digging with a hoe, while Anhai bows before two
mummies. One of these is labelled as 'the Osiris, her
mother Neferiyti', so the scene probably depicts the
reunion of Anhai with her dead parents. Finally, we see
the god Thoth, and Anhai and Nebsumenu again,
paddling a boat towards two unidentified mummiform
figures. This is the only part of Anhai's papyrus in
which she is accompanied by her husband; his
inclusion here may be because this vignette portrays
the use of edged tools, which was a type of depiction
perhaps considered appropriate only to males.

Budge 1899, pl. 6; Faulkner 1985, 10.

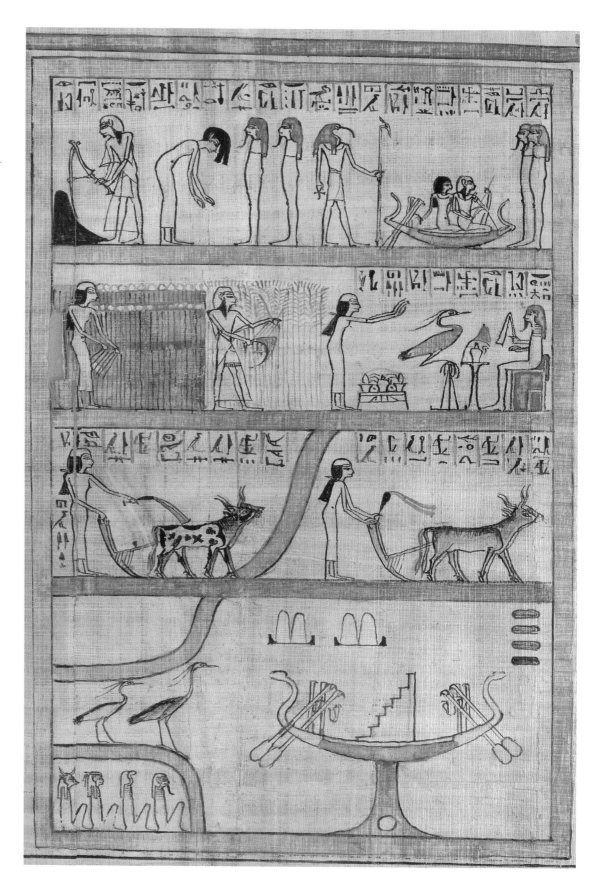

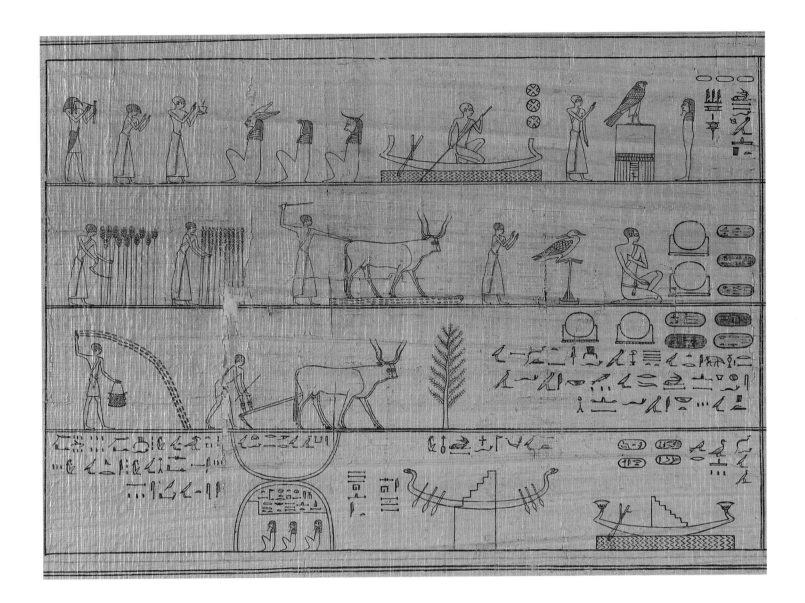

133 A late depiction of the Field of Reeds

Ink on papyrus
H 32.0 cm
Late 26th Dynasty, c. 550–525 BC
Provenance unrecorded (probably Memphite necropolis)
London, British Museum, EA 10558/15

In the Book of the Dead of Ankhwahibra, the vignette of spell 110 is drawn in a stark, academic style. The register lines serve simply to subdivide the main components of the illustration, and no longer represent waterways. Barques, towns and islands are depicted at the bottom. The agricultural operations in the second register now include the casting of seed as well as ploughing. Beyond the solitary tree, the town ovals appear, but the heaps of grain of Ani's papyrus (cat. no. 131) have been reinterpreted as 'horizon' signs, with the sun-disc rising from the mountains. The description of the 'waterway of the white hippopotamus', however, has survived all the changes as the vignette has evolved – although the watercourse itself has disappeared. Above, the deceased harvests and threshes his crops, adores the 'heron of plenty' and sits before his grain supplies (again in the form of the horizon hieroglyph). The top register follows that of Ani's papyrus very closely in its content.

Quirke 1993, 32, no. 23.

134 Shabti figures of Henutmehyt

Painted wood
H 20.0–22.0 cm
19th Dynasty, *c.* 1250 BC
Thebes
London, British Museum, EA 41548

The shabti figure emerged as an important item of funerary equipment in the early Middle Kingdom (see p. 245). A spell to activate these images as substitutes to work on behalf of the dead is first attested in the Coffin Texts, as spell 472. In the New Kingdom this text was incorporated into the Book of the Dead (spell 6) and was often inscribed on the body of the figure. This group is part of a set of forty shabtis (see also p. 245, fig. 74) that was provided for the Chantress of Amun Henutmehyt (see cat. nos 15, 38, 46, 54 and 135). They are typical of their period in representing the owner holding agricultural tools for use in the process of food production in the afterlife. An abbreviated version of the spell is written on the body. Originally each person possessed only one or two shabtis, but during the New Kingdom the number gradually increased; the forty belonging to Henutmehyt reflect not only this trend, but also her high status.

Taylor 1999, 63.

135 Box for shabtis of Henutmehyt

Painted wood
H 34.3 cm; W 18.2 cm; L 33.5 cm
19th Dynasty, *c.* 1250 BC
Thebes
London, British Museum, EA 41549

Early shabtis were stored individually in the tomb inside miniature coffins, but in the New Kingdom these were superseded by specially designed wooden boxes, the shape of which reproduced the form of a shrine. The adoption of this type of container probably reflects the shabti's character as a hypostasis of its owner, who was supposed to have acquired divine attributes after death. This box, one of four made for Henutmehyt (see cat. nos 15, 38, 46, 54 and 134), is in the form of two conjoined shrines, although it contains only one internal cavity. The four sides are inscribed and painted with scenes of a funerary character: on the front, Henutmehyt adores Duamutef and Qebehsenuef, two of the Sons of Horus, and on the back she receives food and water from a goddess (probably Nut) in a tree. This image, a version of the vignette of spell 59 of the Book of the Dead, is common on shabti boxes, perhaps because the shabtis' agricultural labours were a stage in the process of procuring food for the dead.

Aston 1994, 25, 49, pl. 2 (3); Taylor 1999, 63, pl. 17.

136 **Miniature tools for shabtis**

Bronze
Yoke ʟ 14.5 cm; baskets 7.2 x 6.1 cm and 8.5 x 7.3 cm; hoes ʟ 3.9 cm and 5.6 cm
18th Dynasty, *c.* 1400 BC
Abydos
London, British Museum, EA 32693

Some of the larger shabtis are finely crafted pieces of sculpture, and they
were sometimes provided with miniature tools, individually made from
bronze or faience. These examples comprise two hoes (the variable size
suggests that they belonged to different shabtis) and two baskets
suspended from a yoke. Such containers, often carved or painted on the
backs of New Kingdom shabtis, were to be used either for shifting sand or
to hold grain for planting crops. These baskets are inscribed with the name
of Heqareshu, an official. Many shabtis of this man are known, but their
primary purpose was evidently not to work for him in the afterlife. They
were buried not in his tomb but at the sacred site of Abydos, where they
were meant to act as receptacles for the spirit of their owner, enabling him
to participate remotely in the rituals performed there on behalf of Osiris
and to share in the food offerings presented to the god.

EXPLORING THE BOOK OF THE DEAD

11 Making the Book of the Dead

Rita Lucarelli

Assembling a papyrus roll

Among the myriad of ancient Egyptian papyri which have been found and which are on display in museums throughout the world, the most notable are the Book of the Dead rolls, due to their stunning illustrations and harmoniously arranged texts.

Although new papyrus rolls were generally used for this kind of sacral writing as a means of promoting their magical efficacy,[1] those we see in modern exhibitions are generally the best specimens, chosen from amongst the large number of Book of the Dead papyri which are housed in museum collections. In fact, not all the Book of the Dead rolls correspond to our modern aesthetic taste: their appearance varies considerably according to the circumstances of their manufacture. There are also a few cases of reused papyri, such as cat. no. 147, which originally contained a grain account and was later employed as a Book of the Dead.[2]

The Book of the Dead rolls were produced in well-organized workshops, about which we unfortunately possess no archaeological documentation; nor is there any contemporary description of the scribal practices and craftsmanship involved. Hence we can only try to reconstruct these processes by looking carefully at the layout and contents of the papyri themselves.

The dimensions of Book of the Dead papyri vary: there are very long rolls, such as cat. no. 152 of about 40 metres in length (the longest funerary papyrus preserved), as well as rolls which are no more than 1 metre long. They were made by assembling sheets of papyrus whose width was also variable, from 15 to about 45 centimetres, although the average measurement was about 25–35 centimetres. The narrower papyri were made from halved rolls and are more common from the Third Intermediate Period, whereas in the New Kingdom the full height of the papyrus sheet was more often employed.

Scribes and draughtsmen at work

The scribes who had to lay out a Book of the Dead papyrus were generally more careful than those who dealt with non-sacral writings. They attempted to avoid writing on the joints between the sheets and sought to frame the texts within 'pages', leaving margins of a few centimetres at the top and bottom of the roll in order to protect the text from deterioration at the edges. The right and left margins of the roll were also left uninscribed. The external margin could be reinforced by an extra strip of papyrus, a few centimetres long, which on the verso (back) bore the general Book of the Dead title, the standard expression *peret em heru*, 'coming forth by day' (fig. 75). The occurrence of a separate title on individual rolls suggests the existence of an organized storage system for funerary papyri, which were probably kept in temple archives or libraries. This general title on the verso is particularly common on the Book of the Dead papyri of the 21st Dynasty, when the frequent practice of burying the dead with a pair of

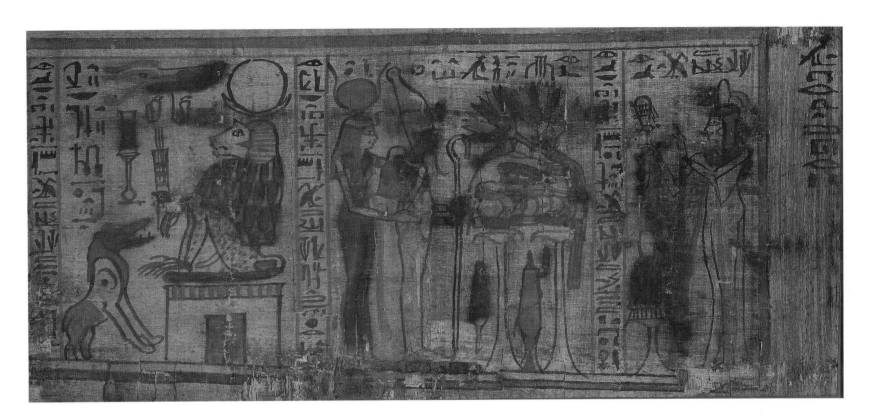

funerary papyri – one of the Book of the Dead type and one of the Amduat – increased the need to catalogue the funerary compositions. There are also a few papyri on which, very unusually, a horizontal line of hieroglyphs containing offering texts appears on the verso (fig. 76).

Apart from the title and other unusual inscriptions, the verso of the papyrus was generally left uninscribed; the few exceptions to this rule may have been originally intended as master copies, such as BM EA 10084, on which the last spell written on the recto (front) continues onto the verso. There is no firm evidence for papyri being used as master copies, but their existence is strongly suggested by the fact that groups of documents can be recognized which were clearly composed in the same period. They contain identical or very similar sequences of spells and vignettes, the composition of which must have been based on a single master copy.

Fig. 75 Strip with general title of the Book of the Dead, 'coming forth by day'. 21st Dynasty, *c.* 1000 BC. EA 10003.

Fig. 76 Papyrus of Amenhotep with a long line of hieroglyphic text, including the offering formula, on the verso. 18th Dynasty, *c.* 1400 BC. EA 10489.

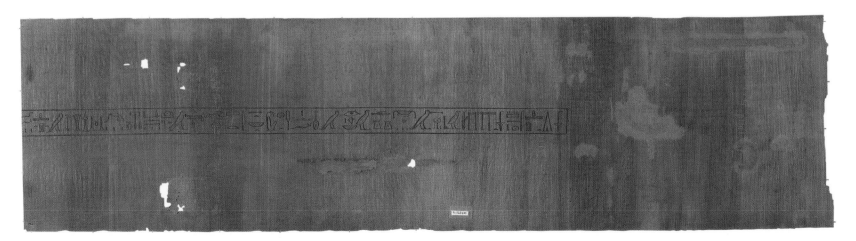

Fig. 77 The papyrus of Tui, an example of a manuscript from the New Kingdom written in retrograde cursive hieroglyphs, with sections in red ink. 18th Dynasty, *c.* 1450 BC. EA 9913/2.

This is certainly the case for the Book of the Dead of Gatseshen (Cairo JE 95838) and for that of Paennestitaui (BM EA 10064), both dating to the 21st Dynasty, which can be considered almost as twin papyri because of the close correspondence of their layouts.[3]

The recto of the roll was filled with texts and illustrations arranged in different layouts. In the papyri of the New Kingdom, generally written in 'cursive hieroglyphs' (a more simplified form of the monumental script), the spells were arranged in columns separated by black lines, similar to the monumental texts carved in tombs and temples from the Old Kingdom onwards (fig. 77). The most common direction of writing was from left to right, but with the hieroglyphs facing right instead of left, which was the beginning of the text. This writing style is called 'retrograde' and its significance is not yet clear; it may have had a magical function or it may be a mere consequence of the process of copying from model papyri written in hieratic, a cursive variant of the hieroglyphs, whose signs always face right. Retrograde writing was also used in many papyri of the Ptolemaic Period. The direction of writing also determined the manner of rolling the papyrus once it was complete: when the retrograde script was used, the right margin was rolled inside and therefore preserved from fraying, while the left one, on the outside, was more vulnerable to deterioration.

The illustrations were inserted in framed sections above, in between, or below the space filled with texts; there are, however, some large-scale vignettes, such as the representation of the Field of Reeds (spell 110) or of the final judgement (spell 125), which may occupy a full page.

In some of the best-illustrated papyri, the borders framing the texts were also painted, such as in the Ramesside papyrus of Ani (for example, cat. no. 131). This papyrus serves as one of the best case studies for understanding how a Book of the Dead was made. Recent pigment analyses have shown that the borders of the various sheets of this papyrus were drawn and then painted in red and yellow before the sheets were assembled. Differences in the colour and width of the borders at the joining points indicate that this roll was made up from sheets which had been prepared earlier (see cat. no. 153).⁴ The sheets comprising the Book of the Dead of Tui (see fig. 77) are even numbered in hieratic on the upper margin, a custom which was to occur more often in the Book of the Dead in the Late Period, especially when the texts were inscribed on mummy wrappings. Exceptionally, the Book of the Dead of Nakht (end of the 18th Dynasty) seems to have been written on two different kinds of material: a leather roll, containing a small portion of spells, and a papyrus (cat. nos 43, 71, 104 and 127–8); the two parts may originally have been joined together.

Many papyri were in fact prepared in advance and kept in stock, as is clear from cases where the name and titles of the owner were written by a different hand, filling spaces in the text which had been left empty. Sometimes the name of the owner was too long for the space which had been allotted, and so the hieroglyphs composing it seem to have been squeezed in. In other cases, the name and titles of the owner were shorter than the space available and consequently the writing in those places is larger than in the rest of the text. In some papyri not all of the name spaces were filled in, probably due to inattention on the part of the scribe; there are also papyri where all the spaces are left blank, as in the Ramesside BM EA 9957. During the copying process, the scribe occasionally found a lacuna or gap in the master copy and indicated this in the papyrus by the notation *gem usher*, 'found missing'.

Hieratic papyri become common from the 21st Dynasty, while in the New Kingdom only a few examples are known, though they include a hieroglyphic manuscript whose last textual section, containing spell 133, was written in hieratic (Louvre E 21324). The layout of these documents is considerably different from that of the earlier hieroglyphic papyri and seems to follow the tradition of the literary manuscripts of the New Kingdom, which were also written in hieratic, with very skilful calligraphy. The hieratic text is written in horizontal lines filling large columns, the so-called 'pages' of the book, which often correspond to the papyrus sheets but whose length can also vary according to the space required for the illustrations inserted in between the text. Sometimes hieratic Books of the Dead contain captions written in hiero-glyphic text, notably when these captions indicate the name and titles of the owner in the larger illustrations, such as the opening scene of adoration of a god (figs 78 and 79), or in the representation of the weighing of the heart (vignette of spell 125).

The style of the vignettes also varies according to local traditions and does not par-ticularly depend on the period of composition. Some papyri of the 18th Dynasty, for instance, may present very simple sketched vignettes, without colour, as in the papyrus of Nebseny (cat. no. 148), but there also exist manuscripts of the same period which contain colourful illustra-tions. However, it is during the Ramesside period that more colourful, very finely executed illustrations seem to be inserted more often in the rolls, some of them even refined with gold leaf. During the 21st and 22nd Dynasties the members of the priestly circle of Amun at Thebes

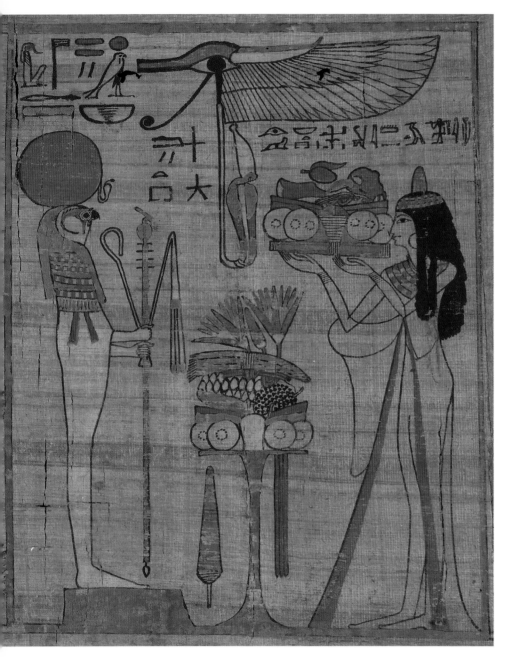

Fig. 78 (above) Scene of Tameni offering to Ra-Horakhty, the opening vignette of her papyrus. 21st Dynasty, *c.* 1069–945 BC. EA 10002/1.

Fig. 79 (above right) Hieratic papyrus of Pinedjem II containing only an opening vignette with the adoration of Osiris, followed by texts. 21st Dynasty, *c.* 970 BC. EA 10793/1.

possessed hieratic Books of the Dead, which were produced according to a variety of different patterns. Some contain no vignettes apart from the opening scene, such as papyrus Campbell (see fig. 79), while others are filled with colourful illustrations, following the earlier Ramesside tradition. The creativity of the Theban workshops of this period also extended to the production of papyri in which only one spell was copied, followed by a series of vignettes without accompanying texts.[5] Finally, in the papyri of the Late and Ptolemaic Periods the vignettes are generally reduced in dimensions and might be placed on the upper register of the roll or in between the texts (figs 80–81).

Texts and vignettes were executed by different craftsmen; some papyri clearly indicate

Fig. 80 Papyrus of Tentameniy of the Theban late tradition with vignettes inserted among the columns of hieratic text. Ptolemaic Period, 305–30 BC. EA 10086/6.

that the scribe copied the text first and left spaces for the vignettes to be filled in by a draughtsman. There are indeed cases in which the work was left incomplete and the spaces for the illustrations remained empty, such as in the 26th-Dynasty papyrus of Nespasefy (cat. no. 151) and in papyrus Marseilles 291 of the Saite Period. In a peculiar papyrus of the 21st Dynasty, belonging to the priestess Ankhesenaset (Paris BN 62–88), the scribe seems to have left some instructions for the draughtsman to follow: on the upper corner of certain pages there are captions, which we might compare to the marginalia of books, indicating what was to be drawn, such as a falcon, a lotus flower or a boat.[6]

Fig. 81 Papyrus of Khonsiu of the Memphite late tradition with vignettes in the upper register. Ptolemaic Period, 305–30 BC. EA 10045/3.

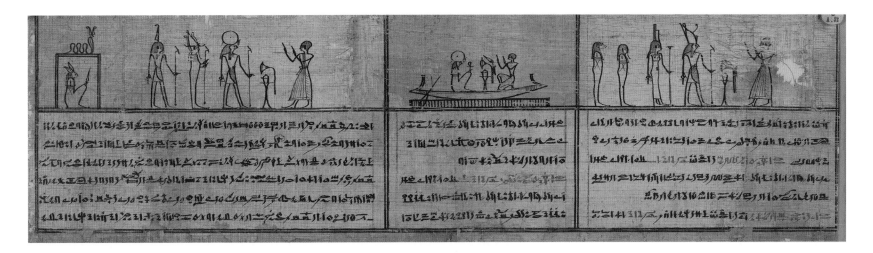

Red and black inks

The texts of the Book of the Dead were written in black ink, with insertions in red, these being the two pigments contained in the scribe's basic palette (which was also the hieroglyph sign for 'writing'). Red ink was used mainly for the titles and opening formulas of the spells; it was also used for the postscripts that close many spells and give ritual instructions on how to recite them, and on what materials they were to be inscribed (see fig. 77). The colour red also had an apotropaic meaning and was therefore used to write the name of dangerous beings such as the snake Apopis, the enemy of the sun-god. Black ink was used in order to highlight the names of other gods when they occurred within textual sections written in red. Red ink was also employed to correct orthographic mistakes, especially in hieratic manuscripts, just as school teachers might do nowadays. A very curious case is that of a papyrus of the 19th Dynasty containing spell 100, written in white ink with a red insertion (cat. no. 15).[7] Red ink was also employed for the glosses (see cat. no. 19), used to explain particularly complex texts, such as spell 17, and also to offer an alternative interpretation of the spell. Hence, the glosses of the Book of the Dead may correspond to what modern philologists call the 'critical apparatus' of a text. Their occurrence shows that before being merely copied by the scribe, the religious texts were also studied and interpreted, probably by the theologians and priests of the temple. Although the scribes themselves might have been experts in theological matters, there are many cases, especially in the Late Period, where the high number of textual mistakes and corruptions clearly indicates that the copyist did not understand his source (for example, cat. no. 154).[8]

The expression *iw=f pw*, literally 'it comes (to the end)' meaning 'it is finished', which represents the colophon at the end of many rolls, is generally written in red. Unlike other kinds of documents such as literary manuscripts, the colophons of the Book of the Dead very rarely include the date or the name of the scribe. The colophon occurring at the end of the papyrus of Yuya of the 18th Dynasty (Cairo CG 51189) is especially indicative of the importance attached to careful and complete scribal work: 'it is finished from beginning to end, as it was found in writing, having been copied, revised, compared and verified sign by sign, for the Divine Father Yuya, justified.'

Authorship and ownership

It is very often possible to establish from the palaeographical analysis of a papyrus that more than one scribe worked on the same manuscript, as in the case of the Book of the Dead of Astemakhbit (cat. no. 150). Sometimes the vignettes contained in one manuscript may also have been drawn by more than one artist, as in the case of the papyrus of Ani. The intervention of different hands on a single manuscript can be noted in short as well as long rolls and therefore did not depend on the amount of time needed to complete a papyrus. This rather reflects the fact that making a roll of the Book of the Dead was considered a collective work, as was the crafting of any other object to be included in the equipment of the tomb.

If the scribe was only a copyist, one might ask who the author was of the Book of the Dead spells. As with other religious books, such as the Bible or the Koran, the authorship of the Book of the Dead was attributed to divine intervention. In the spells there is never any clear information on their original authors, only hints about the antiquity, secrecy and mystery surrounding their

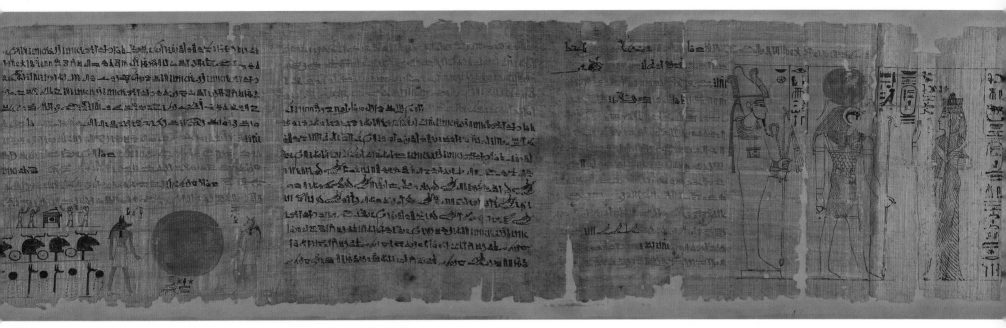

Fig. 82 One of the two funerary papyri of Queen Nodjmet (see also cat. no. 123) showing her in adoration in front of Amun-Ra-Horakhty and Osiris. Unlike her other papyrus, this one contains a selection of Book of the Dead spells interspersed with extracts from the Book of Caverns. The content and style of the document are more characteristic of the later 21st Dynasty; it is possibly an unusually early example of the type, or perhaps it was added to Nodjmet's burial assemblage at the time of her reburial in the Royal Cache. 21st Dynasty. EA 10490/1.

discovery. In the postscript of spell 64, for instance, it is said that the text was found carved on a stone near a temple in Hermopolis, 'and brought it like a marvel to the King Menkaura [4th Dynasty] when he[?] saw that it was a great secret, unseen and unobserved'. However, given the composite nature of the Book of the Dead corpus, we may suppose that the theologians of the beginning of the New Kingdom, who could consult the archives and libraries of the temples, composed the spells by re-editing and revising pre-existing magical texts and rituals, such as the Pyramid Texts and the Coffin Texts, eventually adding new textual sections, titles and illustrations (see pp. 55–7).

It is a point of debate among scholars whether the owner and the scribe of a papyrus might occasionally have been the same person; a few scholars have proposed this for the 18th-Dynasty papyrus of Nebseny (cat. no. 152), who bears the titles of 'copyist of the Ptah temple, draughtsman, copyist in the temples of Upper and Lower Egypt'.[9] In any case, even when not directly involved in the writing process, the owner of the papyrus, who would often have been literate, may have played a role in the selection of the spells and vignettes, suggesting to the atelier's artists which themes and illustrations to insert in his roll. For instance, some of the artisans who lived in the village of Deir el-Medina and worked on the decoration of the royal tombs of the Valley of the Kings possessed Book of the Dead rolls whose texts and vignettes show undeniable similarities with the themes and illustrations to be found in the tombs themselves.[10]

In the 21st Dynasty the number of Book of the Dead papyri belonging to women increased (see p. 63). These owners included female members of the Theban High Priest's family, many of whom were probably well versed in religious matters and who therefore might have edited their own texts.[11] Queen Nodjmet, the spouse of the High Priest Herihor, possessed two papyri, one written in hieroglyphic and the other one in hieratic (fig. 82), containing some peculiar versions of texts which were not attested before and therefore were probably redacted within the priestly sphere to which Nodjmet belonged.[12]

Local traditions of the Late Period

The standardization of the spells brought about by the Saite recension, which seems to have started during the 25th Dynasty and was definitely systematized in the 26th Dynasty (see p. 58), led to a more fixed sequence of spells and vignettes. This appears to have restricted the variety in the layout of the rolls compared to the 'Theban recension' of the New Kingdom. However, this canonic version of the Book of the Dead, which remained in vogue through the Ptolemaic Period, includes groups of papyri that still exhibit different stylistic features; these can be associated with the workshops in which they were made. In general, the papyri composed in the Theban region can be differentiated from those produced at Memphis by means of the arrangement of texts and vignettes. In the Theban papyri the columns of text are not always defined by border-lines, nor are the vignettes placed only above the text, as appears more often in the Memphite papyri. Instead, some vignettes alternate with the text within a single column. However, exceptions to these basic layouts are also known, making it difficult to ascertain the precise provenance of a papyrus on the basis of its layout alone. Recent studies have shown that Akhmim was also a fertile centre of production of Book of the Dead papyri in the Late Period.[13] Some manuscripts of this period, most probably of Theban origin, also include previously unattested texts and vignettes, numbered as spells 162–74. In these apparently newly composed texts, other religious centres, such as Tanis and Napata, are occasionally mentioned as places where the ancient scripts were found. Although we cannot establish on such slender evidence that those cities were also production centres of Book of the Dead papyri, the contents of the spells nevertheless mirror the fertile and wide theological background of the local Book of the Dead traditions at the end of the Pharaonic era.[14]

Therefore, just as in the case of earlier papyri of the New Kingdom, such factors as local traditions, scribal preferences and the personal taste of the papyrus owner seem to have played a role in determining the final layout of each papyrus in later documents.

Selecting texts and vignettes

Within the variety of formal arrangements and textual traditions attested in the Book of the Dead papyri of all periods, it seems clear that spells and vignettes were not copied at random but rather in the context of a carefully considered editing process. Each spell may be present as a more or less abbreviated version, but it can also occur twice within the same manuscript. Moreover, some texts were clearly clustered together in order to form thematic sequences or pairings; the latter are recognizable by their similar titles or vignettes or by their reference to the same general subject. A typical thematic sequence is the group of so-called 'transformation spells', namely spells 76–88, which provided the deceased with the power of multiple manifestations; these occur in almost all the manuscripts of the New Kingdom in a compact textual cluster. Spells 17 and 18 occur instead more often as a pairing and are employed to open the roll. Another peculiar pairing, which in the papyri of the 18th Dynasty is generally copied at the end, consists of spells 149 and 150, describing the so-called 'mounds' of the Netherworld and their inhabitants. Spell 150 is in fact an additional illustration to spell 149, showing the importance that the topography of the Netherworld played in the mortuary religion of ancient Egypt (see Chapter 6).

Another interesting phenomenon of the editing process is the duplication of the same spell within one papyrus. This can be noted especially in the longer rolls and was probably due to the use of more than one papyrus as a model: as he worked the scribe perhaps forgot that he had copied a particular spell already from another source and therefore inserted it a second time. Moreover, we may assume that in some cases the duplication of a text might result from the process of assembling a roll from pre-copied sheets containing similar spell selections; this may have been the case for spell 18 in the papyrus of Ani, which occurs twice in two sections belonging to different sheets. Finally, through duplication, a spell could be present in two variant versions, suggesting an intention to emphasize the particular theme dealt with in the text and vignette. This is the case, for instance, for spells 130–6 illustrating the journey of the deceased in the solar barque, some of which can occur twice, in longer and shorter versions, within the same roll. The vignettes complementing these spells, generally depicting the solar barque carrying the sun-god Ra and the deceased, are often indistinguishable from each other. Among the duplications, we must also count certain spells which were labelled by Richard Lepsius (see pp. 289–90) with different numbers but which in fact present the same or a very similar text, for example spells 100 and 129, which also deal with the solar barque. The thematic sequence dealing with the journey in the barque also provides an example of spells sharing identical passages or very similar postscripts, although the core of their texts differ from each other. In magical and ritual texts from ancient Egypt, the repetition and redundancy of key words, passages and longer texts is indeed a well-known phenomenon, through which the scribes aimed to increase the efficacy of the spell.

In later specimens of the Book of the Dead, the theologians, scribes or even the purchasers of the roll often chose to insert texts and illustrations which did not belong to the traditional corpus but were taken instead from other religious and ritual compositions. So it is not rare to discover, within an apparently 'traditional' Book of the Dead, new compositions which characterize only one or a few rolls produced in the same area. Therefore, despite the great number of manuscripts which have been discovered and studied so far, unrolling and reading a Book of the Dead is always an exciting process.

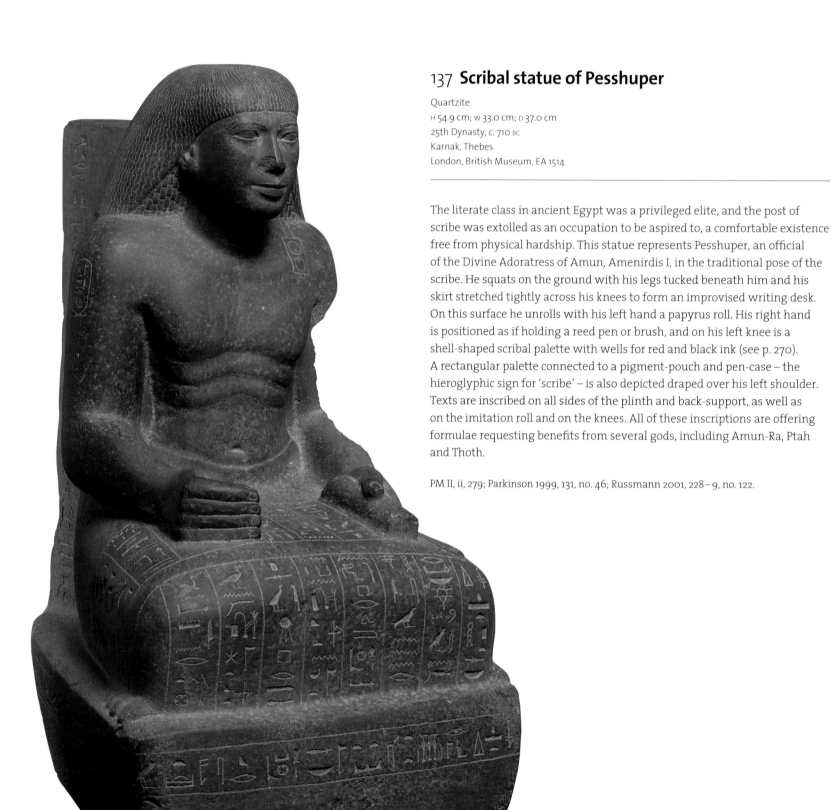

137 **Scribal statue of Pesshuper**

Quartzite
H 54.9 cm; W 33.0 cm; D 37.0 cm
25th Dynasty, *c.* 710 BC
Karnak, Thebes
London, British Museum, EA 1514

The literate class in ancient Egypt was a privileged elite, and the post of scribe was extolled as an occupation to be aspired to, a comfortable existence free from physical hardship. This statue represents Pesshuper, an official of the Divine Adoratress of Amun, Amenirdis I, in the traditional pose of the scribe. He squats on the ground with his legs tucked beneath him and his skirt stretched tightly across his knees to form an improvised writing desk. On this surface he unrolls with his left hand a papyrus roll. His right hand is positioned as if holding a reed pen or brush, and on his left knee is a shell-shaped scribal palette with wells for red and black ink (see p. 270). A rectangular palette connected to a pigment-pouch and pen-case – the hieroglyphic sign for 'scribe' – is also depicted draped over his left shoulder. Texts are inscribed on all sides of the plinth and back-support, as well as on the imitation roll and on the knees. All of these inscriptions are offering formulae requesting benefits from several gods, including Amun-Ra, Ptah and Thoth.

PM II, ii, 279; Parkinson 1999, 131, no. 46; Russmann 2001, 228–9, no. 122.

138 **Thoth, the scribes' patron deity**

Steatite and bronze
H 18.0 cm; W 5.6 cm
19th–20th Dynasties, c. 1295–1069 BC
Provenance unrecorded
London, British Museum, EA 35401

Thoth, the 'Lord of the God's words' (hieroglyphic script), was the patron deity of scribes. They customarily poured a libation to the god before beginning to write in order to invoke his support and aid. Thoth in baboon-form is sometimes depicted in small sculptures which show him watching over a scribe or even sitting on his shoulders. In this example, the precise function of which is unknown, the god squats atop a stepped pedestal and wears a bronze lunar-disc on his head.

Parkinson 1999, 134, no. 49.

139 Model of scribal equipment

Painted wood
H 3.1 cm; W 4.7 cm; D 9.1 cm
First Intermediate Period to early Middle Kingdom, c. 2150–1950 BC
Provenance unrecorded
London, British Museum, EA 35878

This miniature wooden chest probably formed part of a group model of the servants of a nobleman. The sliding lid of the box is shown partly withdrawn, revealing five rolls of papyrus inside. Lying on the lid is a scribal palette, and beside it a tiny peg, to which a circular object – probably a water pot – was originally attached.

Parkinson 1999, 143, pl. 25, no. 56.

140 Scribal knives

Bronze
L 27.2 cm, 22.0 cm
18th Dynasty, c. 1550–1295 BC
Thebes
London, British Museum, EA 65634–5

Egyptian scribes used delicate bronze knives such as these for trimming their brushes, for cutting stalks of papyrus to size before pressing them together into sheets, and for cutting the sheets to the required size for writing on. The handles of these examples end in a duck's head, a type which is depicted in the tomb of Rekhmire at Thebes (c. 1425 BC). Actual examples have been found in the tombs of Neferkhaut and Hatiay at Thebes, and also in tombs at Abydos.

141, 142 Grinding stones

L 12.1 cm (EA 21907), 10.1 cm (EA 64191)
18th Dynasty, c. 1550–1295 BC
Thebes (EA 64191)
London, British Museum, EA 21907 and EA 64191

These stones were perhaps used for grinding pigments. The smaller is inscribed for Benermerut, Overseer of all the Works of the King.

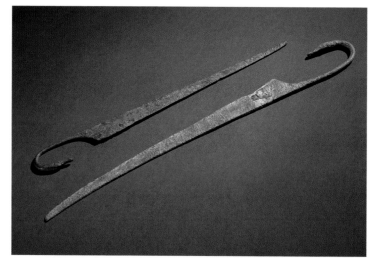

Writing palettes and pens

The typical scribal palette was a narrow strip of wood, containing circular or oval wells for dry cakes of ink, and a central recess for pens. The pens were made from a single rush or reed, the end flattened to create a brush-like tip. Black ink was made from carbon, while red ink was usually iron oxide (ochre) (see p. 270). Water was the medium which enabled the ink to flow.

143 Wooden palette containing reed pens

L 28.8 cm; W 3.5 cm
18th Dynasty, reign of Ahmose I (*c.* 1550–1525 BC)
Provenance unrecorded
London, British Museum, EA 12784

The wells contain red and black inks, and the pens have traces of red and black pigments at the ends.

Parkinson and Quirke 1995, 31, fig. 17; Parkinson 1999, 145, no. 58.

144 Wooden palette containing reed pens

L 28.8 cm
New Kingdom, *c.* 1550–1295 BC
Provenance unrecorded
London, British Museum, EA 12785

145 Wooden palette of the Chief Steward Merire with fourteen wells for ink

L 33.2 cm; W 7.0 cm
18th Dynasty, reign of Thutmose IV, *c.* 1400 BC
Provenance unrecorded
London, British Museum, EA 5512

Parkinson and Quirke 1995, 31, fig. 17; Russmann 2001, 153, no. 65.

146 Basalt pigment grinder and grindstone

Grindstone: 11.9 x 7.2 x 2.6 cm
grinder: H 3.1 cm
New Kingdom, *c.* 1550–1069 BC
Thebes
London, British Museum, EA 5547

This basalt tablet has an oval depression in the centre, on which pigments were crushed using the small grinder. Samples of 'Egyptian blue' (copper calcium silicate) and red ochre pigments are shown.

Parkinson 1999, 146, no. 61.

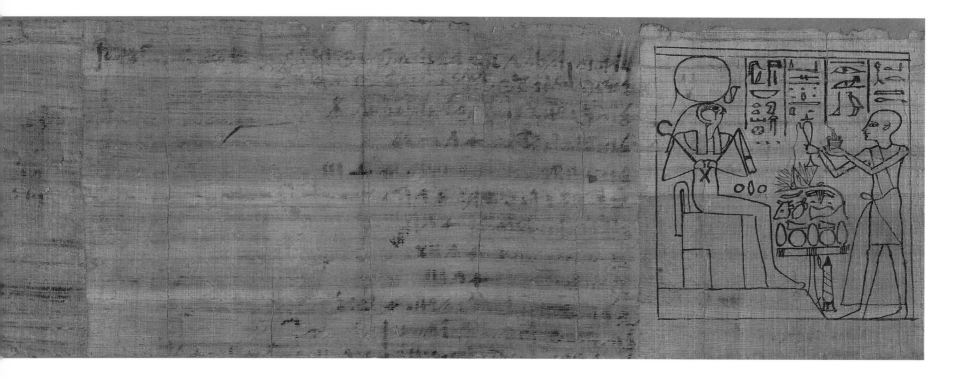

147 Recycling old papyrus: an account document reused as a Book of the Dead

Ink on papyrus
H 11.8 cm
21st Dynasty, c. 950 BC
Thebes
London, British Museum, EA 9974

It was usually the custom for religious texts to be written on a new sheet of papyrus, a recommendation which is actually specified in some parts of the Book of the Dead, such as the colophon to spell 100. In practice, however, this was not always possible. Papyrus was expensive and sometimes an old document might be washed clean and reused. This papyrus bears faint traces of an account of quantities of grain in hieratic script, which had been subsequently erased so that texts from the Book of the Dead could be written in its place. A separate sheet with an introductory vignette (or 'etiquette') was attached, but the actual texts of the spells were never inserted. The intended owner, a man named Buhar, is shown offering to a seated god. Although the deity is not named, his falcon head, surmounted by a solar disc, suggests that he is the sun-god Ra-Horakhty.

Niwinski 1989, 323; Parkinson and Quirke 1995, 48, fig. 33.

148 A Book of the Dead illustrated by its owner?

Ink on papyrus
H 35.8 cm
18th Dynasty, c. 1400 BC
Memphite necropolis
London, British Museum, EA 9900/32

The papyrus of Nebseny is one of the longest and most carefully executed Book of the Dead manuscripts of the 18th Dynasty (see also cat. nos 16, 69 and 103). It is unusual for several reasons. Since Nebseny was himself a scribe and copyist in the temple of Ptah and the temples of Upper and Lower Egypt there is a possibility that he wrote and illustrated his own Book of the Dead. Among the irregular features are the fact that only red and black ink are used, even for the vignettes, and that the texts are written backwards in three places. The vignettes are very finely drawn and are striking for the variation in their details, notably the numerous different poses of the figures of the owner. Nebseny's wife and parents are also named in the papyrus. This in itself is not rare, but it is quite exceptional that three of his children are also named and depicted – perhaps a deliberate innovation made by Nebseny himself. In the scene illustrated, the most elaborate one in the entire papyrus, Nebseny and his wife Senseneb receive offerings from their son Ptahmose, who wears a priestly sidelock and a heart-shaped amulet. Nebseny's titles are included in the text above the scene, and beneath his chair is a container, labelled 'holder for writing', emphasizing the unique prominence of the scribal role in this document.

Parkinson and Quirke 1995, 55, fig. 36; Russmann 2001, 195–6, no. 99; Lapp 2004, pls 95–7.

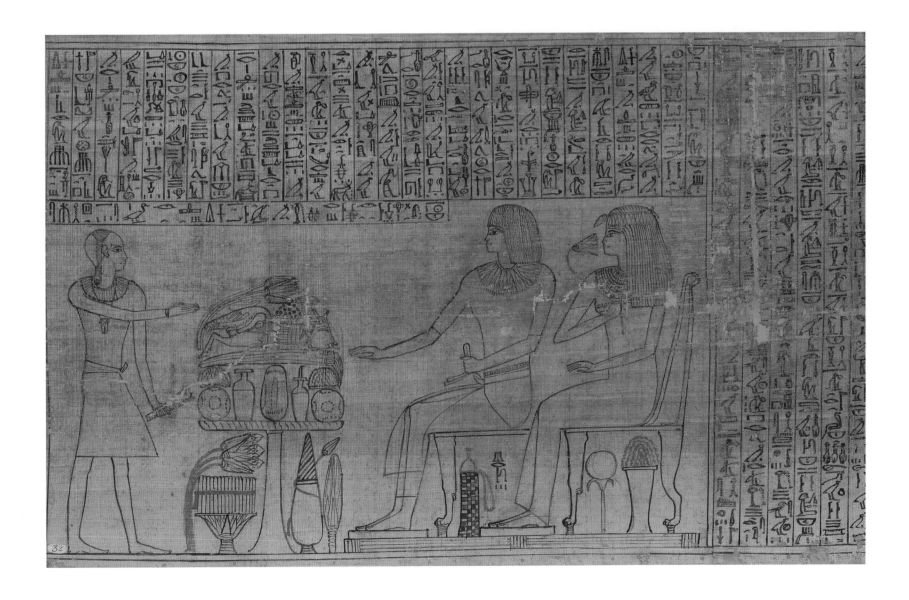

149 **A papyrus with erased names**

Painted papyrus
H 30.5 cm
19th–20th Dynasties, *c.* 1295–1069 BC
Provenance unrecorded
London, British Museum, EA 10478/4

This papyrus contains the short version of the text called the Book of Caverns of the Duat. Although conventionally listed as Book of the Dead spell 168, it is in reality a self-contained composition (see cat. no. 68). The papyrus has been prepared with care, but although it was fully inscribed, the name and titles of the owner were afterwards deliberately obscured by the application of a coat of yellow paint at every spot where they appeared.

By applying the technique of infra-red photography the writing which lies beneath the yellow paint has been revealed, showing that the original intended owner of the papyrus was a man named Bakenmut. His titles are written in several different ways. All of them relate to offices in the temple of the goddess Mut; the commonest title he holds is that of scribe.

The reason for the erasure of Bakenmut's name can only be speculated on. Perhaps his relatives did not pay for the work done by the scribes and painters, and the papyrus was made ready to receive the name of a new owner, which was never inserted.

Piankoff 1974, 41–114, pls 17–33; Quirke 1993, 114.

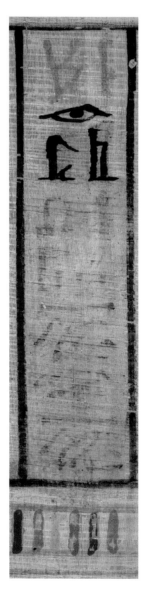

Far left: Detail of the obliterated inscription at lower left opposite. The name 'Osiris' was originally followed by the title and name of the owner.

Left: Infra-red photography of the same inscription. The signs revealed read: 'Scribe, God's [unclear] of Mut, Bakenmut.'

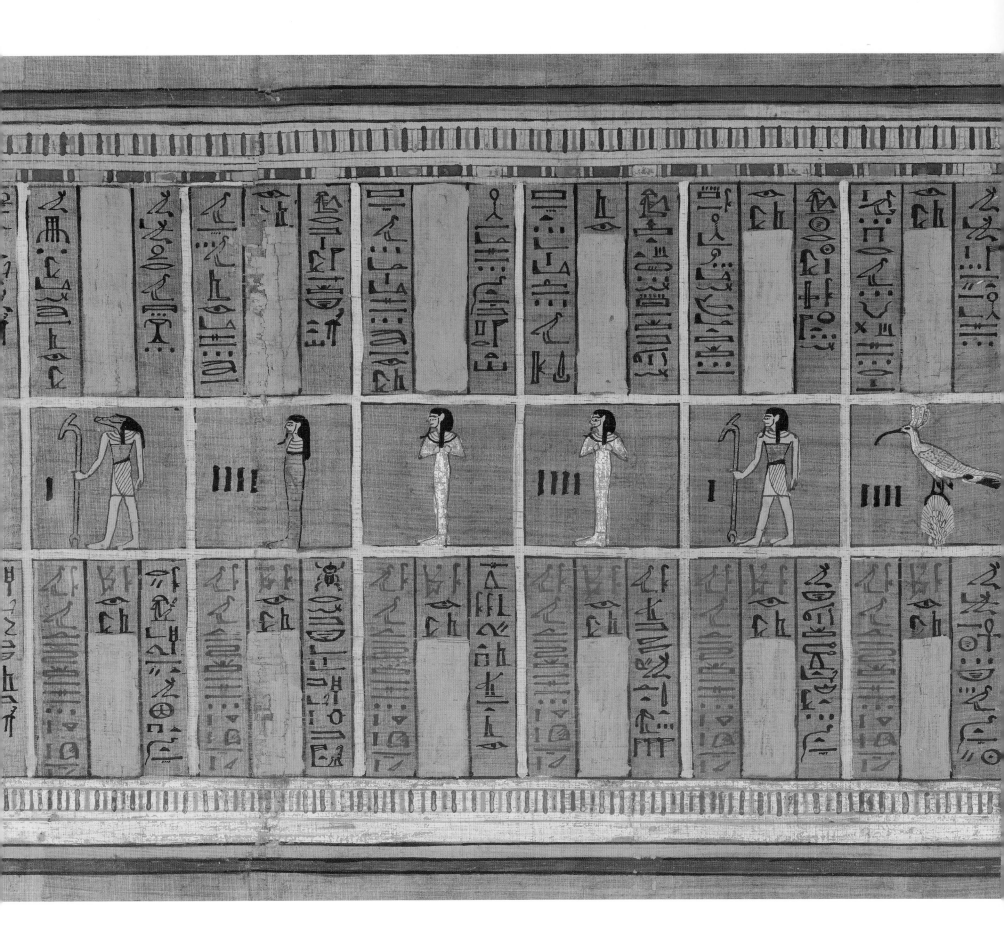

150 Two scribes working on one papyrus

Ink on papyrus
H 30.8 cm; W 75.0 cm
21st–22nd Dynasty, c. 1050–850 BC
London, British Museum, EA 10743/2

The papyrus of the Chantress of Amun and Singer of Mut, Astemakhbit,
is a short Book of the Dead of a type common in the 21st and 22nd Dynasties
(see also cat. no. 116). It consists of an opening vignette showing the deceased
offering to Osiris (not illustrated here) and three 'pages' of hieratic script
containing spells 130, 136A and 134. The handwriting of the third sheet
(at left in the illustration) differs from that of the first two in scale, line-
spacing and style of script (individual signs being drawn in a consistently
different manner). This indicates that the pages were written by two
different scribes and afterwards joined together to form a roll. Possibly the
two scribes collaborated to fulfil a specific commission for Astemakhbit's
relatives, but it is equally possible that the hieratic pages formed part of a
'stock' of prefabricated sheets which could assembled on an *ad hoc* basis
when needed.

Quirke 1993, 33, no. 33.

151 Work in progress: the unfinished Book of the Dead of Nespasefy

Ink on papyrus
H 35–6 cm; L 560.0 cm
26th Dynasty, c. 650–625 BC
Thebes, probably Deir el-Bahri
Marseilles, Musée d'Archéologie Mediterranéenne, Inv. 91/2/1 + 291

The custom of producing Book of the Dead papyri was revived in the 25th Dynasty at Thebes, and from the early 26th Dynasty come the first examples to adopt the new canonical sequence of spells which were a feature of the Saite recension (see p. 58). One of the first of these manuscripts is the papyrus of the priest of Montu Nespasefy, a member of one of the leading Theban families of the time (and a son of Besenmut,

see cat. no. 29). This roll, which is now dispersed between museums in Marseilles, Albany and Cairo (while a further section is untraced), originally contained over 150 spells. The texts have all been carefully written in hieratic, each in a separate compartment, with a space for the appropriate vignette, but these spaces were left blank. They were certainly meant to be filled in, because at one point the scribe has left a note for the draughtsman: 'Add the prescribed images'. The reason why this was never done is unknown. Possibly the editorial process of standardizing the vignettes was not yet complete at the time of the papyrus's production.

The section illustrated here contains the texts of spells 145 and 146. The vignettes, when completed, should have shown figures of the guardians of the various gateways of the Netherworld which are named in the spells.

Brunner-Traut and Brunner 1981, 293, Taf. 126–7; Forman and Quirke 1996, 154–5; Verhoeven 1999, Taf. 35–56, Umschrift-Taf. 43–72.

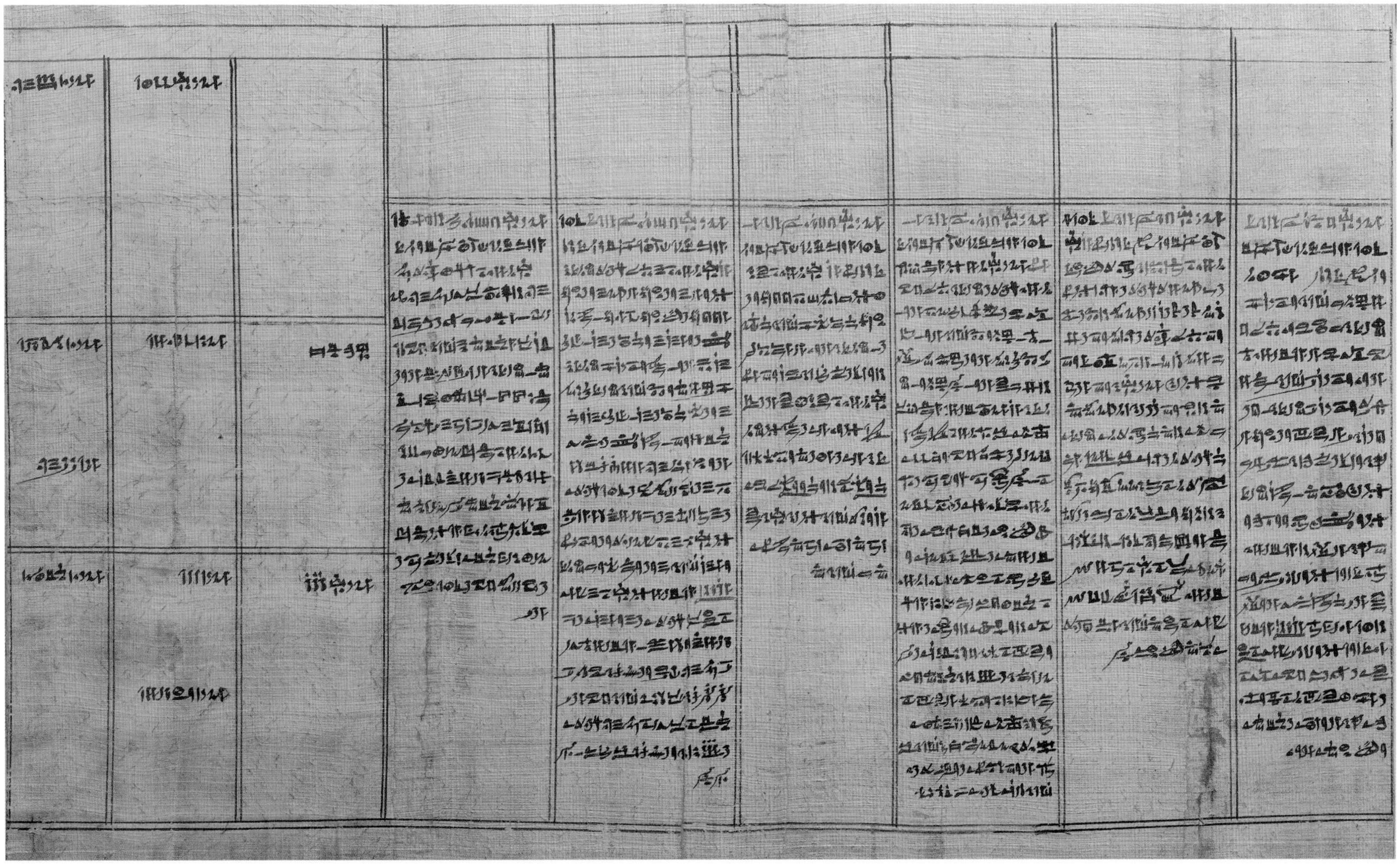

152 **Two different draughtsmen**

Ink on papyrus
H 48.0 cm (10554/19), 47.0 cm (10554/20)
Late 21st or early 22nd Dynasty, *c.* 950–930 BC
Royal Cache, Deir el-Bahri
London, British Museum, EA 10554/19–20

The exceptionally long papyrus of Nesitanebisheru was inscribed and illustrated in separate sections which were then joined together to make a roll 37 metres long (see also cat. nos 93 and 161). The joins are marked by matching pairs of hieroglyphic signs in red at the ends of the adjacent sections. Here the signs take the form of an ibis; others include a bow, a

mouth and a bound prisoner. This point in the roll is also conspicuous for a change in the graphic style of the vignettes in the frieze along the top. Those at the right are consistent in style with the beginning of the papyrus. They have been very carefully drawn, with a fine pen, and the figures have distinctive forms and bodies in proportion. The section to the left is characterized by a less precise line, and by figures with more elongated bodies, thinner limbs, smaller heads with pinched faces and simpler costumes. The distinction evidently reflects the work of two different artists. They probably also wrote the captions – as these also differ – but the main texts below the vignettes seem to be in the same hand on both sides of the join.

Budge 1912, pls XXII–XXIII.

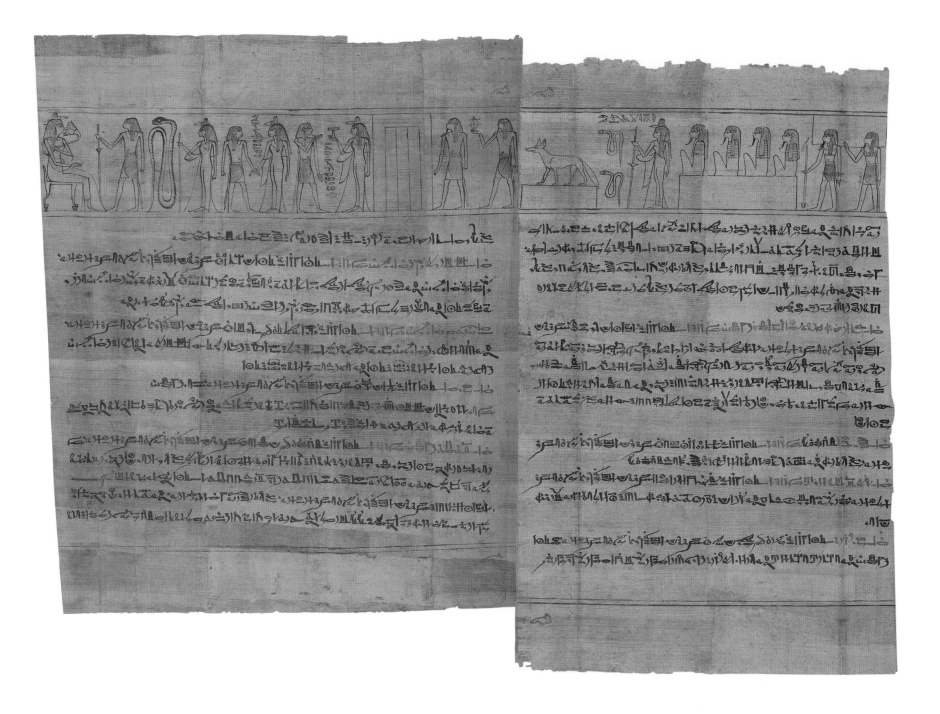

153 Evidence of teamwork production in the Book of the Dead of Ani

Painted papyrus
H 42.0 cm
19th Dynasty, c. 1275 BC
Thebes
London, British Museum, EA 10470/12

Ani's papyrus roll was assembled from separate sections, varying in length from 152 to 540 cm. Several different scribes and painters must have been employed on the production of these sections, since there are variations in handwriting and column widths, as well as in the style of drawing and painting. The handwriting of Ani's name is also distinctly different from the surrounding texts, showing that it was inserted into blank spaces which had been left for that purpose.

When all the component parts of the manuscript had been completed, the sections were joined together (usually overlapping, left over right). Several joins are clearly visible today, where the distance between the top and bottom borders varied and where different pigments had been used to colour the borders (well-preserved red pigments made from iron oxide standing in clear contrast to reds made from realgar, which have faded into yellow due to exposure to light). The uneven height of the borders on different sheets posed a problem for the craftsman who had to assemble the roll. The solution adopted was in some places to erase part of the text and colour at the ends of sheets and to join up the inconsistent borders with sloping lines; at one point sections of text were cut away and a patch of papyrus inserted to make the transition less apparent. This was done in the long spell 17, which had evidently been prepared by two different sets of scribes and painters. The adjustment involved cutting out some text and rewriting it, and the result was far from perfect since a large section of the spell text is missing, having perhaps been removed and discarded. One of the most obvious joins (illustrated) comes after spells 144 and 145 and before spell 18. Here the sheets overlap right over left, and there is a clear change in the position of the borders, which have been clumsily joined by slanting lines and repainted with realgar and orpiment to conceal the adjustment. The distinction in sign-spacing and graphic technique on each side of the join clearly indicates that these sheets were the work of different craftsmen. Despite these interventions, the finished roll, with all its pigments in pristine state, would have appeared generally consistent; the illusion of formal correctness evidently outweighed any possible disadvantages which might result from the incomplete state of the spells.

Parkinson and Leach 2010.

154 Errors and corruptions in the Book of the Dead of Hor

Ink and paint on papyrus
H 36.0 cm
Late first century BC
Akhmim
London, British Museum, EA 10479/4

The papyrus of Hor, stolist of Min and 'scribe of the oracle', is one of a small group of manuscripts from Akhmim, which represent a local tradition of production from the final decades of the use of the Book of the Dead (see also cat. nos 45 and 126). Among the distinctive features of the group is the consistent use of retrograde writing, a peculiarity which had generally fallen out of fashion after the New Kingdom (see p. 266). These manuscripts are also notable for the very corrupt nature of the texts. Hor's papyrus contains hundreds of errors, such as incorrectly copied signs, duplications, words garbled and mistakes arising from faulty transcription from hieratic to hieroglyphic script. In the later sections of the roll (from spell 144 onwards), shown here, even more irregularities occur: signs, words and whole passages of text are missing, and what has been written is often unintelligible. Since the actual signs are drawn with some care, it seems that the scribes who produced these papyri simply copied the texts from a master document without understanding what they were writing. Other papyri from this group show similar errors, suggesting that all of them were based on one or more older manuscripts which were themselves defective – perhaps papyri which had fallen to pieces and had been ineptly reassembled, with parts of the texts in the wrong order. The copyists evidently lacked a sufficiently strong grasp of the meaning of the texts to fill in the gaps or correct mistakes.

Mosher 2001, pl. 9.

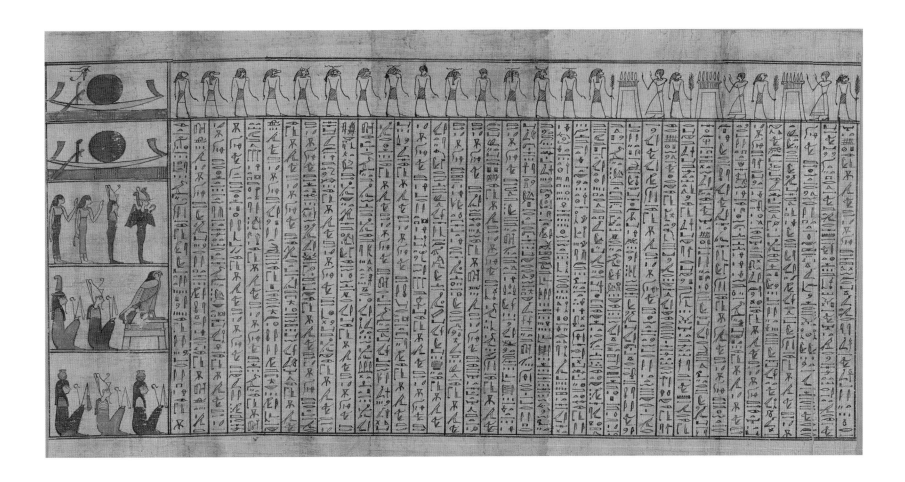

12 Studying the Book of the Dead

Barbara Lüscher

Peret em heru

Three simple words, perfectly unambiguous when taken singly, but by no means easy of explanation when taken together without a context.

(Renouf 1907: CLIII)

The time of the pioneers

In the very early days of Egyptology, before the discovery of the much earlier Pyramid Texts from the Old Kingdom and the edition of the Middle Kingdom Coffin Texts, the compilation of mortuary spells and illustrations now known as the Book of the Dead was long believed to be the oldest and most extensive corpus of religious texts of the ancient Egyptians. Jean-François Champollion (1790–1832), the famous French philologist who in 1822 succeeded in deciphering hieroglyphs, studied the content of some of the papyrus rolls and called it a 'funerary ritual'. Others even saw it as a kind of Bible of ancient Egyptian wisdom, although the original title can best be translated as 'Spells for Coming Forth by Day', referring to the wish to emerge safely from the tomb in a spiritualized form.

Fig. 83 Papyrus of Iuefankh. Late Ptolemaic Period. Turin Inv. 1791.

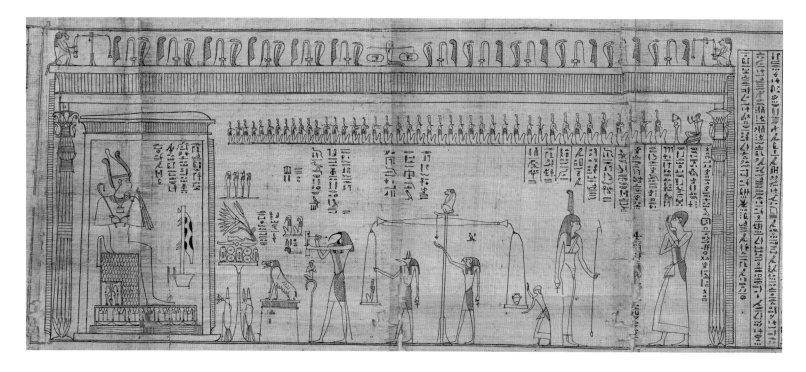

The first facsimile of a complete Book of the Dead manuscript from the Ptolemaic Period had been reproduced as early as 1805[1] and reprinted in the famous *Description de l'Égypte*[2] of the Napoleonic Expedition. But it was Richard Lepsius's publication of the Late Ptolemaic papyrus of Iuefankh[3] (fig. 83) in 1842 which not only introduced the term 'Book of the Dead' for this heterogeneous text corpus, but also established the standard numbering system for its spells that remains in use today, with some additional chapters added by later scholars such as Willem Pleyte, Edouard Naville, Ernest A. Wallis Budge and Thomas G. Allen. At the same time it should be noted that the term 'book' is rather misleading because it is not a codified text with a fixed sequence or a coherent story to be told from beginning to end, but rather a selection of magical spells or groups of spells varying in length and composition, covering the main religious aspects, hopes and fears of the Egyptians concerning the afterlife.

Fig. 84
Richard Lepsius.

(Karl) Richard Lepsius (1810–84) (fig. 84), the pioneer and founder of German Egyptology, who led the famous Prussian Expedition to Egypt and Nubia (1842–5) and thus set a new standard for archaeological documentation, not only confirmed and expanded Champollion's grammatical theories (still much debated at that time), but was also a key figure in the study of the Book of the Dead. As Georg Ebers put it in his biography of Lepsius,[4] there is hardly any monument in the whole field of Egyptology whose foundation stone does not bear the name Lepsius.

After visiting numerous museums and collections Lepsius felt the need for a much wider comparative edition of the Book of the Dead, which he then believed to be the only large corpus of ancient Egyptian texts. He thus presented his project at the Second International Congress of Orientalists in London in 1874, originally aiming to include the texts of all periods of Egyptian history, as explained in the announcement:

> It seemed of special moment for the furtherance of the Egyptian studies, that an edition of the Bible of the Old Egyptians, the Ritual, as Champollion called it, or the Book of the Dead, as Lepsius styles it, as critical and complete as possible should be steadily kept in view. Such edition should present a threefold recension of that most venerable monument of Egyptian speech, archaeology and religion, i.e. it should give us the Book of the Dead as its text consisted – 1. Under the Old Empire, 2. Under the Theban Dynasties of the New Empire; 3. Under the Psammetici (Dyn. XXVI).[5]

Fig. 85
Edouard Naville.

A first comparative edition

To carry out this huge task Lepsius chose his Genevan colleague and former student, the founder of Swiss Egyptology (Henri-)Edouard Naville (1844–1926) (fig. 85), who was later to lead the first excavations of the newly founded British-based Egypt Exploration Fund (later renamed the Egypt Exploration Society). A *circulaire*, signed by a committee consisting of Samuel Birch, Richard Lepsius, François Chabas and Edouard Naville, was sent out in December 1875 to all major museums and private collectors in order to announce the project and ask for support in providing source material. In contrast to Lepsius's original plan, Naville very soon realized that he would have to confine himself to manuscripts from the classical period of the New

Kingdom because of the overwhelming amount of material. He also believed that in order to obtain a correct text of the so-called 'Theban recension' of the New Kingdom, accurate copies of well-preserved papyri had to be published. Comparative studies could then be based on such publications, enabling the ancient text to be amended. But instead of reproducing all texts in full synopsis, Naville decided to copy only one complete version per spell, noting just the main variants from the parallels (fig. 86). In the papyrus of Nebseny (cat. nos 16, 69, 103 and 148) he chose one of the finest manuscripts from the British Museum's collection to serve as his basic version. In several of his letters to Lepsius, Naville mentioned the importance of a first photographic edition of this papyrus[6] which was then realized in 1876 by The Trustees of the British Museum, with Samuel Birch (1813–85) as the department's first keeper in charge. That publication marked the true starting point of the first critical text edition of the New Kingdom Book of the Dead.[7]

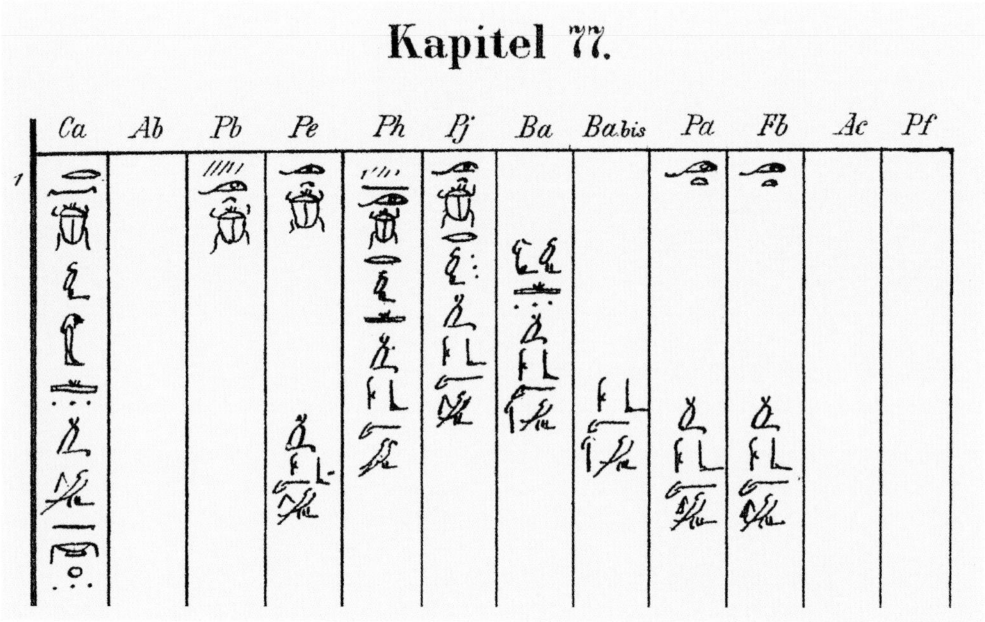

Fig. 86 An example from Naville's text of 1886.

The rest is history: after more than ten years of collecting, studying and copying, Edouard Naville, assisted by his wife Marguerite, a skilled artist who drew all the vignettes, finally presented his extensive publication in 1886. It was to become the standard edition for more than 120 years. It consisted of three parts: volume 1 with selected vignettes for each of the 186 spells given, and volume 2 with the text variants, complemented by an introduction including valuable information about the individual manuscripts. Unfortunately Lepsius did not live to see the final publication, but during his lifetime he always maintained a vital interest in Naville's work.

Lepsius's 1842 publication of the Turin papyrus already served as a basis for early scholarly translations of this text corpus or parts of it, such as the first complete Book of the Dead translation by Samuel Birch.[8] It had been announced by its editor, Baron Bunsen, in the following words:

As to England, Mr. Samuel Birch, in spite of the heavy duties of his office at the British Museum, which to anybody else would not leave even the material leisure, much less the strength and courage required for a great literary work, has crowned his indefatigable and successful researches by what may be called the prize of Egyptological ingenuity and scholarship – a complete translation of the most ancient sacred book in the world; for such we believe the 'Book of the Dead' to be.[9]

Birch himself had already expressed the need for a comparative edition as a basis for accurate translations by stating:

A collation of the best and principal [Rituals] in the museums of Europe would be a most important aid to Egyptian studies; but it is a work requiring the labour of a life, and almost beyond what can be hoped to be realised by private enterprise, and is not likely to be undertaken by governments, which take little interest in any except practical studies and the material sciences.[10]

With Naville's new edition the door was now opened to more detailed studies of the New-Kingdom Book of the Dead tradition.[11] The parallel arrangement of the texts in his volumes allowed easier comparison of the differing versions and thus helped to clarify difficulties and to restore destroyed or broken passages. The oldest Egyptological journal, the Leipzig- (and later Berlin-) based *Zeitschrift für Ägyptische Sprache und Altertumskunde*, which was founded in 1863 by Heinrich Brugsch and then continued by Richard Lepsius and others, published in its first volumes several articles on the Book of the Dead.

Some of the early editions were based on the British Museum's papyrus collection, one of the world's finest and largest. The various works of Ernest A.T. Wallis Budge (1857–1934), successor of Samuel Birch as Keeper of Egyptian and Assyrian Antiquities, are among the most widely reprinted publications of the early days (although nowadays very outdated and often inaccurate). These include publications on papyrus Ani (BM EA 10470), one of the best-known and most exquisitely illustrated Book of the Dead manuscript's from the Museum's collection, which was acquired in Egypt in 1888 by Budge himself. It should be noted here that most of the papyri in today's collections were purchased through local antiquities dealers, early travellers or at auction sales. As a consequence they usually lack any further information, especially about their exact provenance, and their fragments are often scattered today between several current locations (as in the case of the papyrus of Tui, cat. no. 155).

Modern research

Scholarly interest and research in the field of the Book of the Dead has grown and advanced since the early days of Egyptology studies, and the approaches are now manifold. Today's main standard translations are those by Raymond O. Faulkner,[12] Thomas G. Allen,[13] Paul Barguet[14] and Erik Hornung,[15] although numerous chapters will need retranslation once a much wider text basis in the form of new synoptic editions of the proper spells becomes available. Of greatest importance are photographic publications[16] of the original texts on papyri, linen shrouds, tomb walls and various items of the funerary equipment, complemented by detailed studies of particular spells and their accompanying vignettes. As the source material has multiplied since Naville's edition, and continues to grow today through new discoveries either in excavations or auction sales, it becomes increasingly important to make information known and available to scholars worldwide: for example, by easily accessible archives and museum websites including online databases,[17] and by collaborations between international specialists in the field of the Book of the Dead. Following early examples such as the *Göttinger Totenbuchstudien* initiated by Kurt Sethe, Adriaan de Buck and Hermann Kees, several groups of scholars have dedicated their efforts to the study of this text corpus, among them the prominent German Book of the Dead Project, initiated in 1994 as a joint venture between the universities of Cologne and Bonn.[18] Over the years the team of various scholars has not only collected a huge amount of archival material in Bonn and published its own series of Book of the Dead monographs and studies, but also provided useful tools such as an extant bibliography,[19] an online prosopographical database and a word index[20] of the Late Period Turin papyrus. Since information about provenance and dating criteria are lacking for most papyri, international databases and archives can help to find matches and thus reunite scattered fragments in different museums, as mentioned above in the case of the papyrus of Tui.

But publishing, dating and provenancing source material is only one part of current and future work in the field of the Book of the Dead. New translations as well as detailed studies of the history and development of this heterogeneous text corpus must follow. Most of our standard translations are either based on one particular manuscript or go back to Naville's outdated publication of 1886, often combined with the call for a new critical edition with the comparative versions given in full text. Adriaan de Buck, who with his Coffin Texts has set standards for all synoptic editions, commented on Naville's volumes in the introduction of his first Coffin Text volume of 1935:

> Anyone who has seriously worked with Naville's *Todtenbuch* ... will have the experience that such study is much hampered by the fact that Naville gives only the more important variants. What exactly is the situation when Naville is silent? ... In a word, a really sound study of a spell from the Book of the Dead must be continually going back from Naville to the originals.[21]

However, the amount of Book of the Dead material far exceeded that of the Pyramid and Coffin Texts, and the majority of sources still remained unpublished, so a new edition was long regarded as far too large a task for a single person. And although references to Pyramid and Coffin Texts in grammars, religious studies and general secondary literature are quite abundant, the same is not true of the Book of the Dead because of the lack of a sufficiently reliable text basis. It was not until 2004 that plans for such a new edition finally took shape in Basel, Switzerland.[22] While Naville and his contemporaries had to copy all the texts by hand, nowadays scholars can profit from modern technology to faciliate and speed up their work. For example, a new computer software (*VisualGlyph*) was created by the Basel team for the special purpose of accurately writing synoptic hieroglyphic texts, enabling the writer to freely position, scale, rotate or overlap

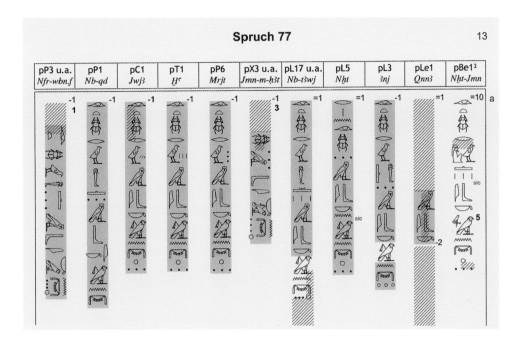

Fig. 87 An example from a modern text edition, 2006.

any chosen signs directly on the computer screen (fig. 87). These are tools Lepsius or Naville could never even have dreamt of!

Tools and techniques

In the early days of Lepsius and Naville, photography – either in the form of the daguerrotype process developed in 1839 by Louis Daguerre or the talbotype/calotype paper negatives introduced in 1841 by Henry Fox Talbot – was still at a formative stage and was available only to specialists. It required a lot of heavy equipment, which was not very practical, particularly when travelling and working in the dust and heat of Egypt. The Englishman Francis Frith (1822–98), one of the early professional photographers in Egypt, had to travel with a specially designed wickerwork carriage which served him as a mobile darkroom.

One of the first technical devices used by modern artists was the so-called camera obscura ('dark chamber'), which ultimately led to the current photographic process. A variant of it was the camera lucida ('light chamber' or 'lit room'), patented in 1807 by the British scientist William Hyde Wollaston (1766–1828) and already in use by the savants of the Napoleonic Expedition at the end of the eighteenth century. This portable optical device helped the artist to accurately draw an object or a whole landscape: it enabled the eye to see the subject and the drawing paper simultaneously by means of a prism with two reflecting surfaces, as in a photographic double exposure. Among the famous artists known to have made good use of this instrument were David Roberts (1796–1864), Robert Hay (1799–1863) and William Edward Lane (1801–76). For printing and distribution the drawings were usually transferred to copper engravings or lithographic plates and then coloured. In contrast to early photography the camera lucida was very light and handy, required no further equipment such as a tent or darkroom, and could be used in most light conditions.

Lepsius, who himself had acquired skills in copper engraving and lithography, seems not to have made use of the young technology of photography for his Prussian Expedition to

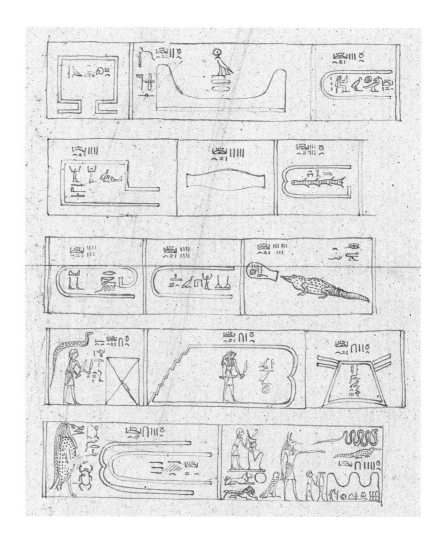

Egypt and Nubia. He relied instead on talented painters and artists such as Jacob Frey and the brothers Ernst and Max Weidenbach, who also lithographed the famous Turin Book of the Dead papyrus (see fig. 83) for publication and were specially trained by Lepsius in copying hieroglyphs. They too used the camera lucida. While some drawings would be made on normal paper, real facsimiles of inscriptions were either done by using semi-translucent tracing paper or – especially for copying inscriptions and reliefs from tombs, temples and museum objects – by taking squeezes (paper impressions). Nowadays this technique is criticized because it has often caused severe damage to the walls and inscriptions by taking off some of the paint (it can still be found on the back of the squeezes). Similar damage was caused by taking wax impressions of the reliefs, as in the case of Giovanni Battista Belzoni's work in the tomb of Sety 1 in the Valley of the Kings.

For his work with funerary papyri Naville mainly used semi-translucent tracing paper to produce his facsimiles (fig. 88). For publication these were then reduced to scale by his wife Marguerite by using a so-called pantograph, an early mechanical device to reduce or enlarge drawings at the same scale. Although tracing paper is still in use in modern archaeology and epigraphy it is now increasingly being replaced by digital photography and its tools.

Another important change can be observed in general printing and typesetting techniques, especially in handling the problem of reproducing the hieroglyphic script. The early monumental publications such as the Napoleonic *Description de l'Égypte*, Champollion's *Monuments de l'Égypte et de la Nubie* or Lepsius's *Denkmäler aus Aegypten und Aethiopien* used engraved facsimiles drawn by skilled artists and epigraphers. Among the members and leading experts of Napoleon's scientific team was the famous physician and engineer Nicolas-Jacques Conté (1755–1805). He invented not only the modern pencil but also a special typographical machine to automate and thus speed up the engraving process, especially of large surface areas such as skies and backgrounds, for the hundreds of large folio-plates of the *Description de l'Égypte*. And even before the time of copper engravings or lithography, woodcuts were being used.

It was and still is essential to accurately render the hieroglyphic script. As mentioned above, in the early days archaeologists had to rely on skilled painters and artists to copy the texts. But the process of making hand copies and lithographs was very costly and time-consuming, especially when editing longer text passages. Therefore already by the first half of the nineteenth century the publishing houses had made the first attempts to create printing types for Egyptian hieroglyphs. The earliest moveable hieroglyphic types were commissioned by Heinrich Julius Klaproth (1783–1835) for a publication of 1829.[23] In Germany the first systematically designed hieroglyphic font was produced in Leipzig in about 1835 at the typefoundry of Friedrich Nies, and first used by Gustav Seyffarth and Moritz G. Schwartze,[24] in large black and rather irregular silhouette shapes (fig. 89). Several other early typefaces followed in different countries, among them the French types commissioned in the middle of the nineteenth century by the Imprimerie Nationale, Paris, under the supervision of Emmanuel de Rougé

Fig. 89 Text examples in earliest hieroglyphic typesets. From Lorck 1879, 148.

Fig. 90 Early hieroglyphic matrices and metal types from the Imprimerie Nationale Paris.

Fig. 91 Example of a hieroglyphic metal type from the Theinhardt font.

(1811–72) and after designs by J.J. Dubois and Eugène Devéria (fig. 90). It was later continued and extended by the French Institute of Oriental Archaeology in Cairo. There were even at this time some hieratic, demotic and coptic typefaces.

One of the most widespread and favoured hieroglyphic typefaces of the time was the German so-called Theinhardt font of 1846 (fig. 91), an outline script produced under the supervision of Richard Lepsius, based on original drawings by Ernst and Max Weidenbach and cut by the engraver Ferdinand Theinhardt on behalf of the Royal Prussian Academy of Sciences at Berlin. This typeface, based on sign forms from the 26th Dynasty, was soon being used in many different countries with its signs continually extended and augmented by their publishing houses. Budge also used this typeface – or more precisely an extension of it by the London publishers Harrison & Son – for his *Hieroglyphic Dictionary and Vocabulary* as well as his translation of the famous Book of the Dead of Ani.

But certainly the most popular and probably the most aesthetic font was the one created at Oxford University Press for the printing of Alan Gardiner's *Egyptian Grammar* of 1927 (fig. 92). Designed by the distinguished Egyptologists and skilled artists Norman and Nina de Garis Davies, these outline hieroglyphs were based on New Kingdom (18th Dynasty) forms. But again, the production of the matrices as well as the typesetting and layout of longer hieroglyphic texts with their varying arrangement was a complicated and very expensive procedure.

With the development of digital technology, book production is currently undergoing a change from offset to digital printing, and it is not surprising that the last two decades have also seen the production of several different word-processing programmes for writing hieroglyphic texts with computer-generated fonts. With the help of such new tools, in combination

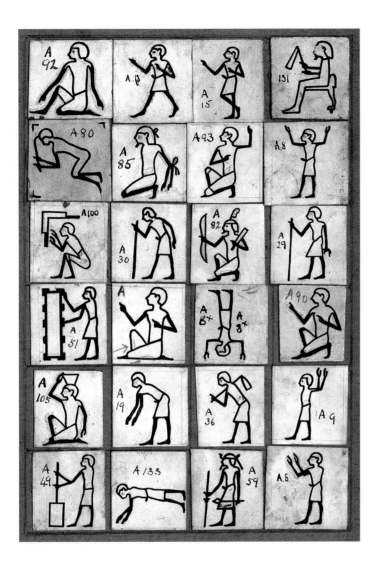

Fig. 92 Drawings by Norman de Garis Davies used for the design of Gardiner's hieroglyphic font.

with digital photography and modern printing technology, the labour and cost of producing large text editions such as the Book of the Dead could be considerably reduced.

Future trends

So where will the future lead us? With the original sources in Egypt, and museum collections slowly but continually and inevitably decaying, there is certainly a need to find methods to somehow preserve the texts. In addition to the skills of museum conservators and papyrologists, photographic publications, archives and databases must continue to be produced, maintained, enlarged and also financially supported. All the text sources should be made available step-by-step in colour photographs to scholars worldwide and more international cooperations established. And as the current digital media are not necessarily as long-lasting as paper prints, publications in book form might still be preferred to CD-ROMs at present. It is to be hoped that exhibitions for the general public such as the present one at the British Museum will also help draw attention to the fascinating religious heritage of the Egyptian Book of the Dead and the importance of its worldwide preservation.

155 The Book of the Dead of Tui

Ink and paint on papyrus
H 25.6 cm (9913/3), 36.7 (79431)
18th Dynasty, *c.* 1450 BC
Thebes
London, British Museum, EA 9913/3 and EA 79431

During the early nineteenth century many papyri were discovered during unscientific digging by local villagers and the agents of European collectors. It was common practice for long documents to be torn into pieces and sold to different purchasers. One of the aims of modern research on the Book of the Dead is to rediscover the connections between such scattered fragments.

Part of this fine early 18th Dynasty papyrus was acquired by the British Museum in 1835 at the sale of the third collection of Henry Salt (1780–1827), former British Consul-General in Egypt. Other portions are today in the Museo Civico, Bologna (Inv. KS 3168). In 2009 the British Museum acquired two further fragments, which had formed part of the collection of William Henry Fox Talbot (1800–77), pioneer of the photographic negative/positive process.

This Book of the Dead was prefabricated, and the name of the eventual owner, Tui, was added in a different hand; it appears on the portion of the papyrus now in Bologna. The papyrus has several unusual features, including the sequential numbering of its individual sections in the upper right-hand corners in retrograde hieratic script. Another rare feature is the presence of a single line of text on the back (verso) in large and elegant hieroglyphs, with spaces left blank for the name of the owner and his mother to be inserted. The section of the manuscript which comes from the Salt collection, illustrated here, shows part of spell 125: Tui and his wife adore the gods of the judgement hall, who are shown in separate compartments, with the words of the 'protestation of innocence' written below them. In front of the gods is an image of the 'Lake of Fire', surrounded by baboons and flaming torches.

The fragment from Fox Talbot's collection includes spell 39, which concerns the defeat of the chaos-serpent Apep by the gods in the entourage of Ra. The vignette of this spell is partly lost, but the remaining portion shows the god Seth standing at the prow of the solar boat, spearing the giant snake, whose body is cut through with knives.

Munro 1988, 288, no. a.55; Quirke 1993, 67, 85, no. 273.

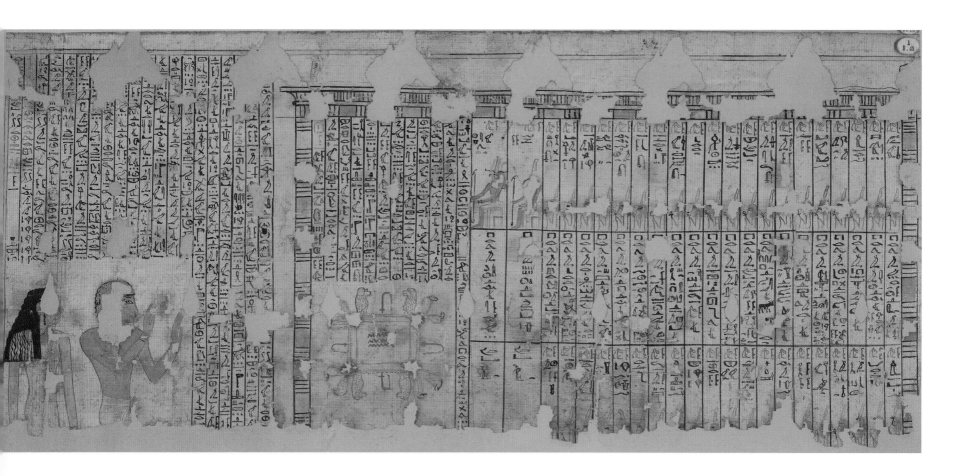

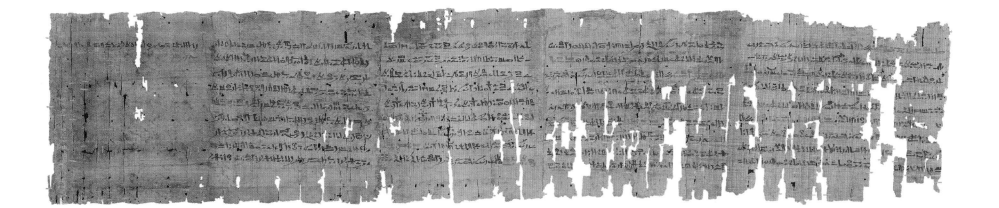

156 Papyrus

H 19.0 cm; W 94.4 cm
Late 21st or early 22nd Dynasty, *c.* 1000–850 BC
Thebes
London, British Museum, EA 74136

157 Base of Osiris figure

Painted wood
L 29.8 cm; W 9.5 cm
Late 21st or early 22nd Dynasty, *c.* 1000–850 BC
Thebes
London, British Museum, EA 9872

This is one of two short Book of the Dead papyri which entered the British Museum in 1843 with the collection of the Earl of Belmore. Each was found inside the base of a wooden Osiris figure. The statuette, which originally stood on the plinth illustrated, is missing. The papyri were extracted from their containers and unrolled in 1988 and 1992. The second of these rolls, illustrated here, was found to be tightly wedged inside a small and roughly hewn cavity in the statue base. It was carefully lifted with the aid of an upholstery needle, and then water vapour was used to relax the dry and brittle papyrus sufficiently for it to be unrolled in approximately 10 cm stages. After a light clean with water vapour, the fragments were mounted between sheets of glass.

Both papyri turned out to be typical short hieratic Books of the Dead of the 21st Dynasty. Each had lost its opening vignette, perhaps torn off by the first discoverer in the early nineteenth century, who then replaced the inscribed portions of the rolls inside the wooden statue bases. The owners were husband and wife: the first papyrus (EA 74135) belonged to a man named Djedkhonsiufankh (whose coffins are today in the Berlin Museum) and the second (illustrated) to his spouse Dimutiudu. The latter document contains only spells 23–6 and 28 of the Book of the Dead.

Leach 1992, 23; Quirke 1993, 35, 72–3, no. 43.

159 Fragments of a Book of the Dead extracted from a fake roll

Painted papyrus
Later 18th or early 19th Dynasty, c. 1400–1250 BC
Probably from Thebes
London, British Museum, EA 70896/3

By dissecting fake rolls such as cat. no. 158, it is sometimes possible to reconstruct portions of the ancient documents from which the forgery was made. These fragments can be dated approximately to the late 18th or early 19th Dynasty, on the grounds of the size and style of the hieroglyphic signs, and the details of some of the vignettes. They formed part of the Book of the Dead of the head tradesman Huy and the texts also mention a woman named Tuia, perhaps his wife. The portion illustrated contains parts of spell 17.

Quirke 1993, 42, 75, no. 91.

158 A fake papyrus roll

L 16.0 cm
Early nineteenth-century forgery, incorporating ancient papyrus
Provenance unrecorded
London, British Museum, EA 76534

Of all the antiquities that were offered for sale to early nineteenth-century collectors and travellers in Egypt, papyri were some of the most highly prized. To augment the demand some local dealers made ingenious forgeries of papyrus rolls. These consisted of fragments of authentic ancient papyri which were too damaged or broken to be accepted by most purchasers, and which were formed into small rolls which purported to be genuine documents. Portions of the inscriptions were sometimes cunningly left exposed to support the deception.

Hunefer and his wife Nasha.
EA 9901/1.

160　The Papyrus of Hunefer

Painted papyrus
H 39.0 cm; L 550.0 cm
19th Dynasty, *c.* 1280 BC
Thebes
London, British Museum, EA 9901/1–8

The papyrus of Hunefer entered the collections of the British Museum in 1852, together with a painted wooden Osiris figure (EA 9861) which had evidently served as the container for the roll. Hunefer's titles are Royal Scribe, Steward (estate overseer) of King Sety I and Overseer of Cattle of the Lord of the Two Lands. His wife, the Chantress of Amun Nasha, is also depicted on the papyrus.

The roll contains spells 15, 183, 30B, 1, 22 and 17 of the Book of the Dead. Between spells 183 and 30B there is a distinct change in the style of writing, noticeable in the contrasting forms of certain common hieroglyphic signs and suggesting that different scribes had worked on these sections of the document. The name and titles of Hunefer were added after the completion of the main texts and were inserted into spaces left for that purpose. The vignettes have been drawn and painted with great care and precision but the texts include numerous errors, perhaps an indication that they had been copied hastily. The final section of the text, spell 17, is incomplete in the papyrus, ending abruptly at the right-hand end of the roll.

Budge 1899, 1-18, pl. 1-11; Munro 1988, 302, no. b.28; Quirke 1993, 41, 75, no. 89.

Above left: The two lions representing
'yesterday' and 'tomorrow'.
Above right: The sun-god, in the form
of a cat, killing his enemy, the serpent.
Left: The deities Heh ('Eternity')
and 'Sea' protecting the Lake of
Natron and the Lake of Maat.
All images from spell 17. EA 9901/5, 6, 8.

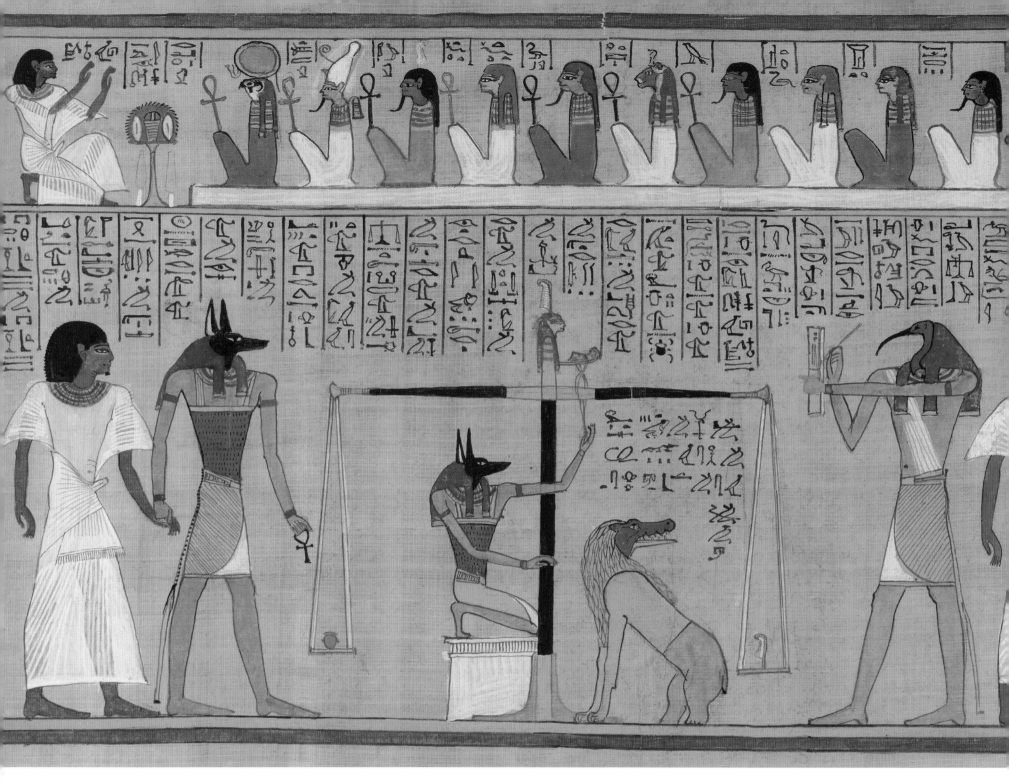

Hunefer undergoing the weighing of
the heart and being presented to Osiris
after his vindication. EA 9901/3.

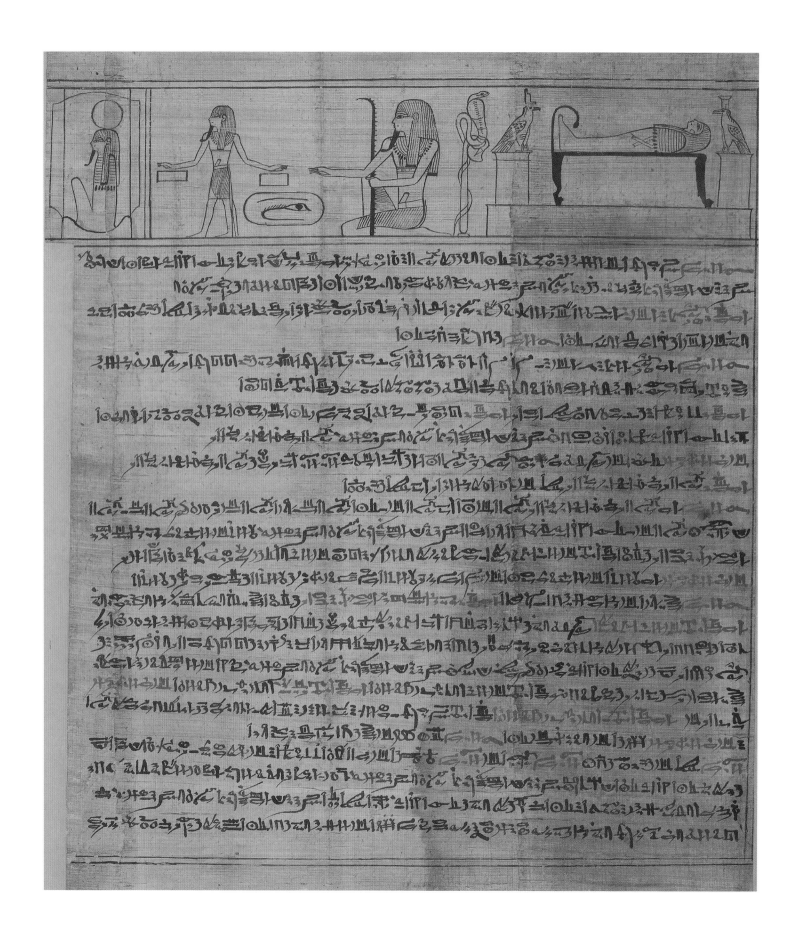

161 The Greenfield Papyrus

Ink on papyrus
H 46–49.5 cm; L 37.0 m
Late 21st or early 22nd Dynasty, c. 950–930 BC
'Royal Cache', Deir el-Bahri
London, British Museum, EA 10554

This papyrus derives its modern name from Mrs Mary Greenfield, whose husband acquired it in the late nineteenth century. Mrs Greenfield presented it to the British Museum in 1910. It was originally made for Nesitanebisheru, daughter of the High Priest of Amun Pinedjem II (fl. c. 990–969 BC). She was one of the most important women in Egypt, holding religious titles at several important cities in Upper Egypt. She was married – possibly to the Third Priest of Amun Djedptahiufankh – and had a daughter, Neskhons 'B'. Nesitanebisheru was buried in the family tomb of Pinedjem II, the 'Royal Cache', which later became the final resting place of many of the pharaohs of the New Kingdom.

Nesitanebisheru's funerary papyrus, at over 37 metres in length, is the longest Book of the Dead known. It is carefully written in a precise hieratic hand and is illustrated with finely detailed vignettes. A few of these extend to the full height of the papyrus, but most are arranged in a continuous strip running along the top of the roll. The texts and vignettes of several of the spells are duplicated, and often the illustrations are not located above the appropriate texts (see cat. no. 93). A number of joins are visible (see cat. no. 152), where prefabricated sections of the document were joined together. These are indicated by matching pairs of marks in red, indicating points at which sections were to be attached.

Besides the familiar Book of the Dead spells, the Greenfield Papyrus contains a number of texts which are not known from other documents. Their inclusion may reflect the personal preference of someone learned in funerary literature who took part in the compilation of the manuscript; this might have been Nesitanebisheru herself or a relative acting on her behalf in the creation of her burial assemblage. Perhaps the same person or persons were responsible for the inclusion of large vignettes such as the 'separation of heaven and earth' and Osiris enthroned above a large serpent, which are also unexpected elements of a Book of the Dead.

Budge 1912; Faulkner 1985, 11, 102, 116, 149, 153; Niwinski 1989, 338; Quirke 1993, 50 (no. 145).

p. 306 A section of spell 17 with vignettes showing the gods Heh and 'Sea', and the mummy on a bier. EA 10554/7.

p. 307, top: Nesitanebisheru adores Ra-Horakhty. EA 10554/61.

p. 307, below: Book of the Dead of the High Priest Amun of Pinedjem II, father of Nesitanebisheru. EA 1079/1.

Left: Nesitanebisheru adores the sun-god in his barque. EA 10554/85.

LIST OF PAPYRI

The following is a list of the British Museum Book of the Dead papyri exhibited and featured in this catalogue.

BM EA 9900 Hieroglyphic funerary papyrus of the Copyist of the Temple of Ptah, and the Temples of Upper and Lower Egypt, Child of the Royal Nursery, Nebseny, son of the Draughtsman Tjenena and the Lady of the House Mutresti. Memphis. 18th Dynasty, *c.* 1400 BC.

BM EA 9901 Hieroglyphic funerary papyrus of the Royal Scribe and Steward of King Sety I, Overseer of Royal Cattle and Scribe of Divine Offerings, Hunefer. Thebes. 19th Dynasty, *c.* 1280 BC.

BM EA 9902 Hieroglyphic funerary papyrus of Tentawy, daughter of Asetweret. Thebes. Ptolemaic Period, 305–30 BC.

BM EA 9904 Hieroglyphic and hieratic funerary papyrus of Lady of the House and Chantress of Amun Astemakhbit, daughter of Maatemheb. 21st Dynasty, *c.* 1069–945 BC.

BM EA 9913 Hieroglyphic funerary papyrus of Tui. Thebes. 18th Dynasty, *c.* 1450 BC.

BM EA 9951 Hieroglyphic funerary papyrus of the Sistrum-player, Mutirdis. Thebes (?). Ptolemaic Period, 305–30 BC.

BM EA 9974 Unfinished funerary papyrus of Buhar. Late 21st or early 22nd Dynasty, *c.* 970–900 BC.

BM EA 9995 Hieratic funerary papyrus of the Nomarch, Kerasher, born of Tasentsenty. Thebes. Reign of Augustus, late first century BC.

BM EA 10002 Hieroglyphic funerary papyrus of the Lady of the House, Chantress of Amun, Tameni. Probably Thebes. 21st Dynasty, *c.* 1069–945 BC.

BM EA 10008 Hieroglyphic funerary papyrus of the Lady of the House, Chantress of Amun, Tameni. Probably Thebes. 21st Dynasty, *c.* 1069–945 BC.

BM EA 10009 Hieroglyphic funerary papyrus of the Scribe, Userhat, son of Lady of the House Sat [...]. 18th Dynasty, *c.* 1450 BC.

BM EA 10010 Hieroglyphic funerary papyrus of the Chantress of Amun, Muthetepty. Thebes. 21st Dynasty, *c.* 1050 BC.

BM EA 10063 Hieratic funerary papyrus of the Chief Baker of the domain of Amun, Padiamenet. Probably from Thebes. Late 21st or early 22nd Dynasty, *c.* 950–900 BC.

BM EA 10086 Hieratic funerary papyrus of Tentameniy, daughter of Neshorpakhered. Ptolemaic Period, 305–30 BC.

BM EA 10470 Hieroglyphic funerary papyrus of the Royal Scribe, Accounting Scribe for the Divine Offerings of all the gods, Overseer of the Granaries and of the Lords of Tawer, Ani. Thebes. 19th, *c.*1275 BC.

BM EA 10471, 10473 Hieroglyphic funerary papyrus of the Royal Scribe and Chief Military Officer, Nakht. Late 18th or early 19th Dynasty, *c.* 1350–1290 BC.

BM EA 10472 Hieroglyphic funerary papyrus of the Chief of the Musicians of Osiris, Chief of the Musicians of Nebtu and Khnum, Chantress of Amun, Anhai. Probably from Thebes. 20th Dynasty, *c.* 1100 BC.

BM EA 10477 Hieroglyphic funerary papyrus of the Steward of the Chief Treasurer, Nu, son of the Steward of the Chief Treasurer, Amenhotep and the lady Sensenb. 18th Dynasty, *c.* 1400 BC.

BM EA 10478 Hieroglyphic funerary papyrus of the Scribe and priest of Mut, Bakenmut. 19th Dynasty, *c.* 1250 BC.

BM EA 10479 Hieroglyphic funerary papyrus of the Stolist and Scribe of the Oracle, Hor, son of the Stolist Djedhor and the Lady of the House Sebat. Akhmim. Late first century BC.

BM EA 10541 Hieroglyphic funerary papyrus of the King's Mother, Lady of the Two Lands, Nodjmet, daughter of the King's Mother Herere. Thebes. Early 21st Dynasty, *c.* 1050 BC.

BM EA10554 Hieratic funerary papyrus of the First Chief of the Musicians of Amun, Prophetess of Mut, of Anhur-Shu, of Min, Horus and Isis at Akhmim, of Osiris, Horus and Isis at Abydos, of Horus of Djufy, of Amun at Iurudj, Nesitanebisheru, daughter of the High Priest of Amun Pinedjem II and Neskhons. Thebes. Late 21st or early 22nd Dynasty, *c.* 950–930 BC.

BM EA10558 Hieratic funerary papyrus of Ankhwahibra. Late 26th Dynasty, *c.* 550–525 BC.

BM EA 10743 Hieratic funerary papyrus of Lady of the House, Chantress of Amun-Ra, King of the Gods, noblewoman, Singer of the reach of Mut, Astemakhbit. Probably Thebes. 21st Dynasty, *c.* 1069–945 BC.

BM EA 74136 Hieratic funerary papyrus of Chantress of Amun, Dimutiudu. 21st Dynasty, *c.* 1069–945 BC.

NOTES

PREFACE
1   Munro 1988, 160–2; Lüscher 1998, 12.

CHAPTER 1
1   Assmann 2005, 23–225.
2   Assmann 2005, 142.
3   Assmann 2005, 23–38.
4   For the meaning of 'Osiris of X', see Smith 2006.
5   DuQuesne 2006, 25–6.
6   Assmann 2005, 407.
7   Adapted from Assmann 2005, 163.
8   Pinch 2006, 148–9.

CHAPTER 2
1   Pinch 2006, 12.
2   For the distinction between these two categories of texts, see Assmann 1990.
3   Niwinski 1989, 13–17.
4   Allen 1974, 214.
5   Translation adapted from Faulkner 1985, 27–8; see comments in Assmann 2005, 29–30.

CHAPTER 3
1   Hornung 1997.
2   Gestermann 2003.
3   Hornung 1997.
4   Geisen 2004.
5   Parkinson and Quirke 1992.
6   Grimm and Schoske 1999.
7   Niwinski 1989.
8   Lucarelli 2006; Niwinski 1989.
9   Quack 2009.
10 Lesko 2003.
11 Gestermann 2005.
12 Munro 2010.
13 Lesko 2003.
14 Lepsius 1842.
15 Kockelmann 2008.
16 Mosher 1992.
17 Coenen 2001.
18 Lejeune 2006; Quirke 1999b.
19 Saleh 1984.
20 Perraud 2006.
21 Žabkar 1985.
22 Kockelmann 2008.
23 Kockelmann 2008.
24 Illés 2009.
25 Raven 1979.
26 Cooney 2007; Janssen 1975.
27 Cooney 2007.
28 Munro 1994.
29 Gabolde 2008.

30 Quirke 1999a.
31 Munro 2009.

CHAPTER 4
1   Lloyd 1989, 124–5.
2   Assmann 2005, 304–5.
3   Assmann 2005, 301.
4   Assmann 2005, 309.
5   Text on an early 18th Dynasty stela: Assmann 2005, 301.
6   Assmann 2005, 318.
7   Lloyd 1989, 125–6.
8   Roth 2001, 605–9.
9   Assmann 2005, 324.
10 Roth 2001, 607.

CHAPTER 5
1   Roth 1992, 146.
2   LLoyd 1989, 124.
3   Lüscher 1998, 74–7.
4   Regen 2010.
5   Roth and Roehrig 2002, 138.
6   PT 519.
7   Assmann 2005, 107.
8   Adapted from Assmann 2005, 107–8.
9   Andrews 1994, 8, fig. 2.
10 PT 526.

CHAPTER 6
1   Allen 2003, 25–7.
2   Assmann 1989, 147.
3   Assmann 1989, 147.
4   Borghouts, 1988, 131–9.
5   Assmann 1989, 148.
6   Quirke 2003, 168–9, 172–3.
7   Quirke 2003, 173.
8   Quirke 2003, 174.
9   Assmann 1989, 198–9.

CHAPTER 7
1   Fabian 1988, 256.
2   Fabian 1988, 252, 256.
3   Lloyd 1989, 128.
4   Lloyd 1989, 128.
5   Assmann 2005, 215.

CHAPTER 8
1   Spell 41B. Lucarelli 2001–2, 44, 46.
2   Assmann 2005, 192.

CHAPTER 9
1   Lloyd 1989, 128

2   Grieshammer 1970.
3   Quirke 2002, 173–4.
4   Seeber 1976, Abb. 23–4.
5   Adapted from Assmann 1989, 150.
6   Seeber 1976, 65–6.
7   Assmann 1989, 151.
8   Assmann 1989, 151.
9   Seeber 1976, 179.
10 Seeber 1976, 167–71.
11 Seeber 1976, 170.
12 Roth and Roehrig 2002, 137.

CHAPTER 10
1   Quirke 2003, 176.
2   Allen 2003, 24.
3   Hays 2004, 181, 187, 199.
4   Allen 2003, 24.

CHAPTER 11
1   Caminos 1986.
2   Parkinson and Quirke 1995.
3   Munro 2001; Lucarelli 2006.
4   Parkinson and Leach 2010.
5   Niwinski 1999, pls 11–16.
6   Ragazzoli 2010.
7   Taylor 2001, 197, fig. 139.
8   Gasse 2002.
9   Lapp 2004.
10 Milde 1992; Lüscher 2007.
11 Lesko 1992.
12 Lenzo 2010.
13 Lüscher 2000; Mosher 2001.
14 Wüthrich 2010..

CHAPTER 12
1   Cadet 1805.
2   Pancoucke 1821, pls 72–5. For additional (late) Book of the Dead manuscripts published in the *Description de l'Égypte* see the preceding pls 60–71 in the same vol. II and pls 44–6 in vol. V.
3   Turin Museum Inv. 1791, Lepsius 1842.
4   Ebers 1885, 136.
5   Transactions of the second session of the Second International Congress of Orientalists, p. 442, cited in Naville 1886 (Introduction), 5f.
6   Nebseni 1876. For a new publication of this papyrus see Lapp 2004. A first translation of papyrus Nebseny was published in French by Massy 1885. An even earlier photographic reproduction of a Book of the Dead manuscript was that of papyrus Hunefer (BM EA 9901) by the British photographer Stephen Thompson, in *Egyptian Antiquities* 1872.

7   Naville 1886. A detailed study on Edouard Naville and his time, with special reference to early Book of the Dead studies, is being prepared by the present author.

8   Samuel Birch's 'Funereal Ritual' in Bunsen 1867, 123–333, followed by a dictionary of hieroglyphics on pp. 335–586, printed with England's first hieroglyphic typefaces, cast from designs drawn by Joseph Bonomi. An early French translation was published by Pierret 1882 and later translated into English by Davis 1894.

9   In his Appendix of Bunsen 1867, 110.

10   In Bunsen 1867, 132f.

11   A translation based on Naville's publication (edited and completed by Naville) was provided by Renouf 1907. For a detailed and extensive bibliography on the Book of the Dead see Backes 2009.

12   Faulkner 1985.

13   Allen 1974.

14   Barguet 1967.

15   Hornung 1979.

16   With the British Museum as forerunner (see note 6). Other early publications presented the papyri in coloured facsimiles, such as for example the works of Devéria and Pierret 1872, or Leemans 1882, and others.

17   As very good examples the websites of London's British Museum and Petrie Museum can be mentioned here.

18   Under the direction of Ursula Rössler-Köhler and Heinz-Josef Thissen, with Irmtraut Munro as main member of the staff.

19   Backes 2009.

20   Backes 2005. A first Book of the Dead word index had already been published by Lieblein 1875, followed by Budge 1911.

21   De Buck 1935, XIVf.

22   As a collaboration between Günther Lapp and the present author. For their publications see the series *Totenbuchtexte* from Orientverlag Basel.

23   Klaproth 1829.

24   A first one was used and designed by Seyffarth 1840, another one by Schwartze 1843.

BIBLIOGRAPHY

Allen, J P 2003. The Egyptian Concept of the World. D O'Connor and S Quirke (eds), *Encounters with Ancient Egypt. Mysterious Lands*. London, 23–30.

Allen, T G 1974. *The Book of the Dead or Going Forth by Day. Ideas of the Ancient Egyptians Concerning the Hereafter as Expressed in their Own Terms*. Studies in Ancient Oriental Civilization 37. Chicago.

Altenmüller, H 1985. *Die Apotropaia und die Götter Mittelägyptens: eine typologische und religionsgeschichtliche Untersuchung der sogenannten 'Zaubermesser' des Mittieren Reichs*. Thesis. Munich.

Andrews, C 1994. *Amulets of Ancient Egypt*. London.

Andrews, C 1998. *Egyptian Mummies* (2nd edn). London.

Andrews, C 1998. *Eternal Egypt*. Treasures from the British Museum. Hong Kong and Singapore.

Andrews, C 2000. *Egyptian Treasures from the British Museum*. Santa Ana.

Assmann, J 1990. Egyptian mortuary liturgies. S Israelit-Groll, *Studies in Egyptology Presented to Miriam Lichtheim*. Jerusalem. I, 1–45.

Assmann, J 2005. *Death and Salvation in Ancient Egypt*. Translated from the German by David Lorton. Ithaca and London.

Aston, D A 1994. *The Shabti Box: a Typological Study. Oudheidkundige Mededelingen uit het Rijksmuseum van Oudheden te Leiden* 74, 21–54.

Backes, B 2005. *Wortindex zum späten Totenbuch (pTurin 1791)*. Unter Mitarbeit von I Munro und S Stöhr. Studien zum Altägyptischen Totenbuch 9. Wiesbaden.

Backes, B 2009. *Bibliographie zum Altägyptischen Totenbuch. 2, erweiterte Auflage*. Bearbeitet von B Backes, S A Gülden, H Kockelmann, M Müller-Roth, I Munro und S Stöhr. Studien zum Altägyptischen Totenbuch 13. Wiesbaden.

Barguet, P 1967. *Le Livre des Morts des anciens Egyptiens*. Paris.

Barthelmess, P 1992. *Der Übergang ins Jenseits in den thebanischen Beamtengräbern der Ramessidenzeit*. Studien zur Archäologie und Geschichte Altägyptens 2. Heidelberg.

Bohleke, B 1997. An Oracular Amuletic Decree of Khonsu in the Cleveland Museum of Art. *Journal of Egyptian Archaeology* 83, 155–67, pl. XIX.

Borghouts, J F 1988. A new Middle Kingdom Netherworld Guide. *Studien zur Altägyptischen Kultur. Beihefte* 3, 131–9.

British Museum 1890. *The Book of the Dead. Facsimile of the Papyrus of Ani in the British Museum*. London.

British Museum 1894. *The Book of the Dead. Facsimile of the Papyrus of Ani in the British Museum* (2nd edn). London.

Brunner-Traut, E and Brunner, H 1981. *Die Ägyptische Sammlung der Universität Tübingen*. Mainz am Rhein.

Budge, E A W 1895. *The Book of the Dead. The Papyrus of Ani in the British Museum*. London.

Budge, E A W 1899. *The Book of the Dead. Facsimiles of the Papyri of Hunefer, Anhai, Kerasher and Netchemet, with supplementary text from the Papyrus of Nu*. London.

Budge, E A W 1911. *A Hieroglyphic Vocabulary to the Theban Recension of the Book of the Dead. With an Index to All the English Equivalents of the Egyptian Words*. Books on Egypt and Chaldaea 31. London.

Budge, E A W 1912. *The Greenfield Papyrus in the British Museum*. London.

Budge, E A W 1913. *The Papyrus of Ani. A Reproduction in Facsimile edited, with Hieroglyphic Transcript, Translation and Introduction*. London and New York.

Buhl, M-L 1947. The Goddesses of the Egyptian Tree Cult. *Journal of Near Eastern Studies* 6, 80–97.

Bunsen, C C J (ed.) 1867. *Egypt's Place in Universal History. An Historical Investigation in Five Books*. Translated from the German by C H Cottrell, with additions by S Birch. Vol. V. London.

Cadet, J M 1805. *Copie figurée d'un rouleau de papyrus trouvé à Thèbes, dans un tombeau des rois*. Paris.

Caminos, R A 1986. Some comments on the reuse of papyrus. *Papyrus Structure and Usage*. British Museum Occasional Paper 60, 43–61.

Coenen, M 2001. On the demise of the Book of the Dead in Ptolemaic Thebes, *RdE* 52, 69–84.

Cooney, J D 1976. *Catalogue of Egyptian Antiquities in the British Museum, IV. Glass*. London.

Cooney, K M 2007. *The Cost of Death. The Social and Economic Value of Ancient Egyptian Funerary Art in the Ramesside Period*. Egyptologische Uitgaven 22. Leiden.

Davis, C H S 1894. *The Egyptian Book of the Dead. The Most Ancient and the Most Important of the Extant Religious Texts of Ancient Egypt*. New York.

Dawson, W R and Gray, P H K 1968. *Catalogue of Egyptian Antiquities in the British Museum, I. Mummies and Human Remains*. London.

De Buck, A 1935. *The Egyptian Coffin Texts*. Vol. 1. Chicago.

de Cenival, J.-L. 1992 *Le livre pour sortir le jour. Le livre des Morts des anciens Égyptiens*. Le Bouscat.

Devéria, T and Pierret, P 1872. *Le papyrus de Neb-qed (exemplaire hiéroglyphique du Livre des Morts). Reproduit, décrit et précédé d'une introduction mythologique*. Paris.

Dunham, D 1931. A Fragment from the Mummy Wrappings of Tuthmosis III. *Journal of Egyptian Archaeology* 17, 209–10, pls XXXI–XXXVI.

Eaton 2005–2006. A 'Mortuary Liturgy' from the *Book of the Dead* with comments on the nature of the 3h-spirit. *Journal of the American Research Center in Egypt* 42, 81–94.

Ebers, G 1885. *Richard Lepsius. Ein Lebensbild*. Leipzig.

Edwards, I E S 1960. *Oracular Amuletic Decrees of the Late New Kingdom*. Hieratic Papyri in the British Museum. Fourth series. London.

Egyptian Antiquities 1872. *Egyptian Antiquities*. British Museum. London.

Fabian, Z I 1988. Heart-chapters in the context of the Book of the Dead. *Studien zur Altägyptischen Kultur. Beihefte* 3, 249–59.

Faulkner, R O 1985. *The Ancient Egyptian Book of the Dead*. C Andrews (ed.), revised edition. London.

Forman, W and Quirke, S 1996. *Hieroglyphs and the Afterlife in Ancient Egypt*. London.

Germer, R 1997 *Das Geheimnis der Mumien. Ewiges Leben am Nil*. Munich and New York.

Gabolde, L 2008. Des Livres des Morts qu'on cherché sans les trouver et d'autres qu'on trouvé sans les chercher. À propos du linceul et du papyrus du Musée de l'Imprimerie de Lyon (MIL 1204 et 429). *Kyphi. Bulletin du Cercle lyonnais d'égyptologie Victor Loret* 6, 25–42.

Gasse, A 2002. *Un papyrus et son scribe*. Paris.

Geisen, C 2004. *Die Totentexte des verschollenen Sarges der Königin Mentuhotep aus der 13. Dynastie*. SAT 8. Wiesbaden.

Gestermann, L 2003. Neues zu Pap. Gardiner II (BM EA 10676). Z Hawass (ed.) *Egyptology at the Dawn of the Twenty-first Century. Proceedings of the Eighth International Congress of Egyptologists*. Cairo, Vol. 1: Archaeology, 202–8.

Gestermann, L 2005. *Die Überlieferung ausgewählter Texte altägyptischer Totenliteratur ('Sargtexte') in spätzeitlichen Grabanlagen*. ÄA 68. Wiesbaden, 403, 435.

Glanville, S R K 1927. Note on the Nature and Date of the 'Papyri' of Nakht, BM 10471 and 10473. *Journal of Egyptian Archaeology* 13, 50–56, pl. XIX–XXI.

Grimm, A and Schoske, S 1999. *Im Zeichen des Mondes. Ägypten zu Beginn des Neuen Reiches*. München.

Habachi, L 1976. The Royal Scribe Amenmose, son of Penzerti and Mutemonet: his monuments in Egypt and Abroad. J H Johnson and E F Wente (eds), *Studies in Honor of George R Hughes. Studies in Ancient Oriental Civilization* 39. Chicago, 83–103.

Hawass, Z 2006 *Bilder der Unsterblichkeit. Die Totenbücher aus den Königsgräbern in Theben*. Mainz.

Hays, H M 2004. Transformation of Context: the Field of Rushes in Old and Middle Kingdom Mortuary Literature. S Bickel and B Mathieu (eds), *D'un monde à l'autre. Textes des Pyramides & Textes des Sarcophages. Bibliothèque d'Étude* 139. Cairo, 175–200.

Herbin, F-R 2008. *Books of Breathing and Related Texts. Catalogue of the Books of the Dead and other Religious Texts in the British Museum*, IV. London.

Hornung, E 1979. *Das Totenbuch der Ägypter*. Zürich and München.

Hornung, E 1997. *Altägyptische Jenseitsbücher. Ein einführender Überblick*. Darmstadt, 5–33.

Illés, O 2006. Single spell Book of the Dead papyri as Amulets. B Backes, I Munro and S Stöhr (eds) Totenbuch-Forschungen. Gesammelte Beiträge d*es 2 Internationalen Totenbuch-Symposiums 2005. Studien zum Altägyptischen Totenbuch 11*. Wiesbaden, 121–30, pls 1–3.

Illés, O 2009. Fragment of a Book of the Dead manuscript. T A Bács, Z I Fabián, G Schreiber and L Török (eds) *Hungarian Excavations in the Theban Necropolis. A Celebration of 102 Years of Fieldwork in Egypt*. Budapest, 135–6.

James, T G H 1970. *The British Museum. Hieroglyphic Texts from Egyptian Stelae etc*. IX. London.

Janssen, J J 1975. *Commodity Prices from the Ramesside Period*. Leiden, 291.

Kemp, B 2007. *How to Read the Egyptian Book of the Dead*. London.

Kitchen, K A 2000. *Ramesside Inscriptions Translated and Annotated*. Translations III. Oxford.

Klaproth, J 1829. *Collection d'antiquités égyptiennes, recuellies par M. le Chevalier de Palin, publiées par MM. Dorow et Klaproth en 33 planches, auxquelles on en a joint une trente-quatrième représentant les plus beaux scarabées de la collection de M. J. Passalacqua, précédée d'observations critiques sur l'alphabet hiéroglyphique découvert par M. Champollion le jeune, et sur le progrès fait jusqu'à ce jour dans l'art de déchiffrer les anciennes écritures égyptiennes. Avec deux planches*. Paris.

Kockelmann, H 2008. *Untersuchungen zu den späten Totenbuch-Handschriften auf Mumienbinden*. SAT 12, 2 vols. Wiesbaden, 85–9, 232–6.

Landa, N and Lapis, I 1974. *Egyptian Antiquities in the Hermitage*. Leningrad.

Lapp, G 1997. *The Papyrus of Nu (BM EA 10477). Catalogue of the Books of the Dead in the British Museum*, I. London.

Lapp, G 2004. *The Papyrus of Nebseni (BM EA 9900). Catalogue of the Books of the Dead in the British Museum*, III. London.

Leach, B 1992. Behind the Scenes. British Museum Magazine 11 (Autumn 1992), 23.

Leemans, C 1882. *Aegyptische hiëroglyphische Lijkpapyrus (T. 2) van het Nederlandsche Museum van Oudheden te Leyden*. Leyden.

Leahy, L M 1989. Wahibreemakhet at Giza. *Journal of Egyptian Archaeology* 75, 239–43, pl. XXXV.

Legrain, G 1893. Textes recueillis dans quelques collections particulieres. *Recueil de Travaux relatives a la Philologie et a l'Archeologie Egyptiennes et Assyriennes* 15, 1–20.

Lejeune, B 2006. A study of pLouvre N. 3125 and the end of the Book of the Dead tradition. B Backes, I Munro and S Stöhr (eds), *Totenbuch-Forschungen. Gesammelte Beiträge des 2. Internationalen Totenbuch-Symposiums 2005*. SAT 11. Wiesbaden, 197–202.

Lenzo, G 2010. The two funerary papyri of Queen Nedjmet. *Proceedings of the Book of the Dead Colloquium/BMSAES*, forthcoming.

Lepsius, R 1842. *Das Todtenbuch der Ägypter nach dem hieroglyphischen Papyrus in Turin*. Leipzig (reprint Osnabrück 1969).

Lesko, L 1992. Some further thoughts on chapter 162 of the Book of the Dead. E Teeter and J A Larson (eds), *Gold of Praise. Studies on Ancient Egypt in Honor of Edward F. Wente*. Chicago, 255–9.

Lesko, L H 2003. Nubian influence on the later versions of the Book of the Dead. Z Hawass (ed.), *Egyptology at the Dawn of the Twenty-first Century. Proceedings of the Eighth International Congress of Egyptologists*. Cairo. Vol. 1: Archaeology, 314–18.

Lieblein, J 1875. *Index alphabétique de tous les mots contenus dans le livre des Morts publié par R. Lepsius d'après le papyrus de Turin*. Paris.

Lloyd, A B 1989. Psychology and society in the ancient Egyptian cult of the dead. J P Allen, J Assmann, A B Lloyd, R K Ritner and D P Silverman, *Religion and Philosophy in Ancient Egypt*. Yale Egyptological Studies 3. New Haven, 117–33.

Lorck, C B 1879. D*ie Herstellung von Druckwerken. Praktische Winke für Autoren und Buchhändler. Dritte, umgearbeitete und vermehrte Auflage*. Leipzig.

Lucarelli, R 2001–2. Ch. 41B of the Book of the Dead. *Jaarbericht Ex Oriente Lux* 37, 41–51.

Lucarelli, R 2006. *The Book of the Dead of Gatseshen. Ancient Funerary Religion in the 10th Century BC*. Egyptologische Uitgaven 21. Leiden, 23, 39.

Lüscher, B 1998. *Untersuchungen zu Totenbuch Spruch 151*. Studien zum Altägyptischen Totenbuch 2. Wiesbaden.

Lüscher, B 2000. *Das Totenbuch pBerlin P. 10477 aus Achmim (mit Photographien des verwandten pHildesheim 5248)*. HAT 6. Wiesbaden.

Lüscher, B 2006. *Die Verwandlungssprüche (Tb 76–88). Synoptische Textausgabe nach Quellen des Neuen Reiches*. Totenbuchtexte 2. Basel.

Lüscher, B 2007. *Totenbuch-Papyrus Neuchâtel Eg. 429 und Princeton Pharaonic Roll 2: zur Totenbuch-Tradition von Deir el-Medina*. Beiträge zum Alten Ägypten 1. Basel.

Massy, A 1885. *Le papyrus de Nebseni. Exemplaire hiéroglyphique du Livre des Morts conservé au British Museum*. Gand.

Milde, H 1991. *The Vignettes in the Book of the Dead of Neferrenpet*. Egyptologische Uitgaven 7. Leiden.

Mosher, M 1992. Theban and Memphite Book of the Dead traditions. *Journal of the American Research Center in Egypt* 29, 172.

Mosher, M 2001. *The Papyrus of Hor (BM EA 10479) with Papyrus MacGregor: The Late Period Tradition at Akhmim*. Catalogue of the Books of the Dead in the British Museum, II. London.

Munro, I 1988. *Untersuchungen zu den Totenbuch-Papyri der 18 Dynastie*. London and New York.

Munro, I 1994. *Die Totenbuch-Handschriften der 18. Dynastie im Ägyptischen Museum*. ÄA 54. Wiesbaden, 31–5.

Munro, I 2001. *Das Totenbuch des Pa-en-nesti-taui aus der Regierungszeit des Amenope (pLondon BM 10064)*. HAT 7. Wiesbaden.

Munro, I 2009. *Der Totenbuch-Papyrus der Ta-schep-en-Chonsu aus dem späten 25. Dynastie (pMoskau Puschkin-Museum I, 1b, 121)*. Mit Beiträgen von John H Taylor. HAT 10. Wiesbaden.

Munro, I 2010. Evidence of a master copy transferred from Thebes to the Memphite area in the 26th Dynasty. J H Taylor (ed.). *British Museum Studies in Ancient Egypt and Sudan* 15. London.

Nagel, G 1949. Le Linceul de Thoutmes III. *Annales du Service des Antiquites d'Egypte* 49, 317–29, pls I–III.

Naville, E 1886. *Das aegyptische Todtenbuch der XVIII. bis XX. Dynastie*. 3 vols. Berlin.

Nebseni 1876. *Photographs of the Papyrus of Nebseni in the British Museum*. London.

Nelson, M 1978. *Catalogue des Antiquités Égyptiennes. Collection des Musées d'Archéologie de Marseille*. Marseilles.

Niwinski, A 1988. *21st Dynasty Coffins from Thebes. Chronological and Typological Studies*. Theben V. Mainz am Rhein.

Niwinski, A 1989. *Studies on the Illustrated Theban Funerary Papyri of the 11th and 10th Centuries BC*. Orbis Biblicus et Orientalis 86. Freiburg and Göttingen.

Pancoucke, C L F (ed.) 1821. *Description de l'Egypte ou Recueil des observations et des recherches qui ont été faites en Egypte pendant l'expédition de l'armée française*. Seconde édition dédiée au Roi. Antiquités, Vol. II. Paris.

Parkinson, R and Quirke S 1995. *Papyrus*. London.

Parkinson, R B 1999. *Cracking Codes. The Rosetta Stone and Decipherment*. London.

Parkinson, R and Leach, B 2010. Creating borders: observations on pigments and fading on the Papyrus of Ani (EA 10470). Forthcoming.

Parkinson, R and Quirke, S 1992. The coffin of Prince Herunefer and the early history of the Book of the Dead. A B Lloyd (ed.) *Studies in Pharaonic Religion and Society (FS J G Griffiths)*. Occasional Publications 8. London, 37–51.

Parkinson, R and Quirke, S 1995. *Papyrus*. London.

Payraudeau, F 2003. La Désignation du Gouverneur de Thèbes aux Époques Libyenne et Éthiopienne. *Revue d'Égyptologie* 54, 131–153.

Perraud, M 2006. Untersuchungen zu Totenbuch Spruch 166: Vorbemerkungen. B Backes, I Munro and S Stöhr (eds), *Totenbuch-Forschungen. Gesammelte Beiträge des 2. Internationalen Totenbuch-Symposiums 2005*. SAT 11. Wiesbaden, 283–96.

Piankoff, A 1974. *The Wandering of the Soul*. Egyptian Religious Texts and Representations 6. Princeton.

Piccione, P A 2007. The Egyptian Game of Senet and the Migration of the Soul. I L Finkel (ed.), *Ancient Board Games in Perspective*. London, 54–63.

Pierret, P 1882. *Le Livre des Morts des Anciens Egyptiens. Traduction complète d'après le Papyrus de Turin et les manuscrits du Louvre*. Paris.

Pinch, G 2006. *Magic in Ancient Egypt* (2nd edn). London.

Pusch, E B 1979. *Das Senet-Brettspiel im Alten Ägypten. 1.1. Das inschriftliche und archäologische Material. Münchner Ägyptologische Studien* 38. München Berlin.

Quack, J F 2009. Redaktion und Kodifizierung im spätzeitlichen Ägypten. Der Fall des Totenbuches. J Schaper (ed.), *Die Textualisierung der Religion*. Tübingen, 11–34.

Quirke, S G J 1993. *Owners of Funerary Papyri in the British Museum*. Occasional Paper 92. London.

Quirke, S 1999a. Women in ancient Egypt: temple titles and funerary papyri. A Leahy and J Tait (eds), *FS H S Smith*, Occasional Publications 13. London, 227–35.

Quirke, S 1999b. The last Books of the Dead? W V Davies (ed.), *Studies in Egyptian Antiquities. A Tribute to T G H James*, BMOP 123. London, 83–98.

Quirke, S G J 2002. Judgment of the Dead. D B Redford (ed.), *The Ancient Gods Speak. A Guide to Egyptian Religion*. Oxford, 173–7.

Quirke, S 2003. Measuring the Underworld. D O'Connor and S Quirke (eds), *Encounters with Ancient Egypt. Mysterious Lands*, London. 161–81.

Quirke, S and Spencer, A J (eds) 1992. *The British Museum Book of Ancient Egypt*. London.

Ragazzoli, C 2010. Traces of a workshop production? The Book of the Dead of Ankhesnet. *Proceedings of the Book of the Dead Colloquium/BMSAES*, forthcoming.

Raven, M 1979. Papyrus-sheaths and Ptah-Sokar-Osiris statues, *OMRO* 59–60, 251–96.

Reeves, N and Taylor, J H 1992. *Howard Carter before Tutankhamun*. London.

Renouf, P 1907. *The Life-work of Sir Peter Le Page Renouf. First Series, Volume IV: The Book of the Dead*. Translation and Commentary. Continued and completed by Prof. E. Naville. Paris and Leipzig.

Roberson, J 2009. The early history of 'New Kingdom' netherworld iconography: a late Middle Kingdom apotropaic wand reconsidered. D P Silverman, W K Simpson and J Wegner (eds), *Archaism and Innovation: Studies in the Culture of Middle Kingdom Egypt*. New Haven and Philadelphia, 427–45.

Roth, A M 1992. The PSS-KF and the 'Opening of the Mouth' ceremony: a Ritual of Birth and Rebirth. *Journal of Egyptian Archaeology* 78, 113–47.

Roth, A M 2001. Opening of the Mouth. D B Redford (ed.), *The Oxford Encyclopedia of Ancient Egypt* 2, 605–9.

Roth, A M and Roehrig, C H 2002. Magical Bricks and the Bricks of Birth, *Journal of Egyptian Archaeology* 88, 121–39.

Russmann, E R 2001. *Eternal Egypt. Masterworks of Ancient Art from the British Museum*. London and New York.

Saleh, M 1984. *Das Totenbuch in den thebanischen Beamtengräbern des Neuen Reiches, Texte und Vignetten*. AV 46. Mainz.

Säve-Söderbergh, T 1994. *De l'Assassif a Terijoki. La 'Pierre Perovski' de l'Ermitage*. C Berger, G Clerc and N Grimal (eds), *Hommages à Jean Leclant, 4. Varia*. Bibliothèque d'Etude 106/4. Cairo, 337–54.

Schneider, H D 1999. *Life and Death under the Pharaohs. Egyptian Art from the National Museum of Antiquities in Leiden, The Netherlands*. Perth.

Schwartze, M G 1843. *Das alte Aegypten oder Sprache, Geschichte, Religion und Verfassung des alten Aegyptens nach den altägyptischen Original-Schriften und den Mittheilungen der nicht-ägyptischen alten Schriftsteller. Erster Theil: Darstellung und Beurtheilung der vornehmsten Entzifferungs-Systeme der drei altägyptischen Schrift-Arten*. Leipzig.

Seeber, C 1976. *Untersuchungen zur Darstellung des Totengerichts im Alten Ägypten. Münchner Ägyptologische Studien* 35. München Berlin.

Seyfried, K-J 1990. Das Grab des Amonmose (TT 373). *Theben* 4. Mainz am Rhein.

Seyffarth, G 1840. *Alphabeta genuina Aegyptiorum. Beitraege zur Kenntniss der Literatur, Kunst, Mythologie und Geschichte des alten Aegypten*. Leipzig.

Shore, A F 1979. Votive objects from Dendera of the Graeco-Roman period. J Ruffle, G A Gaballa and K A Kitchen (eds), *Glimpses of Ancient Egypt. Studies in honour of H W Fairman*. Warminster, 138–60.

Stadelmann, R 1985 *Die ägyptischen Pyramiden. Vom Ziegelbau zum Weltwunder*. Mainz.

Strudwick, N 2006 *Masterpieces of Ancient Egypt*. London.

Strudwick, N and Taylor, J H 2005. *Mummies. Death and the Afterlife in Ancient Egypt. Treasures from the British Museum*. Santa Ana.

Szpakowska, K 2003. *Behind closed eyes: dreams and nightmares in ancient Egypt*. Swansea.

Taylor, J H 1995. Tracking down the past. *British Museum Magazine* 21 (Spring 1995), 8–11.

Taylor, J H 1996. An Egyptian mummy-mask in the British Museum. A new date and identification of the owner, *Apollo* (July 1996), 33–8.

Taylor, J H 1999. The Burial Assemblage of Henutmehyt: inventory, date and provenance. W V Davies (ed.), *Studies in Egyptian Antiquities. A Tribute to T G H James*. British Museum Occasional Paper no. 123. London, 59–72, pl. 14–21, col. pls IX–XVI.

Taylor, J H 2001. *Death and the Afterlife in Ancient Egypt*. London.

Taylor, J H 2003. Theban coffins from the Twenty-second to the Twenty-sixth Dynasty: dating and synthesis of development. N Strudwick and J H Taylor (eds), *The Theban Necropolis. Past, Present and Future*. London, 95–121, pls 42–75.

Verhoeven, U 1999. *Das Totenbuch des Monthpriesters Nespasefy aus der Zeit Psammetichs I*. Handschriften des Altägyptischen Totenbuches 5. Wiesbaden.

Waitkus, W 1987. Zur Deutung einiger apotropäischer Götter in den Gräbern im Tal der Königinnen und im Grabe Ramses III, *Göttinger Miszellen* 99, 51–82.

Wüthrich, A 2010. *Théologie Thébaine Tardive: Les Chapitres Supplémentaires du Livre des Morts*. SAT. Wiesbaden. Forthcoming.

Zabkar, V L 1985. Correlation of the Transformation Spells of the Book of the Dead and the Amulets of Tutankhamun's Mummy. F Geus and F Thill (eds.), *Mélanges offerts à Jean Vercoutter*, 375–88.

Ziegler, C 1982. 'Livre des morts appartenant au scribe Nebqed', in Naissance de l'ecriture. Cuneiformes et hieroglyphs. Paris, Editions de la Reunion des musees nationaux, 288-9.

Ziegler, C 2008. *Queens of Egypt. From Hetepheres to Cleopatra*. Monaco and Paris.

ILLUSTRATION ACKNOWLEDGEMENTS

All illustrations are copyright the Trustees of the British Museum except for the following:

Fig. 4 photo. akg-images/De Agostini Picture Library;
Fig. 14 photo. akg-images /Andrea Jemolo; Fig. 15 Musée
du Louvre/George Poncet; Fig. 16 RMN All rights reserved;
Fig. 17 Private collection, photo. I. Munro; Fig. 18 Private
collection; Fig. 19 photo. Sandro Vannini; Fig. 20
Universität zu Köln, Seminar für Ägyptologie; Fig. 21
Courtesy of PM Image and Alexandra Küffer; fig. 22 Cairo
Museum; Fig. 23 Royal Ontario Museum, Toronto (photo.
Wolfgang Schade); Fig. 31 Musée du Louvre / Christian
Larrieu; Fig. 34 Musée du Louvre / Christian Larrieu;
Cat. no. 41 Musée du Louvre / Christian Larrieu; Fig. 35
Soprintendenza per i Beni Archelogici dei Piemonte e del
Museo Antichità Egizie; Fig. 38 Sandro Vannini; Cat. nos
52–3 CAM, Marseille; Fig. 41 John H. Taylor; Fig. 46 Sandro
Vannini; Cat. no. 74 RMN / Hervé Lewandowski; Fig. 60
Sandro Vannini; Fig. 69 bpk / Ägyptishches Museum and
Papyrussammlung, Staatliche Museen zu Berlin; Cat. no.
151 CAM, Marseille (photo. David Giancatarina); Fig. 83
Fondazione Museo Antichita Egizie di Torino; Fig. 84
photo. Ernst Milster, Berlin 1874; Fig. 85 Naville
Foundation, Geneva (photo. Musée D'Art et D'Histoire,
Ville de Genève); Fig. 86 From Naville 1886 (vol. 2), 160;
Fig. 87 from Lüscher 2006, 13; Fig. 88 Griffith Institute,
University of Oxford, Davies MSS (Wishart donation);
Fig. 89 From Lorck 1879, 148; Fig. 90 Atelier du Livre
d'art et de l'Estampe-Imprimerie Nationale, Paris;
Stiftung Deutsches Technikmuseum Berlin (photo.
Dietmar Ruppert).

INDEX